The Complete Guide to
CONSERVATORY PLANTS

The Complete Guide to
CONSERVATORY PLANTS

ANN BONAR

TIGER BOOKS INTERNATIONAL
LONDON

This edition published in 1995 by
Tiger Books International PLC, Twickenham

First published in Great Britain 1992
by Collins & Brown Limited
London House
Great Eastern Wharf
Parkgate Road
London SW11 4NQ

British Library Cataloguing-in-Publication Data.
A catalogue record for this book
is available from the British Library.

ISBN 1-85501-687-7

Conceived, edited and designed by Collins & Brown Limited

Editorial Director **Gabrielle Townsend**

Editor **Susan Berry**

Art Director **Roger Bristow**

Designer **Steven Wooster**

Filmset by Bookworm Typesetting, Manchester
Reproduction by Scantrans, Singapore
Printed and bound in Hong Kong by Dai Nippon

Contents

ACQUIRING A CONSERVATORY

THE ACQUISITION of a conservatory or garden room is a delight, with some unforeseen pleasures as well as the obvious ones. It will certainly give you the best of both worlds, enabling you to bring the garden into the living-room and to enjoy it all year round.

Practical considerations

Once the conservatory is established, you will wonder how you lived without it. In summer it becomes *the* place to sit and relax and, above all, to garden, as you explore the possibilities of growing even the most exotic of tropical and subtropical plants. But summer is not the only season of use for a conservatory in a cool-temperate climate; provided it is heated to some degree in winter, it can be of value all year round.

One of the unexpected benefits of growing plants in these kinds of surroundings is that they grow twice as well as they would in normal domestic conditions owing to the great increase in available light. They grow taller, and larger, flower where they perhaps did not flower at all or double their former flowering ability. Fruiting becomes a common occurrence rather than an unexpected bonus so that, for example, oranges, peaches or melons mature, their time of ripening depending on whether the conservatory is heated or unheated.

The nature of the planting in a conservatory or garden room is dictated to some extent by the orientation. Blinds or shading will help to cool down a south-facing conservatory, such as the one left, while those with a north- or east-facing aspect, like the conservatory, right, are ideal for a range of large-leaved foliage plants which prefer cooler conditions. The different areas of the conservatory can be exploited for growing plants with varying cultivation needs, so that the back or side walls of the conservatory can be put to good use for shade lovers, while the more exotic, sub-tropical species benefit from being closest to the source of light.

Deciding what to grow

As with houseplants, it pays to consider a little first, ideally before the conservatory is built, what effects you can obtain and what plants you can grow, given the aspect, size and heating potential of the proposed conservatory. Do you actually like growing plants? Because if so, you will try to fill all the available space with them, and that will lead to quite a lot of work in looking after them and in keeping the conservatory tidy. If you want plants chiefly for decoration, the answer is to limit yourself to a few large slow-growing varieties which will supply a lot of attractive greenery without much effort on your part.

Lean-to conservatories are normally the cheapest to construct. Where they are long and narrow, it pays to position the plants to break up the length. This particular conservatory has a wide range of plants, most of them with decorative foliage, as well as some interesting Mediterranean plants such as citrus and oleander.

Aspect and size

The aspect – the direction in which the conservatory faces – can affect the choice of plants; for instance if the conservatory or garden room faces north, it will be shaded all day – cool in summer and chilly in winter. Ferns, begonias, Cape primroses (*Streptocarpus*) and ivies are typical of the plants that can be grown in such a conservatory, but the choice for such a situation is limited. It would be better, if you have the choice, to ensure that the long axis of the conservatory runs north/south, at right-angles to the house-wall, rather than east/west, running along it in the form of a lean-to.

A south-facing position means that the conservatory will become extremely hot in summer, and the temperature, light and humidity will be much harder to manage. Certainly, it would have the advantage of warmth in winter, and the best available light, so if you were planning to use it in winter, this might well provide the best aspect. The plant display in winter in it would be better than in conservatories facing in other directions, and the spring and autumn displays should be good, too. East- and west-facing positions each have their advantages, but the choice of plants is not affected a great deal – there will be plenty that can be grown in either – and it is more a case of considering your own preferences and uses.

The size of the conservatory makes some difference to the choice of plants. Remember that plants grow rapidly owing to the increase in light and the provision of shelter, and climbers like jasmine, *Hoya carnosa* and stephanotis will reach the roof in no time. Mimosa and *Grevillea robusta* will do their best to turn themselves into their normal size as rapidly as possible – the latter makes a 30m (100ft) tree in its native Australia – and you could easily be crowded out by the vegetation even in an area of, say, 3.6 by 2.4m (12 by 8ft).

However, there are plenty of well-behaved decorative plants for areas of this size or smaller, giving you room to enjoy the surroundings as well. If your preference is for large plants, the more slowly growing varieties are the most suitable, with a few chosen to provide greenery and colour for as much of the year as possible.

Heating

The third variable, heating, can make a considerable difference to the diversity of the plant collection. In cool-temperate climates, artificial heat is usually needed during the winter to keep the conservatory temperature above freezing. A generally accepted minimum temperature for what are known as cool conditions is 7°C (45°F). This should still permit a considerable range of plants to be grown, without being exorbitantly expensive to heat. Another minimum for sub-tropical plants is 10°C (50°F), and a third level, for tropical plants, is a minimum of 16°C (60°F). For normal use, the temperatures will need to be well above the last-quoted minimum during the day, and perhaps in the evening as well; with luck the sun will provide the extra lift some of the time.

ASPECT AND CONDITIONS

The direction in which a conservatory faces – its aspect – will to some extent govern the appearance of the conservatory. North-facing garden rooms and conservatories, like the one shown left, will have proportionately more foliage plants, while south- and west-facing conservatories allow you to grow more exotic flowering plants.

Flowering interest can always be introduced into a cooler conservatory on a short-term basis. The waxy white-flowered orchid (*Phalaenopsis*), below, set off so well against the dark leaves of *Tradescantia zebrinuas* 'Purpusii', would probably have to be grown in a sunnier, warmer conservatory but survives if brought in as a fully grown plant, although cymbidium orchids, which thrive in cooler conditions, will cope well with a north-facing aspect. Geraniums, including the attractive ivy-leaved pelargonium, shown below, are not fussy about aspect, and make a brilliant splash of colour.

ORIGINS OF PLANTS

T HE POTENTIAL number of plant species suitable for conservatory cultivation runs into many thousands, though as yet relatively few nurserymen specialize in this type of plant. Nevertheless the plants are available, thanks to the efforts of the plant hunters who risked their lives bringing plants back from all over the world.

Serious plant-hunting started in the 1600s, when John Tradescant, a professional gardener, was sent by his employers, the Cecils, to Europe to look for new varieties of fruit and vegetables. He eventually became Charles 1's gardener, after undertaking many plant-hunting expeditions to Russia, North Africa, Greece and the Mediterranean countries, as well as Continental Europe. His son, also John, took on his father's post on the latter's death, and began plant collecting in Virginia. Father and son, between them, discovered hundreds of species and opened the gates to what eventually became a flood of new plants, introduced for cultivation in both private and commercial circumstances, including covered gardens.

From the start of the eighteenth century and right through the nineteenth, plant hunters were sent by their employers all over the world. Some were gardeners, some employed by the new nurseries, some were botanists, and some were simply very enthusiastic amateurs. The desire for plants to furnish the gardens that were appearing everywhere, attached to the houses that the new merchant class were building, helped to prompt the expeditions, although often a simple thirst for exploration was the only excuse needed. The need was further fuelled by the appearance of, first, orangeries, and then conservatories and greenhouses where tropical plants could be grown in safety in frost-ridden climates.

The plant-hunters not only faced adverse conditions. They also had to cope with the problems of sending plants home. This was made more difficult by the fact that most of the plants needed considerable warmth, as well as a rooting medium and care, and the journey home was long. An invention called the Wardian Case proved to be their salvation. Introduced in 1833 by Dr Ward, a medical practitioner and a botanist, it was effectively a miniature greenhouse, enabling the majority of plants grown in it to survive until they could be planted under protection.

Many of these new plants came from hot countries; some from areas of high humidity such as the tropical rain forests, others from the opposite extreme like the desert fringes. Some of the trees and shrubs from China were completely hardy, as indeed, were most of the rhododendrons. Some plants flowered during the winter, such as the bulbs from the Cape of South Africa, where the seasons are reversed. Provided they were given a little artificial heat, they grew perfectly well.

Dramatic effects can be created by using contrasting forms and colours of foliage. This particular group comprises a tree fern, Cibotium chamissoii, Colocasia, Ficus benjamina *and hydrangea, all of which need plenty of humidity to do well.*

The new conservatories

Concurrently with all this exploration of land and nature, came the Industrial Revolution and its many technological achievements. Among them were the uses to which cast iron could be put in conjunction with glass to create an entirely new class of building. The architectural concepts that then took shape during this period must have seemed as novel as the design of the Sydney Opera House in this century, and probably had a similarly mixed reaction.

As time went on and wrought iron was introduced into the construction as well, the designs of the new glass buildings became more complex, resulting in the production of theatres, market halls, such as that at Covent Garden, and conservatories and winter gardens purely for housing plants.

The elegant outline, left, of the Palm House at the Royal Botanic Gardens, Kew. One of the great conservatories of the Victorian era, it was designed by Decimus Burton and Richard Turner, an engineer from Dublin.

The exotic trumpet-like flowers of Brugmansia arborea (syn. Datura arborea) 'Knightii' will fill the air in the conservatory with a delicious scent.

Although cast iron had been manufactured since near the end of the eighteenth century, the way in which glass was made until early in the nineteenth century had limited its use in plant-house construction. By 1833 a method for manufacturing good sheet glass was perfected, and in 1845 an iniquitous tax on glass, in place since the seventeenth century, was abolished with the result that the price nose-dived overnight. The way was then open for the relatively cheap production of conservatories (both public and private), winter gardens and greenhouses of all sizes and shapes. By the end of the nineteenth century, architects were designing houses with conservatories as an integral part of the overall plan.

Timber continued to be used a good deal in the construction, but cast iron and wrought iron in particular were used in the larger buildings. Because wrought iron had intrinsically more strength and flexibility it was possible to manufacture comparatively delicate glazing bars and to make them curved, so helping them to improve the design and the entry of light. The Great Conservatory built at Chatsworth between 1836 and 1840, in the shape of a trefoil leaf, was one of the first of the really large private conservatories. It was designed by the head gardener, Sir Joseph Paxton, with the help of the architect Decimus Burton. Paxton later went on to create his masterpiece – the Crystal Palace – built in 1851 in Hyde Park to cover the Great Exhibition. Its dimensions were approximately 560 by 120 by 20m (600 by 130 by 20yd); it was later removed and rebuilt at Sydenham, in 1854, where it acted as a cover to a garden with fully grown trees in it, besides pools, statues, glades and fountains.

A vast conservatory was also built in Brussels in the late nineteenth century by Leopold II, covering nearly 2ha (5 acres), with 4ha (10 acres) of glass; at Buckingham Palace not one but three conservatories were built. In 1845, a Winter Garden was made in Regent's Park: it was described as "a veritable fairyland, transplanted into the heart of London" where "the most exquisite odours wafted to and fro with every movement of the glass doors".

The Victorian heyday

The Victorians had a passion for foliage in their conservatories. Any plant that was large, curiously shaped or unusually coloured was certain to find a place under glass, and at the time there were plenty of plants of this nature being shipped home. Although some were relatively tough and easy to grow, others needed high humidity and a lot of warmth. But there was a cheap and plentiful source of heat in the coal-fired boilers that heated the water for the cast-iron pipes running beneath grilles in the conservatory floor. Water tanks, frequent watering and overhead spraying supplied the humidity, so that it was easy to grow, for instance, the fragile caladiums, their leaves delicately netted with coloured veining.

In direct contrast to these was the foliage of the banana plant, massive, glossy and at least 1.5m (5ft) long. Whether the bananas fruited or not was immaterial, though it was a satisfying bonus if they did. Palms were fantastically popular, and one nursery, the Hackney Botanical, listed between 150 and 170 different kinds. Cycads, too, found a place in the Victorian conservatory. A relic from the fossil age, they grow slowly into frondy plants like green shuttlecocks – a halfway-house between palms and tree ferns.

One hundred and fifty years ago a lot of plants grown under cover were the same as those we grow today as houseplants rather than conservatory plants. Because they had the advantage of a great deal more light in such places, they grew twice as well. Calatheas, marantas, the rubber plant and other ficus species, *Dizygotheca* and *Dieffenbachia*, a mass of different varieties of ivies and all sorts of ferns were just a few of the other foliage species seen in the average domestic Victorian conservatory – some heated, some unheated, just as now. In fact, the craze for outdoor ferneries spread indoors, and an entire conservatory might be devoted to ferns in a naturalistic setting with waterfalls, pools and grottoes. *Begonia rex* figured largely and variously in many collections, its exotically coloured leaves as bright as many flowers, and longer lasting.

To start with, many of the species which were sent home from abroad were assumed to need temperatures above 21°C (70°F), but as time passed, it was realized that these were too high for some plants. Camellias, in particular, which were widely grown, were thought to be tender, though they can survive frost. New honeysuckles (*Lonicera*), hydrangeas, cytisus and daphne were grown under cover, as were rhododendrons and azaleas, which were in fact hardy, and some of the new roses. But the heavenly pink trumpets of *Lapageria* did need warmth, as did bougainvillea, *Ixora* and *Passiflora angularis*.

Flowering shrubs included the bottlebrushes (*Callistemon*) from Australia, fuchsias (which reached their apogee in the ways in which they were pruned and shaped), *Abutilon*, myrtle, mimosa and *Sparmannia africana*, grown for its white flowers that are easily produced in the good light of a conservatory. For herbaceous plants Victorians could choose

The large golden fruit of Citrus 'Ponderosa'. All members of the citrus family provide good conservatory plants, with the bonus of glossy evergreen foliage, attractive flowers and edible fruit.

Spectacular flowers, in this
example the bracted flowerheads of
Protea repens *(syn.* P.
mellifera*), distinguish many of the
plants introduced from the sub-
tropical climates of the world.*

from lilies, pelargoniums, orchids, cinerarias, hyacinths, chrysanthemums and primulas. Hot-water plants (*Achimenes*) were so popular there were hundreds of different hybrids.

Later, as the nineteenth century advanced, more exotic plants still began to be seen: the sarracenias (insectivorous pitcher plants), succulents including cacti, and ginger plants (*Zingiber*) among them. Perhaps the plant which best characterizes the period is the giant waterlily, *Victoria amazonica*, from tropical south America, whose flat, circular leaves were at least 1.8m (6ft) wide, with a vertical edge up to 15cm (6in) deep all the way round them. The arrangement of the veins on the leaf under-surface is said to have been the source of Paxton's inspiration for the roof of the Chatsworth conservatory.

The conservatory revival

But the First World War destroyed much of this civilized beauty and charm. The price of coal soared, the labour became gun-fodder, and the plants were untended, with the result that many species were permanently lost.

Between the two world wars and following the second one, the flag of protected cultivation was kept flying by greenhouse owners, who have somehow managed to salvage and retain some of the old varieties of conservatory plants. In the last decade conservatories have started to appear again, some of them replicas of their predecessors, some of them of modern design, taking advantage of the new building fabrics. Now that leisure time is increasing, they are beginning to form an integral part of house design once again, as their considerable advantages become more and more apparent.

DISPLAYING THE PLANTS

No matter how well grown and well cared for your plants may be, unless you can display them to advantage you will fail to get true value from your conservatory. This chapter explains how to combine and group plants to achieve the best effects, taking into account the various attributes of different plants, such as foliage, form and colour, flowering season, and preferred light conditions. It also discusses the types of container available, and the furniture and equipment most suitable for displaying the plants.

NEEDS OF LIGHT AND SPACE

T HE DIFFERENCE that a conservatory or garden room can make to everyday life is enormous, not least because you then have the opportunity to enjoy what is, truly, an indoor garden. Houseplants are merely decorative additions to the home, dotted about here and there, in the same way that flower arrangements are, but lasting longer. But the great and unavoidable drawback to growing plants in a house is the shortage of light, since it is rarely received from more than one direction.

In a conservatory, light pours in from many angles: from the transparent roof above the plants as well as from two or three sides, depending on the conservatory's shape. Consequently the plants grow twice as well and much more quickly; non-flowering houseplants that are meant to flower will, if moved into a conservatory, immediately improve their growth and leaf colouring and in most cases start to bloom.

Conservatory aspect

One factor above all others that makes such a fundamental difference to plant growth is light, both in quantity and quality, as I point out on pp. 152–3. One of the variables affecting the quality of light is the direction in which the conservatory faces. For instance, attached to a west-facing wall, the conservatory receives sunlight in summer from about midday until sunset. Thus it receives sun directly from the south for an hour or so, from the south-west for somewhat longer, and from the west in the afternoon and evening.

This means that it will become very hot between about two and five o'clock in the afternoon in summer, and will remain warm until well into the night, provided the windows and ventilators are closed in good time. But from dawn until midday it will be shaded and comparatively cool, which can be a drawback in winter. Conversely, an east-facing aspect – with the axis of the conservatory running north to south, facing the rising sun – it will be much less warm in the afternoon, but will warm up quickly after a chilly start.

South-facing conservatories have the best light of all, but get extremely hot in summer – unacceptably so for many plants, and especially for their owners. First-class shading and ventilation are essential for these conditions, but, of course, they also have the best light transmission in winter, and offer a better opportunity to grow a varied selection of plants, both for foliage and flowering.

When planning a planting scheme for the conservatory, it pays to consider the vertical dimensions as carefully as the horizontal ones. Here, a dramatic grouping has been created using rocks to provide a backdrop for the fronds of the miniature date palm, Phoenix roebelenii, *colourful* Impatiens New Guinea hybrids, *and campanula in the hanging basket.*

In many cases the would-be conservatory owner does not have a choice as to aspect. If the only space available at ground-level faces north, flowering plants could be difficult to grow and the choice limited; heating costs could be high if there is no protection from the north and east winds. If you have a choice, west- or east-facing positions are generally the best and, for my money, the west wins, because such a conservatory gets the benefit of the evening sun.

Conservatory design and shape

Although the aspect may well be decided by the situation of the house, the choice of conservatory design is r
under your control, being limited only by availab.
by cost. If you have the height of a house wall, or if y.
a design with an octagonal roof, or even with a cupola, you will find it much easier to grow large climbing plants and shrubs successfully, and it will be much easier to show them off.

Naturally the conservatory design itself can enhance the display of the plants and, in my opinion, some of the Victorian replicas now available are particularly appealing. These glass rooms – octagonal, rectangular or gable-ended in shape – decorated with finials, cresting, pilasters and moulded iron-work, and with clear or coloured glazing, curved or angular in outline, cannot be anything other than ornamental, and make perfect showcases for their floral contents.

Arranging and combining plants

One of the great joys of having a conservatory lies in combining the plants so that they complement one another in the best possible way. Colour, size and shape are some of the variables that need to be taken into account, as well as cultivation needs, such as temperature, light and humidity, together with your own requirements of the conservatory. But there is one factor that always seems to be overlooked: plants are living objects, and their appearance is constantly changing.

Not only is the size and aspect of the conservatory an important consideration, so too is the style. It pays to try to keep the architecture in style with that of the house. The proportions and form of this Victorian-style conservatory blend well with those of the house.

Mostly they enlarge, rather than diminish (although the bulbs die down after flowering) and their colouring alters with maturity in many cases. Leaves become brilliantly coloured, or flowers appear, so that what started out as a splendid colour scheme may well have to be adjusted a few weeks later. Equally, a collection of plants that fitted comfortably into a corner to make an eye-catching feature, becomes unacceptably crowded after a couple of months and has to be split up.

Plants need regular re-arrangement, maybe only in small ways, but about once a week some, at least, will need to be shifted, and sooner rather than later one or another will have to be moved to a completely new position if it is to have room to grow and flourish. However, as the plants will also need tidying up every few days – removing dead flowers and withered or discoloured leaves – any repositioning needed can be done at the same time. In this respect conservatory gardening does have a unique advantage over most outdoor gardening: plants in containers are easily moved if they grow too big for their space.

Shapes of plants

To the uninitiated, plants may often appear to be just a generally amorphous, rounded mass of green, patched with other colours when they flower. In fact, they fall into several

Lean-to east-facing conservatory
In this small conservatory the plants have been grouped for maximum impact with the focus on spiky- and slender-leaved plants, like dracaenas and rushes. Colour can be provided as needed by different varieties of pelargonium or impatiens.

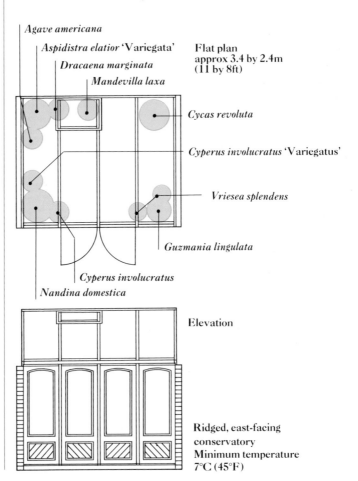

Agave americana
Aspidistra elatior 'Variegata'
Dracaena marginata
Mandevilla laxa

Flat plan
approx 3.4 by 2.4m
(11 by 8ft)

Cycas revoluta

Cyperus involucratus 'Variegatus'

Vriesea splendens

Guzmania lingulata

Cyperus involucratus
Nandina domestica

Elevation

Ridged, east-facing
conservatory
Minimum temperature
7°C (45°F)

21

specific groups as regards their shape. Although many are bushy and rounded, for instance the Rex begonias, prayer plants (*Maranta*), and most ferns, some are basically upright, with a central main stem or trunk, sometimes several of these stems. The rubber plant (*Ficus elastica*) is an example, as are the cane begonia and *Abutilon*.

Climbing plants are another group, of great use in a conservatory for covering the vertical areas provided by back walls, or for training around supporting pillars or doors and windows. Summer-flowering jasmine is not an ideal plant for the living-room, being a mighty grower and a sun-lover, but in a conservatory it can fully extend itself, and the better light in there will ensure it produces its heavenly scented flowers all summer. Also in this group are the trailers and creepers, which are usually nowhere near as vigorous as the climbers, but nevertheless look exceedingly attractive in hanging pots and baskets or cascading down from shelves or wall brackets.

The spider plant (*Chlorophytum*) is a good subject for a conservatory as it then has room for its arching stems to hang naturally; as a houseplant it so often finishes up resting on the

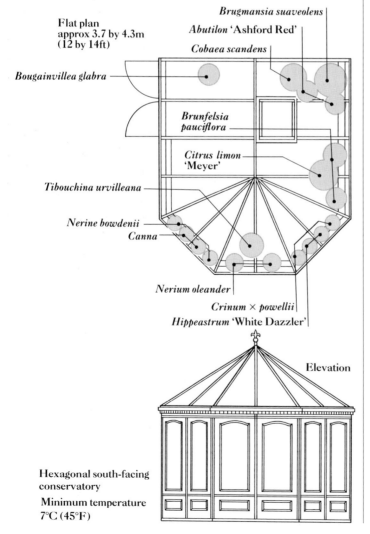

Flat plan approx 3.7 by 4.3m (12 by 14ft)

Brugmansia suaveolens
Abutilon 'Ashford Red'
Cobaea scandens
Bougainvillea glabra
Brunfelsia pauciflora
Citrus limon 'Meyer'
Tibouchina urvilleana
Nerine bowdenii
Canna
Nerium oleander
Crinum × *powellii*
Hippeastrum 'White Dazzler'

Elevation

Hexagonal south-facing conservatory

Minimum temperature 7°C (45°F)

Hexagonal south-facing conservatory

Conservatories that get a lot of sun make an ideal environment for exotic flowering plants that benefit from the high light levels, including oleanders, bougainvillea and daturas (now Brugmansia*). Shading and ventilation are particularly important for south-facing conservatories as the temperatures can otherwise rise to uncomfortable heights in summer.*

furniture and marking it. The variegated ivies are pretty trailers, as is the old-fashioned *Pelargonium* 'L'Elegante' – a hybrid left over from Victorian plantings, with its trailing ivy-shaped pink-flushed leaves and purple-veined flowers.

Another group – "rosette" plants – are a good way of covering compost and providing a horizontal dimension, as are the creeping plants. Rosette plants include African violets, bromeliads such as the earthstars (*Cryptanthus*) and the echeveria with the incredible blue-grey-pink leaves, *Echeveria glauca*. Similarly the creepers can be used as background in a border or a trough, or given prominence because they have eye-catching foliage. The snakeskin plant (*Fittonia argyroneura* 'Nana') has net-like white veining on its oval leaves, and *Episcia cupreata* has pale green to white veining on its dark green leaves, set off all summer by tubular vermilion flowers.

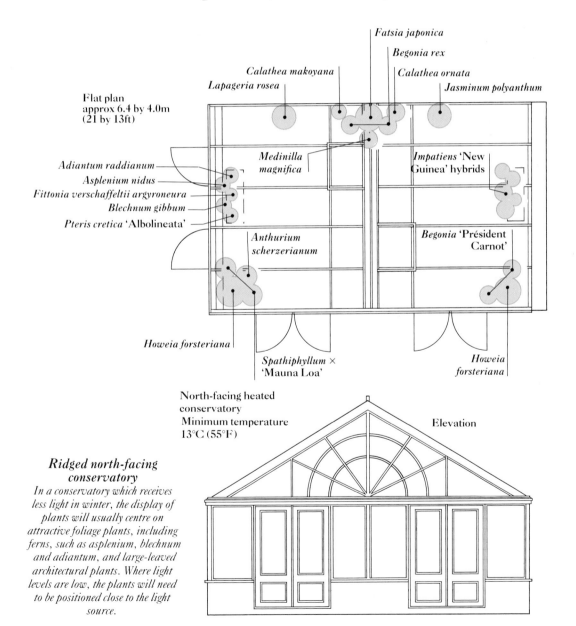

Flat plan
approx 6.4 by 4.0m
(21 by 13ft)

Fatsia japonica

Begonia rex

Calathea makoyana
Lapageria rosea

Calathea ornata
Jasminum polyanthum

Adiantum raddianum
Asplenium nidus
Fittonia verschaffeltii argyroneura
Blechnum gibbum
Pteris cretica 'Albolineata'

Medinilla magnifica

Impatiens 'New Guinea' hybrids

Anthurium scherzerianum

Begonia 'Président Carnot'

Howeia forsteriana

Spathiphyllum × 'Mauna Loa'

Howeia forsteriana

North-facing heated conservatory
Minimum temperature
13°C (55°F)

Elevation

Ridged north-facing conservatory
In a conservatory which receives less light in winter, the display of plants will usually centre on attractive foliage plants, including ferns, such as asplenium, blechnum and adiantum, and large-leaved architectural plants. Where light levels are low, the plants will need to be positioned close to the light source.

TYPES OF PLANT

THE MAJORITY of plants grown in conservatories are perennials, living for several or even many years. Some are herbaceous or soft-stemmed like the Zonal and Regal pelargoniums and the Italian bellflower (*Campanula isophylla*), purple tradescantia (*Tradescantia zebrina*) and the Cape primrose (*Streptocarpus*), but most are hard-wooded shrubs and are grown in conservatories because they make such a good display from a young age. Camellias will flower in their second or third year, as will the smaller rhododendrons and azaleas. *Citrus sinensis* is an enthusiastic (and scented) flowerer; hibiscus, oleander, medinilla and heliotrope also flower profusely under cover.

Many climbing plants are hard-stemmed, too, and are often ideal for conservatory conditions as they naturally grow in shade. It is because of this that they have adopted a climbing habit, enabling them to get to the top of forest trees into the sunlight. Stephanotis can be a rampant climber in the right conditions, with its masses of heavily scented white flowers; *Allamanda cathartica* has brilliant yellow flowers, and *Lapageria rosea* large rose-pink trumpets, which are best appreciated when the stems run along just below the conservatory roof.

Trees also have their place in the conservatory. They are one of the most useful groups for creating the impression of an authentic, lush, tropical forest. The weeping fig (*Ficus benjamina*) is much more suited to a conservatory than the living room, which cannot allow it to do justice to its potential height and decorativeness. It will grow as tall as room allows, and makes a graceful small tree clothed in small glossy leaves. Palms manage to grow surprisingly tall in containers that look too small for them, and the Australian silk oak (*Grevillea robusta*) has large, feathery leaves which clothe it right from the base of the stem.

Bulbs, corms and tubers include some of the most decorative of the smaller flowering plants. They include gloxinias (*Sinningia*), large-flowered begonias and *Achimenes* for summer, together with the hardy outdoor spring-flowering bulbs that can be brought on early. Bulbs make ideal conservatory plants; they have conspicuously ornamental flowers and are no trouble once they have finished flowering, provided they can be kept dry and frost-free until their rest period is complete.

Other groups of plants include cacti and succulents, those curious perching plants, the bromeliads (whose dramatic leaf and flower formation is in a class of its own), and the orchid family; once you are hooked on orchids you will have neither time nor inclination to grow anything else – they are addictive.

Careful grouping is the key to all successful plant displays. Here, the spiky leaves of Phormium *contrast well with the variegated leaves of scented geraniums. Good use has also been made of the vertical dimension with rampant climbers like jasmine and stephanotis.*

EASY CONSERVATORY PLANTS

This large lean-to conservatory, which faces north, houses a splendid collection of plants, both in pots and planted directly into a border, which was created when the conservatory was built. The pelargoniums in the foreground are a particularly good selection, with the red and white *P.* 'Fringed Aztec', *P.* 'White Bonanza' and the pink-flushed *P.* 'Break o' Day' making an attractive display, against the velvety dark red flowers of *P.* 'Fifth Avenue' behind. The walls host a range of climbers, including a "climbing" variegated-leaved geranium, *Trachelospermum jasminoides* and *Jasminum polyanthum* and a mimulus in flower on the end wall. The vine trained across the roof regularly produces a good crop of wine grapes each autumn. In another corner of the conservatory, *Abutilon* 'Kentish Belle', below, makes a particularly worthwhile subject, with its profusion of attractive gold and bronze drooping flowers in late summer.

POSITIONING PLANTS

WHILE THE plants in a conservatory are chosen largely for their decorativeness, they can also be made to work for their keep. A line of them can act as a living divider to cut a dining area off from a sitting area; two or three of the larger plants can hide the equipment of conservatory care, or a group consisting of trailers, hangers and plants on vertical stands can block off an unprepossessing view.

Conversely, they can also be used to draw attention to a view, by framing it, or you can go one step further and group them round a *trompe l'oeil* on a wall to make the illusion even more credible. If the conservatory is long and rectangular, rather than rounded, the plants can be used to break up the length, and prevent it from looking like a railway carriage.

With so many shapes, sizes and types of plants, the possible combinations and permutations for display are endless. Leaves can figure largely in it as many plants are grown purely because they have outstandingly shaped foliage, and the protection of the conservatory ensures that this is grown and seen at its best. In fact, leaves have almost more to offer than flowers; certainly they have as much, as they are not necessarily plain green, but can easily be coloured, in addition to being interestingly formed. Furthermore, in the warmth of the conservatory most species keep their foliage all year round.

It is hard to believe that the border, right, is in the conservatory, not outside it. The huge flower spires of Campanula pyramidalis *in blue and white combine well with the pink-flowered variegated "climbing" geranium, to create a cottage-garden feel.*

Much of the impact made by the plants in a conservatory depends on how they are positioned, below. Here, a central feature is planted up with a group of Spathiphyllum wallisii, *the large glossy green leaves and white sail-like flowers making a suitably architectural display.*

PLANT SIZE

ON THE WHOLE, plants in conservatories look best if they are on the medium-to-large size, say 45cm (18in) tall and upwards; smaller ones are best grouped, otherwise their impact is lost. Trailing plants used in hanging pots and baskets do not need to be large; the medium or small ones are ideal and, when hanging from the roof, can add to the illusion of a jungle as they mingle with the plants in containers growing up towards them.

A few large specimens, well-grown and sited in strategic spots, can give the illusion that the whole conservatory has been filled with plants, while allowing plenty of space both for furniture and to move about between it and the plants. Climbing plants do this job even better, being more or less flat against the wall, but they are more trouble to maintain, since they need supporting, tying-in, and pruning; also, renewing the compost can be awkward. This is where a gap in the conservatory floor is so useful, to allow a border to be provided in which plants can be directly grown.

Large plants will inevitably be placed on the floor, but anything smaller will need to be higher, perhaps on shelves attached to the walls, on ledges by the windows, hanging from the walls or roof, or on display stands. Groups catch the eye; single plants will do so only if there is something special about them – striking flower colour or "architectural" leaves. Incidentally, if you do collect them together, whether free-standing or planted together in troughs or planters, group only those that need the same growing conditions.

Large-leaved foliage plants help *to give the conservatory a lush, jungle-like atmosphere. The bird's nest fern,* Asplenium nidus, *with its curiously unfernlike leaves, thrives in the shadier part of a conservatory (left) while the huge palm,* Chrysalidocarpus *(right), does best in direct, but filtered, light.*

COLOUR CONSIDERATIONS

T HE TENDENCY when dealing with conservatory plants is simply to grow a mixed collection, often as a background to the furnishings. But it is perfectly possible to use colour and to blend, complement and contrast a variety of shades and tints in the same way as you would in a good herbaceous border. With a knowledge of the flowering seasons, you could, for example, create a scheme based on cool blues and lilacs, together with grey and blue-grey leaves, and touches of white, for a south-facing conservatory in summer. Alternatively plain green-leaved plants and nothing but white flowers would help to give a cooler, sophisticated impression.

Yellow-variegated leaves, and yellow, cream and orange flowers, combined with plain green foliage, help to lighten in the morning a conservatory which faces west, and would not be too dazzling in the afternoon if the shading was in place. For east-facing aspects, there are several species of plants with truly purple leaves, which look particularly good in cool morning sunlight, and which would look warm on a dull evening. Flowers to mix with them, along with green leaves, could be pink, lilac and blue, perhaps with white.

Coloured leaves

I cannot help feeling that coloured leaves are of more use than flowers as far as conservatory plant decoration is concerned because they are all-year-round, especially in the warm conservatory. Most native cool-temperate climate plants, even when evergreen, are mostly plain green, with some variegated and blue-grey exceptions, notably among the conifers and heathers. But plants from tropical regions often have brilliantly coloured leaves, and are also mostly evergreen. Take the flame nettles (*Solenostemon* hybrids), for example, from Java; nothing could be more flamboyant and gaily coloured than their leaves. Then again, the Rex begonias come in a variety of subtle foliage shadings of plum, wine, rose-pink, grey, lilac, crimson and silver, and the crotons (*Codiaeum*) are another colourful-foliage group. One of the most beautiful of foliage plants is the caladium *C.* × *hortulanum*, and there are many others with beautifully marked leaves.

Purple-leaved plants figure largely amongst varieties suitable for conservatory growing. Purple is an overpowering colour, but it can be toned down by combining it with blue-grey leaved plants, such as *Sedum sieboldii*. Equally good for conservatories are plants with interestingly marked leaves, such as irregular yellow, cream or white markings on the foliage. The ivies in particular go in for this kind of marking, but there are many more plants, including *Impatiens* 'New Guinea' hybrids, *Fittonia*, variegated *Schefflera*, and so on.

Sometimes the simplest planting scheme is the most effective. Here, the dramatically veined leaves of Anthurium crystallinum *make an eye-catching feature, framed in summer by the bougainvillea above.*

FLOWERING BY SEASON

The majority of conservatory planting schemes tend to concentrate on creating the best show in midsummer, but with a certain amount of planning you can create a good backdrop all year round using interesting foliage plants with good leaf form and colour, and then focus attention on one or two spectacular accent plants in each season. Pelargoniums have a long season and come in so many forms, with excellent flower and leaf qualities, that they make invaluable conservatory plants. *Solenostemon* (formerly *Coleus*) is another worthwhile conservatory plant with its long display of brilliantly coloured leaves. Star performers – in this case the brilliant scarlet flowers of *Hibiscus rosa-sinensis* – can be found for most seasons of the year (see pp 182–5 for suggested plants).

SPECIALIST DISPLAYS

W HATEVER PLANTS you put in a conservatory, and however you arrange them, they will always help to improve the link between the house and the garden. Rather than just assembling a heterogeneous collection of plants, it can be fun, and more stylish, to combine them to form a feature, or deliberately use all of them to create a particular effect. Carefully chosen hardware, as opposed to the software of plants, is useful for enhancing these effects and includes statues, busts and containers chosen for their shape and colouring, as well as display stands.

Borders

Since the conservatory is an indoor garden, there is no reason why you should not create a border in its floor, into which plants are directly planted. It is well worth incorporating at the time the conservatory is being constructed; indeed, many conservatory owners wish they had thought of it at the outset.

When grouping plants, *right, a more unified effect is created by limiting the colour palette. Here white and pink pelargoniums provide the colour, against a backdrop of contrasting foliage shapes, including spiky-leaved phormiums and the filigree-like fronds of ferns.*

The inclusion *of a water feature, left, helps to improve the humidity in a conservatory, making an ideal situation for many of the foliage plants which prefer a moist atmosphere, such as spathiphyllums and ferns, left.*

If it is practicable, it has all sorts of advantages: it provides unlimited root-room, bypasses the need to repot and to buy new compost frequently, and in particular makes an easier place in which to grow climbing plants if it is sited at the foot of the house wall. If the conservatory is large enough for the border to be in the centre, small trees can be planted in the middle, such as palms, the weeping fig or one of the scheffleras, surrounded by flowering shrubs, such as camellias and hibiscus.

Where pillars are used as a support for the conservatory, they can be covered with twining climbers like jasmine and *Philodendron scandens*, which would naturally use tree trunks to support themselves, and will require less work than on the flat surface offered by a house wall.

Water gardens

Water makes a good centrepoint and is particularly welcome in the heat of summer, as well as being good for the plants growing there. If a fountain is installed, there is no more beguiling sound on a hot day than the gentle splashing of water. The pool can be sunk in the floor and planted with varieties of waterlilies not normally grown in cool-temperate climates, or can be a simple affair such as a large tub filled with water and planted up.

Whatever the size, a fountain can be fitted to it. The smallest models are suitable for dining-tables, so there would be no difficulty with a conservatory pool, and with some clever construction work with rocks, a trickling stream could be added, to flow continually into the pool.

The curious forms and brilliant flowers of cacti and succulents, above, make a particularly striking display in a conservatory, as does the brilliant red-flowered Echinopsis *'Ruby'.*

Desert plants

If you are entertained and amused by the cactus family, as I am, and by the other desert plants usually known as succulents, there is no reason why a replica in miniature of a desert scene should not be created, perhaps in one corner, or along the back of a south-facing conservatory. Cacti are celebrated for their flowering capacity, while succulents are admired for the colourfulness and the bizarre shaping of their leaves, so a mixture of the two could be highly decorative. Obviously, other plants in the rest of the conservatory would have to accept the same temperature range and light, and could include, for instance, geraniums (*Pelargonium*), passionflowers (*Passiflora*), *Strobilanthes*, bougainvillea, *Strelitzia* and canna lilies.

Belonging to another large group of cacti, Parodia claviceps *(syn.* Notocactus claviceps*) has attractive large sulphur yellow flowers in summer. Ideally, cacti and succulents need to be displayed in an organized group, with a successional display of flowers.*

PLANT ACCESSORIES

T HE CONSERVATORY is designed as much for humans as for plant protection and the plants in it are performers rather than workhorses, earning their keep by their looks. The equipment used for plant cultivation should not be apparent; all should appear to have been "born" as adult flowering or foliage plants, decorative, uninfested by pest or disease, and tidy. In a conservatory the ways in which they arrived at this state need to be discreetly hidden (see pp. 166–7). In the meanwhile, there is a variety of ways in which the appearance of the plants can be enhanced.

A conservatory is for plants as well as humans; it is easy to lose sight of this fact and import a collection of furniture and artefacts which barely leave room for the plants. This would be a pity since an ideal environment in which to grow plants has been constructed, and it is well worth making use of it accordingly, if only because plants are so decorative.

There are a number of devices which can be employed to improve any display of plants. For instance, reflections can increase the apparent size of the conservatory and the number of plants in it, so a mirror or mirrors judiciously placed on a wall will double the interior space. To a lesser extent, a pool will do the same.

Screens are coming into their own, too, in conservatories as their usefulness is discovered for shielding draughts from necessarily open windows or ventilators, or for dividing areas with different uses. There are some distinctive and highly unusual designs available, including orientally inspired styles.

As with outdoor gardens, there is hardware available in the literal sense, in the form of statues and busts. How many you have and how you dispose them is entirely a personal judgement; much depends on the style of the conservatory and the type of plants. Some conservatories are now taking the form of the classic and much older orangeries, and these certainly lend themselves to displays of sculpture.

Treillage, or trellis-work is, like screens, also making a come-back, and wooden or plastic trellis coloured green or white – or just plain brown wood – can be obtained in various lengths and widths. It is attractive in its own right, uncovered, but is also ideal for supporting climbers, remembering that, for this purpose, it needs to be fixed so that there is a space between it and the wall, to allow air to circulate. Otherwise problems occur in the shape of pest infestations and diseases such as mildew.

Trellis can also be obtained which is purely decorative, and misleading, such as an arch, inviting one to walk through it, to the garden beyond, another *trompe l'oeil*, or into what is apparently an extension of the conservatory, except that the arch frames a mirror.

It is important, *when planning the arrangement of the plants, to consider varying the levels to get the best effects from the different groups. Tables and windowsills can be used for plant display, along with specialist conservatory accessories.*

Display supports

Unless they are large, most of the plants need to be put on a stand of some kind so that they are raised up off the floor. Originally, there was only the kind of support called staging, commonly used in greenhouses, but new designs do the same job while looking much more presentable.

Display staging

This consists of a framework of aluminium tubing on to which aluminium trays are fitted; the tubing is held together with black nylon joints that are easily put in place with a mallet. The staging can be supplied in standard designs with one, two or three steps; as a corner unit – one of the most useful – or as trough holders, again singly or in steps. Alternatively, you can ask for your own designs to be made up, to suit your needs.

Tables

There is a wide selection including purpose-built tables for plants, and household versions intended for drinks and meals. Tables for plants include white- or green-painted models in three tiers, with carved legs, each table top being smaller than the one below it. There are also plant benches nearly a metre (3ft) long, which can double up as coffee tables or seats.

Larger tables, like small kitchen tables or even marble-topped washstands, make good supports in lieu of staging,

An antique jardinière, left, filled with variegated ivy and small-flowered pelargoniums makes an attractive free-standing display, which can easily be moved around, as required, to bring a touch of colour to an area of the conservatory where the display is dying down.

where a block display of plants is wanted. A trolley is particularly convenient, as it allows you to move a group of plants about to provide a display wherever one is most wanted. Whatever is used, it should either be waterproof or be easy to mop up water from, and must also be easy to clean.

Hanging containers

Nothing adds more to the effect of a lush tropical jungle than overhead vegetation, and plant containers suspended from the roof can provide this in luxuriant profusion without any effort on your part. Hanging baskets in various diameters, starting at 30cm (12in), and made of galvanized wire, plastic-coated wire, recycled cellulose or compressed peat, have room for several plants, some of which should be trailing. They do, however, generally need twice-daily watering in the height of summer.

A better alternative to hanging baskets, and just as decorative, is a hanging pot. Like ordinary pots, they first appeared coloured in the standard terracotta, but are now supplied in a variety of pastel colours, and may also have coloured patterns on them. They are sold with their own plastic hangers that snap easily onto the rim of the pot, with a hook at the other end.

Some plants grow satisfactorily only when hanging in the air, for instance the stag's-horn fern (*Platycerium bifurcatum*), and many orchids, and for these you will find that rafts or platforms made of slatted wood are the most suitable, to which the special fibrous composts they need can be bound. Such composts absorb a great deal of water, rather like sponges, do not drip and require only moderate watering.

Wall containers and brackets

Another way of covering bare walls is to use containers that are attached directly to the brick or stonework. These are flat-backed and therefore semi-circular, mostly in terracotta, although some are made of reconstituted white marble. There are no drainage holes in these planters; they have to be tightly attached to the wall, and watering must be carefully controlled so that just enough is given to be soaked up by the compost.

An alternative to wall planters is to fix brackets to the wall, and put pots or other containers on or in them. There are wrought-iron styles, painted white or black, from which pots can be hung and there are also brackets that have a pot-shaped wire framework attached, into the base of which a pot saucer can be inserted.

Alternatively, if your conservatory has a Victorian feel you can use *jardinières* or small antique tables.

Other vertical supports and containers

Stands of various descriptions can be used. Some are wooden, carved to resemble doric columns, some are quite heavy, being made of terracotta or reconstituted stone; some are short, forming pedestals rather than columns. Whatever their shape, they provide a much more solid and chunky impression, while still making use of the third dimension.

Hanging baskets, above, often look more attractive surrounded by foliage, rather than dangling in isolation from the conservatory roof. Here pelargoniums have been combined with the spiky leaves of Trachycarpus fortunei.

In the plant group, right, a stone bust provides a focal point for a group of delicate-looking plants that would otherwise lack impact, making a perfect contrast with the drooping heads of fuchsia, the small blue flowers of Campanula *and the fine filigree leaves of* Grevillea robusta.

The style and form of containers and ornaments can make or mar a display of plants in a conservatory. They should be chosen with both the style of planting and the architecture of the conservatory in mind. In the conservatory, left, an old terracotta oil jar and a stone mask blend with the stone floor and the predominantly foliage plant grouping, the flowering accent provided by a cymbidium orchid.

Quite a different concept is the tall container with holes in the sides as well as in the top, such as the strawberry barrel. The herb or parsley pot can look particularly attractive planted up with the bromeliads called earthstars (*Cryptanthus*), house-leeks, sedums or rock plants.

Pots, troughs and tubs

Plain terracotta clay pots have come back into fashion and are being made again in some quantity. The bigger ones are also likely to be ornamented with swags and flowers in relief on the outside of the pot, with decorated rims, or made in different shapes, and with small or large pedestals, together with all sorts of other refinements.

There are specialist potters producing these containers (the addresses of whom are given on pp. 186–7). Amongst their collections are "baskets", boxes, oval pots, amphorae and sassanian jars, any of which can as well be used in a conservatory as out of doors.

Reconstituted stone was discovered to have considerable possibilities for moulding, and is now used to produce a range of decorated urns, troughs and planters.

Large tubs made of clay or stone will be heavy, even when empty, and, if needed, are better made of painted or unpainted timber (oak, teak or cedar are long-lasting) or a synthetic material which is light in weight. The classic four-sided orange-tree tubs are now being made again in wood, or copies can be obtained in white fibreglass, which are impossible to distinguish from the originals.

There are also many fibreglass planters and troughs, which exactly imitate the handsome outlines of the Italian carved lead originals, even to the dark grey colouring, while weighing a fraction of the amount.

Shelving

Most conservatories have an expanse of back wall, particularly if the conservatory is a lean-to design. One of the ways of dealing with this is to attach shelving. A width of 20–23cm (8–9in) for each shelf is usually about right; if you grow plants in containers with a larger diameter than this, the plants will become very large, and heavy.

The vertical spacing between shelves is important, too, since too narrow a gap will make it difficult to accommodate the majority of the plants as they grow and extend. To make anything of a display, a plant needs about 45cm (18in) headroom, though much depends on the kinds of plants you will be growing, as some are naturally small.

Portable shelving is an ideal way of providing a mobile divider, to separate a dining area from a sitting area, or to cut off the working part of the conservatory from the rest of it, or simply to define spaces.

Wooden shelving at differing heights and with varying widths helps to add variety to the plant display. Here, kalanchoe, canna lilies, begonias and camellia have been set off on a dense carpet of mind-your-own-business (Soleirolia soleirolii *syn.* Helxine soleirolii).

A-Z
DIRECTORY
OF PLANTS

Organized as a clear, simple reference guide to
the best and most popular conservatory plants.
Chosen with as wide a range of plants as possible
– from bromeliads to orchids, cacti to foliage
plants – it covers every aspect of each plant's
habit and cultivation needs, including size,
flowering season, light requirements, watering
and humidity, feeding, propagation, and any
special requirements that each plant has.
The information on watering, humidity, and light
requirements has been standardized to make it as
brief as possible. An explanation of the terms
used is given in the section on Conservatory
Management. (See page 153 for light and
humidity, and page 154 for watering).

A. 'Cannington Red'

A. *armata*

MALVACEAE
Abutilon

LEGUMINOSAE
Acacia

ONSERVATORY ABUTILONS are rapidly growing and easily cultivated flowering shrubs
from South America. They have distinctive, bell-like flowers and maple-like, lobed
leaves; flowering can continue all summer.

The popular cultivar A. 'Ashford Red' has been
derived from A. × *hybridum*. It has striking
rose-red flowers, 4cm (1½in) wide, throughout
the summer on a branching plant 1–2m (3–6ft)
tall. A. 'Cannington Red' is similar but with
golden variegated leaves. A. *megapotamicum* is
smaller, at about 90cm (3ft), evergreen, and with
red and yellow flowers, with protruding red
stamens. A. *m.* 'Variegatum' has golden-yellow
blotched leaves, and is a smaller and more
delicate, twiggy plant. Flowering for both is
continuous from mid-spring into autumn.

Light Good with some sun, but not midday sun.
Temperature Minimum 7°C (45°F) for short
periods only; 16–27°C (60–80°F) in summer.
Moisture Normal humidity; water freely while
growing, sparingly in winter while resting.
Feeding Liquid feed from early summer if in
soil-less compost.
Propagation Semi-hardwood cuttings in
midsummer.
Problems Greenfly; whitefly; red spider mite.
Special needs Deadhead regularly; cut away dead
growth, and cut back by about half, or to fit the
space available, in early spring.

HERE ARE WELL over 500 species of acacia,
many of them from Australia, but those
best known and most cultivated are the
mimosas, whose small fluffy balls of yellow
flowers cover the plants so attractively in late
winter and spring.

Acacia armata, the kangaroo thorn, has deep
golden-yellow flowers in mid-spring; its average
height in the wild is 3m (10ft), which is comparatively small, and makes it much easier to manage
than the silver wattle, A. *dealbata*, which will
make up to 30m (100ft) when fully grown. The
flowers of the latter species are scented, and can
be fully open from mid-winter right through until
spring. The flower clusters start to form in late
summer. The silver wattle has elegant, fern-like
leaves which fold up at night, showing their
silvery backs.

Light As much as possible.
Temperature Minimum 4°C (40°F), but can be
lower for short periods if dryish; 16–27°C (60–
80°F) in summer.
Moisture Normal humidity; water moderately
from spring to autumn, sparingly in winter.
Feeding Liquid feed occasionally in summer.
Propagation Heel cuttings in summer under
frame.
Problems Scale insects (rarely); yellow leaves
from too much water or cold.
Special needs Cut hard back from beginning in
late spring to prevent legginess.

Achimenes hybrid

A. capillus-veneris

GESNERIACEAE
Achimenes

THESE SMALL, easy-to-cultivate plants have beautiful open trumpet-shaped flowers mostly in blue, purple and pink, and shades of these colours, though yellow-, orange-, white- and red-flowered hybrids are available. Some hybrids are upright growing (to about 30cm/12in), and some are trailing, looking pretty in hanging containers. Flowering starts about three months after planting, and continues throughout summer. Currently there are more than 50 hybrids available: the following is just a small selection: 'Camberwell Beauty': pink; 'Clouded Yellow': pale yellow with darker markings; 'Margarita': white (1856); 'Pendant Purple': deep purple, trailing; 'Prima Donna': vivid coral red; 'Topsy': light blue.

Light Good but not direct sun.
Temperature Minimum 10°C (50°F); 16–27°C (60–80°F) in summer.
Moisture Normal humidity; water freely; do not allow to dry out.
Feeding In late summer and early autumn with potash-high fertilizer.
Propagation From tubers; choose the biggest; plant in early spring about 2.5cm (1in) deep, three to a 10-cm (4-in) pot, in 16°C (60°F); water well with warm water; growth appears about three weeks later.
Problems Greenfly occasionally.
Special needs Nip out the tips of shoots at third pair of leaves for extra bushiness; supply split canes for support.

ADIANTACEAE
Adiantum

THE MAIDENHAIR FERN, *A. capillus-veneris*, belongs to this genus, and each delicate leaflet, or pinnule, is shaped like a miniature fan, forming a lacy frond borne on a wiry black stem. It grows to about 23cm (9in), and arches over when fully grown. *A. raddianum* looks much like it but has even more delicately cut leaves and needs a minimum temperature of 13°C (55°F); there is also a scented form called *A. r.* 'Fragrantissimum'. *A. hispidulum* is sometimes called the rose maidenhair, as its young fronds are a pronounced pink, forked at their base into three or four segments; it needs more warmth.

Light Shade or good light.
Temperature Minimum 4°C (40°F) or 10°C (50°F) depending on species; 16–27°C (60–80°F) in summer.
Moisture Very high/humidity, with frequent misting as well (the fronds dry up rapidly without a really moist atmosphere); water freely in temperatures above 27°C (80°F); sparingly in winter; otherwise normally.
Propagation Short sections of rhizome, half buried, in early to mid-spring; spores spread naturally in damp warm conditions.
Problems Scale insect; mealy bug; brown withered fronds from dry air or lack of water; sudden collapse from drop in temperature or too much water.
Special needs Acid compost; provide drainage material 2.5cm (1in) deep in base of container.

A. africanus

BROMELIACEAE
Aechmea

ONE OF THE MOST commonly cultivated aechmeas, *A. fasciata*, an epiphyte from Brazil, is extremely colourful. The grey-green, strap-shaped leaves which can be up to 60cm (24in) long are transversely banded with silver and form a stiff, somewhat upright and open rosette 30–38cm (12–15in) tall, from which it derives its common name, the urn plant. From the centre of this rosette the flowering stem emerges when the plant is fully mature – usually about two to three years old. It carries a bright pink head of bracts about 15cm (6in) long which remains colourful for many weeks. When it finally dies, the parent plant dies too, but by then offsets will have been produced from the base. These can be detached once they have acquired roots, normally when they are about 15cm (6in) tall. They can be potted up, to flower approximately 18 months later.

There are two variegated forms of *Aechmea*: *A. f.* 'Albomarginata', which has cream-coloured borders to each leaf and *A. f.* 'Variegata' in which the cream stripes run vertically up the leaves.

Light Good.
Temperature Minimum 10°C (50°F), preferably higher; 16–30°C (60–85°F) in summer.
Moisture Normal humidity; keep centre of rosette (funnel) full of water from spring to autumn; quarter-full in winter; use soft water at air temperature.
Feeding Liquid feed occasionally via the funnel.
Propagation By offsets in 7.5cm (3in) pots of compost. These should be potted up once they have grown to their final size of 12–15cm (5–6in). Try to keep them as warm as possible in summer – for example, around 21–30°C (70–85°F), to ensure eventual flowering.
Problems Cold conditions cause discoloured leaves with brown markings; occasionally susceptible to scale insect.
Special needs See general bromeliad cultivation, p. 164.

A. fasciata, opposite

LILIACEAE
Agapanthus

THE GENERIC NAME comes from the Greek *agape* (love) and *anthos* (flower) although the lily-of-the-Nile, as it is commonly called, is in fact a beautiful flowering perennial from South Africa. It is late-flowering, in late summer, lasting several weeks. It needs winter protection from frost, but is nearly hardy, particularly the deciduous forms, although the majority of the species are evergreen.

Agapanthus africanus produce a mass of strap-shaped leaves, and many flowering stems 45–75cm (18–30in) long. The tubular flowers are blue, though some hybrids are white-flowered, and are held in clusters at the end of the stems. Even a single plant makes a magnificent show. The Headbourne hybrids are almost hardy, with flowers in varying shades of blue.

Light As good as possible.
Temperature Minimum 4°C (40°F); 16–30°C (60–85°F) in summer.
Moisture Water freely in summer, but allow to become almost dry in winter.
Feeding Liquid feed from early summer if in soil-less compost.
Propagation By division in spring.
Problems Leaf spot – rarely.
Special needs Good drainage of compost, together with drainage material in base of container; deadhead.

A. americana 'Mediopicta'

A G A V A C E A E
Agave

COMMONLY CALLED the century plant, because it was originally thought to flower only once every hundred years, *A. americana*, in fact, flowers about every seven years and then dies. *A. a.* 'Mediopicta' has a wide central yellow stripe marking each leaf, on the margin of which there are short pointed teeth – the leaf also ends in a sharp spine. There is also a variety called *A. a.* 'Marginata', with irregularly marked yellow leaf margins.

Rosette-shaped in habit, these variegated agaves grow very slowly, and can conveniently be grown under cover, unlike the plain green-leaved ones which are larger, with a spread of 1.8m (6ft).

A native of Mexico, it also grows in other parts of the world with a suitably hot and arid climate.

Light As much as possible.
Temperature Minimum 4°C (40°F); 16–30°C (60–85°F) in summer.
Moisture Normal humidity; water moderately while growing; keep almost dry in winter while resting.
Feeding Liquid feed very occasionally in summer.
Propagation Use basal offsets.
Problems Discolouration or wilting while resting indicates over-watering; slow growth and a "grey" look may be caused by root aphis or scale insect on the under-surface of the leaves.
Special needs Soil compost with extra grit; drainage layer in base of container; repot every four to five years.

A. cathartica

A. comosus variegatus

APOCYNACEAE
Allamanda

THE GOLDEN TRUMPET vine, *A. cathartica*, is one of the most attractive of the South American climbers, with evergreen leaves and bright yellow, funnel-shaped flowers from early to midsummer; they are 7.5cm (3in) wide in the cultivar *A. c.* 'Grandiflora'. It twines to a height of about 3m (10ft), maybe more in ideal conditions, and will make a good job of decorating a pillar.

It is not difficult to grow, provided it has the warmth it needs in winter. It will do best if planted in a border, otherwise it needs a tub at least 30cm (12in) in diameter, preferably more. If the stems grow particularly vigorously, they can be trained along the underside of the conservatory roof to produce an attractive display.

Light Good, with some direct sun daily, if possible.
Temperature Minimum 13°C (55°F); 16–30°C (60–85°F) in summer.
Moisture High humidity; water moderately from spring to summer, less in autumn, sparingly in winter.
Feeding Liquid feed from early summer if using soil-less compost.
Propagation Tip or hardwood stem cuttings in spring in 21–27°C (70–80°F).
Special needs Night temperatures must not drop below minimum in spring and autumn; in late winter cut back previous season's new growth to within two leaf-joints; alternatively prune by half only, if there is plenty of space for the plant.

BROMELIACEAE
Ananas

PINEAPPLE FRUITS ARE obtained from the plain-leaved species, *A. comosus*, of this tropical plant, and indeed from the variegated form *A. c. variegatus* though the former is used for commercial cropping. As a bromeliad, *A. c. variegatus* has the rosette of leaves common to such plants; they are green with a wide, irregularly creamy-yellow edge, flushed with pink. The leaves are about 90cm (3ft) long, and they are narrow and spiny.

The pink-purple flowers in late spring to early summer are small. From the cone-shaped 7.5–15cm (3–6in) long flowerhead small pink fruits develop, edible but bland, when the plants are about two years old. They mature five to seven months after setting if temperatures are kept continuously high – a minimum of 18°C (65°F) while resting, and in the range of 32°C (90°F) in summer – together with high humidity.

Light Good with some daily sun.
Temperature Minimum 16°C (60°F), but as high as possible while growing.
Moisture Very high humidity; water the roots, freely in summer, moderately in winter; also keep the water level topped up in the funnel.
Feeding Liquid feed from start of flowering until the fruit matures.
Propagation By basal offsets as for *Aechmea* (p. 51).
Problems Mealy bug; scale insect; basal rot from cold and/or wet compost.
Special needs Rich, acid compost; no draughts.

A. flavidus

AMARYLLIDACEAE
Anigozanthos

IF YOU LIKE ODDITIES, the kangaroo paw from Australia is an interesting genus. The leaves of *A. flavidus* are like iris leaves in miniature, and the roots are fleshy, but the flower consists of a bent tube with a collection of petals at its extremity, resembling a hand at the end of an arm. A cluster of four or five flowers is carried in late spring, each on a stem, with several clusters at the end of each main flowering stem.

In this species, the 4cm (1½in) long flowers are yellow-green and reddish, and the whole flower-head, besides being unusual in its own right, seems a most unlikely one to emerge from the leaves described. Height in the wild is about 1.2m (4ft), but about 60cm (2ft) in containers.

Light Good, with some sun, especially while growing.
Temperature Minimum 4°C (40°F), 16–30°C (60–85°F) in summer.
Moisture Water freely in spring and summer, moderately in autumn and winter.
Feeding Liquid feed from midsummer.
Propagation By seed or division in spring.
Problems Slow to establish in containers after dividing; fleshy roots need careful handling.
Special needs Grows best in soil-containing compost; deadhead if seed is not required.

ARACEAE
Anthurium

THE FLAMINGO FLOWER is brilliant red and has a central, twisted yellow-orange spike. Besides being exotic in colour, the flower of this herbaceous perennial is exotic in formation, too. It is surrounded by a scarlet blade called a spathe, which is wax-like, flat and roundish, and carried on a long stem. The spike consists of the true flowers, tiny and tightly packed.

The species *A. scherzerianum*, from Costa Rica, flowers from late winter to midsummer, and grows into a plant about 38cm (15in) tall and as much across. Its leaves add to its attraction, being dark green, oblong and up to 20cm (8in) long by 5cm (2in) wide. Varieties of it are rose-pink or white.

Another beautiful species, *A. andreanum*, known appropriately enough as the painter's palette, is less easy to grow. It has a 10cm (4in) long heart-shaped bright crimson spathe, with a straight cream-coloured spike, and the whole flowerhead is carried on a stem 30cm (12in) long in summer, lasting for several weeks.

Anthurium crystallinum has spectacularly veined large dark green leaves. It makes a plant about 75cm (2½ft) tall.

Light Good in summer; good with some sun in winter.
Temperature Minimum 16°C (60°F); 16–30°C (60–85°F) in summer.
Moisture High humidity, mist overhead above 24°C (75°F); water freely when growing, moderately at other times.
Feeding Liquid feed while plants are actively growing.
Propagation Divide in midwinter or early spring, and keep divisions at 24–27°C (75–80°F); keep moist until obviously growing.
Problems Yellowing leaf edges from cold/dry air; lack of flowers, curling of leaves or brown leaf tips from insufficient humidity; brown leaf spots from minor fungus disease.
Special needs Soil-less compost with a half-part of sphagnum moss added; grow in pans or baskets with drainage material in the base; use soft, lukewarm water when watering; no bright summer sun; avoid injury to the roots when dividing; if flower spikes of *A. andreanum* begin to bend, tie them to very thin stakes with soft or plastic-covered wire.

A. scherzerianum, opposite

CACTACEAE

Aporocactus

A CURIOUS CACTUS, *A. flagelliformis* is usually found growing on rocks or trees, rather than directly out of the ground, though it still grows happily in conventional cactus compost. Its common name is the rat's tail cactus, and indeed its long cylindrical hanging stems make it quite unlike the majority of cacti in appearance. It was thought to have completely disappeared from the wild, so its origin was not known until it was rediscovered in Mexico.

The crimson tubular flowers, about 2.5cm (1in) wide at the mouth and 5cm (2in) long, appear in mid- to late spring, and each lasts for several days, giving an overall flowering period of three or four weeks. It occasionally produces round red fruits covered in bristles.

The stems can grow to about 1.8m (6ft) in the wild, although in cultivation they are generally much shorter.

Light As much as possible.
Temperature Minimum of 7°C (45°F), 16–27°C (60–80°F) in summer.
Moisture Normal humidity; water normally in summer; keep compost just moist in winter.
Feeding Use high-potash liquid feed between midsummer and early autumn.
Propagation By rooted offsets, which look like small new stems.
Problems Mealy bug; shrivelling roots from lack of water or cold.
Special needs Cactus compost; does well in hanging containers; see also section on cacti, p. 165.

ARAUCARIACEAE

Araucaria

T HE COMMON NAME of *A. heterophylla* is the Norfolk Island pine, derived from its home, a tiny Pacific island belonging to Australia. It is related to the monkey puzzle (*A. araucana*), though it is much more graceful, its frond-like branches held out horizontally, and regularly arranged around the trunk in tiers. In fact, it resembles a fern with a central trunk. In the wild it becomes a 60m (220ft) tall tree, but in containers does not grow appreciably beyond 1.8m (6ft), making a good-sized specimen without becoming unwieldy. Its awl-shaped leaves are unlike the conventional conifer needles, and are up to 1.5cm (½in) long.

Light Light shade in summer; good light in winter.
Temperature Minimum 4°C (40°F); plenty of ventilation to lower the temperature to below 27°C (80°F) in summer, if possible.
Moisture Normal humidity; water moderately while growing, sparingly in winter.
Feeding Only needed if grown in soil-less compost, from midsummer.
Propagation Difficult – by seed sown in autumn or spring.
Problems Leaves falling or discolouring from too much warmth/sun/dry atmosphere, although the lowest branches fall naturally on old plants.
Special needs Repot every three to four years; keep slightly potbound to maintain juvenile growth habit; prune to shape if necessary, in late summer.

A. setaceus 'Nanus'

A. elatior

LILIACEAE
Asparagus

APART FROM THE common edible asparagus, there are several ornamental kinds. *A. densiflorus* 'Sprengeri' is the one with long trailing stems covered with fine, narrow leaves, looking rather like green tinsel. The stems can be anything up to 60cm (2ft). *A. setaceus* 'Nanus' (syn. *A. plumosus* 'Nanus') is the florist's asparagus fern. It is the complete opposite, a somewhat rounded plant with wiry stems about 30cm (12in) tall and horizontal, triangular fronds made up of leaves finer than needles. The fronds are produced at different levels, owing to the irregular length of the stems, and the whole plant has an air of delicacy, setting off the blooms of flowering plants such as freesias and nerines. Both forms of asparagus are evergreen.

Light Good, or light shade.
Temperature Minimum 10°C (50°F), 16–30°C (60–85°F) in summer.
Moisture Normal humidity; water normally while growing, sparingly in winter while resting.
Feeding Liquid feed from midsummer if in soil-less compost.
Propagation By division in spring or summer.
Problems Greenfly if in too dark a position; yellowing and/or falling leaves from dry compost/high temperatures/dry air.
Special needs Do not overwater, but keep compost moist; soil-containing compost preferable, with one part extra grit added; keep mature plants in containers 15–25cm (6–10in) in diameter; prune only to fit the space available.

LILIACEAE
Aspidistra

THE ASPIDISTRA acquired the common name of the cast-iron plant because it could withstand practically any adverse environmental condition. *A. elatior* was especially popular with the Victorians since it survived the pollution caused by coal fires, oil lamps and gas mantles amongst other things.

The handsome leaves are dark green, leathery and shiny, and can be as much as 50cm (20in) long, ending in a point. A mature, well-grown plant can be nearly 90cm (3ft) wide, and about 38cm (15in) tall. If you like variegated leaves, *A. e.* 'Variegata' has leaves irregularly striped and spotted with cream.

The aspidistra can flower unexpectedly from late winter to early spring. Its flowers are a muddy purple, barely rising above the surface of the compost among the leaf stems, and only about 1cm (½in) wide. Flowering is by no means frequent – once every seven years is normal.

Light Good to shade.
Temperature Minimum just above frost; summer preferably 16–24°C (60–75°F).
Moisture Normal humidity; water normally while growing, moderately in winter.
Feeding Liquid feed occasionally in summer.
Propagation In spring, by dividing the rhizomes and putting each division with a leaf attached in a 15cm (6in) container.
Problems Brown leaf spotting (rarely) caused by extreme overwatering; will die if repotted too frequently.
Special needs Repot only every four to five years.

A. nidus

Asplenium

Two species of this plant are easily grown and decorative: one is *A. bulbiferum*, the mother spleenwort or hen and chieken fern. The feathery fronds can be 30–60cm (1–2ft) long, and 30cm (12in) wide at the base, narrowing to a pointed tip. They are very feathery in appearance; as the fronds mature they develop bulbils in such quantity that the fronds are weighed down.

The second species is *A. nidus*, the bird's-nest fern, which has fronds that look exactly like the leaf-blades of conventional plants. Each is a shiny light green, up to 1.2m (4ft) long in the wild, and 20cm (8in) wide, tapering to a point, and narrowing to a short stem. All the leaves come from the base, forming a kind of giant rosette, and emerge from a fibrous base, the "bird's-nest".

Light Light shade or good light.
Temperature Minimum 10°C (50°F) for *A. bulbiferum*; minimum 16°C (60°F), for *A. nidus*; 16–30°C (60–85°F) in summer for both.
Moisture High humidity; water freely in summer, moderately in winter.
Feeding Liquid feed from early summer.
Propagation *A. bulbiferum* by plantlets produced from bulbils at any time; *A. nidus* by division in spring; both by spores.
Problems Scale insect; browning of fronds from dry air or dry compost.
Special needs Humidity is important – either mist or stand out in warm summer showers; acid compost.

B. 'Burle Marx, B. rex, B. masoniana

B. rex

BEGONIACEAE

Begonia

THE BEGONIA family is a large and diverse one, cultivated both for its foliage and its flowers. Some begonia flowers are amongst the most richly coloured there are, while foliage varieties add to their charms, and some species and varieties flower in winter.

Begonias were named after Michel Begon, a French patron of botany who lived during the seventeenth century. They like damp/cool to tropically-hot tropical conditions, and are found wherever these obtain, except Australia. One of their characteristics is their asymmetrically sided leaves; most of their flowers are small except for the much bred, large, double-flowered ones, which grow from a tuber. Although their root systems vary between tuberous, rhizomatous and fibrous, their needs for temperature, light and humidity are similar; water requirements do vary depending on type.

Foliage begonias

Among the begonias grown for their ornamental leaves, there are small, bushy, rounded types, and tall shrubby kinds, the "cane" begonias; they are patched, veined or spotted with different colours on a mostly green background though some appear to have lost this colour completely.

SMALL SPECIES There are some easily grown, tidy plants in this group; *B. bowerae*, the eyelash begonia, is one, with deep green, rather rounded leaves, about 2.5–5cm (1–2in) wide. Black or dark brown markings trim the leaf edges, from which grow the long curling hairs responsible for its name. In winter it has small white flowers in clusters. There is a hybrid of it, called *B.*

'Cleopatra', with much larger leaves, patched with a metallic brown and edged with hairs. It has the bonus of small pink flowers in spring.

There are various other hybrids, in particular the Caribbean Islands Mixed, of which *B.* 'Cleopatra' is one, whose leaves are spotted and blotched in various shades of brown. They have been specially bred for growing under cover, and grow quickly to about 15 by 30cm (6 by 12in).

The "iron cross" begonia, *B. masoniana*, has deeply corrugated and somewhat hairy leaves, and its green colouring is overlaid in the centre with a dark chocolate marking in the shape of the German medal, hence the common name. Fully grown leaves are about 12.5cm (5in) long and nearly as wide.

The outstanding coloured-leaved begonias in this group are the Rex begonia hybrids. The original *B. rex* came from Assam, where it grows amongst rocks, and was discovered in 1858; it has olive-green leaves with a metallic sheen and a broad white stripe close to the leaf margin. It has been crossed repeatedly with other species, in particular *B. decora*, which introduced the shades of crimson, bronze and pink to the markings.

The heart-shaped and lobed leaves can be as much as 30cm (12in) long, and plants up to 45cm (18in) wide, and about 23cm (9in) tall.

Colouring consists of infinite combinations of rose, green, wine red, maroon, pink, purple, yellow and silver, and the plants will carry pink or white flowers in summer, though these are best removed. Some hybrids are quite different, in that they are simply light or dark green and silvery white, such as *B.* 'Silver Queen'.

B. scharfii

All these small leafy plants are rhizomatous – they have thick, fleshy, creeping underground stems just below the compost or soil surface, on which the true roots are carried.

CANE BEGONIAS The bush or cane begonias are large plants, growing quickly to 1.5 or 1.8m (5 or 6ft) tall in appropriately sized tubs, 30cm (12in) diameter and upwards, and spreading to 60–75cm (2–2½ft) wide. Mainly grown for their leaves, some of them do have clusters of small flowers as well, in summer or winter. All those described here are fibrous-rooted.

Begonia coccinea is the angel's-wing begonia, with shiny green leaves, edged with red and, in its hybrid *B.* 'Président Carnot', large white spots on the upper leaf surface. Light red flowers in large clusters last from late spring into autumn.

Begonia scharfii (syn. *B. haageana*) has such large leaves, between 20 and 25cm (8 and 10in) long, that it is called the elephant's-ears begonia; the olive-green upper surface is veined with red and

backed by a deep red reverse, the red being echoed in the stems, and the whole plant being covered in short white hairs. Height can rapidly achieve 1.5m (5ft). From late autumn to mid-spring it produces large clusters of light pink flowers, and altogether it makes a handsome and useful plant.

Begonia maculata has white-spotted olive-green leaves, coloured red on the underside; it is a smaller plant, with 17.5cm (7in) long leaves and a height of about 90cm (3ft) only, decorated in summer with clusters of pale pink or white flowers.

Flowering begonias

The outstanding varieties in this group are undoubtedly the large, double-flowered hybrids, which grow from tubers. These are the show begonias, as much as 60cm (2ft) tall, and with 15cm (6in) wide flowers, brilliantly coloured in shades of red, orange, yellow and crimson, as well

Flowering begonias   *B. sutherlandii*

as white. The average plant is, however, not as large as this, being about 30cm (12in) tall, and with flowers 7.5–12.5cm (3–5in) wide. There are some particularly pretty varieties with picotee edges. Named varieties are available, or unnamed mixed hybrids can be obtained.

Another variation on these tuberous flowering begonias is the pendulous group, which have long drooping stems with single or double pointed petal flowers in a range of colours. They also flower throughout the summer, and are one of the best of the "air" plants for hanging containers. The latest offering amongst these has flowers on sideshoots as well as at the stem ends.

RIEGER BEGONIAS This is a new strain of begonias from Germany, which have been cross-bred from the Hiemalis (winter-flowering) types. They have a mass of small flowers about 2.5cm (1in) wide, usually double, though single ones are available, in dark and light pink, red, yellow, crimson and orange, and a lot of glossy, densely packed foliage; height and spread are about 23cm (9in), and they can remain in flower all year. All are fibrous rooted.

B. fuchsioides is one of many attractive fibrous-rooted species – its flowers mimic those of the fuchsia to a remarkable degree and indeed, the whole habit of growth is reminiscent, too. Height can be 1.2m (4ft), though is often less, and the glossy, deeply toothed leaves, 4cm (1½in) long, are profusely produced. Flowering is in winter and spring, when a lot of pink or red flowers appear on drooping stems.

B. sutherlandii is not often seen, though easy to grow, and is rather different from the others. It grows from a tuber to produce deep red, slender, branching stems arching over to form a mound like a crinoline about 30cm (12in) wide and nearly as high. Small, single, bright orange flowers appear in early summer and continue until well into autumn; it is almost hardy. The leaves are pointed and light green, also with red stems.

Light Light shade to good light; avoid direct-sun.
Temperature Minimum 10–13°C (50–55°F), preferably the higher; *B. sutherlandii*: minimum 7°C (45°F); 16–27°C (60–80°F) in summer.
Moisture High humidity in summer with misting on very hot days; normal in winter; water moderately in summer, sparingly in winter for most fibrous and rhizomatous-rooted kinds, except the large cane begonias, which need to be watered freely for most of the year, the exception being from late winter to mid spring. Tuberous-rooted varieties need watering freely while flowering. If in doubt with begonias, give less rather than more.
Feeding Heavily flowering kinds need liquid feeding from about four weeks after flowering until they start to die down in autumn.
Propagation Tuberous and fibrous-rooted begonias: seed sown in 18–21°C (65–70°F) in late winter to spring; *B. sutherlandii*: detach bulbils from stems and plant in summer; leaf cuttings for ornamental-leaved type; soft stem cuttings for large-flowered hybrids and fibrous-rooted kinds, including Rieger begonias; division in spring for rhizomatous begonias – each section should have several growing points or "eyes" on it.
Problems Mildew; fungal tuber rot from overwatering; grey mould; leaf withering if dry and in low temperatures; greenfly; whitefly; scale insect; mealy bug and broad mite; in general, however, main troubles are mildew and tuber rot.
Special needs Start tubers in late winter-early spring in 16–18°C (60–65°F) and transfer to permanent containers when shoots are 1.5–2.5cm (½–1in) tall; keep dry and store in containers when they have died down at 10°C (50°F); supply stakes to support cane and large, double-flowered begonias; cut back cane begonias to fit space from early to mid spring, and to remove dead growth.

B. nutans

B. gibbum

BROMELIACEAE
Billbergia

NONE OF THE bromeliads is really difficult to grow, and *B. nutans*, an epiphyte from Eastern Brazil, must be the easiest of them all. It has the rather fanciful common name of queen's tears, and is grown purely for its flowers, unlike the majority of the genus. The familiar rosette of leaves is tall, to about 30cm (12in), the grass-like arching leaves being long and narrow. Handle the plant with caution as there are small spines on the leaf edges.

The flowerheads appear in mid- to late spring and consist of a narrow sheath of rose-pink bracts, from which the long dangling flowers emerge, coloured yellow, navy blue, green and pink, lasting for several weeks. The bracts remain colourful for longer but, as with all the family, the plant dies after flowering, and is replaced by the offsets produced prolifically round its base.

Light Good, with some sun.
Temperature Minimum 7°C (45°F), but will survive light frost for short periods if the compost is dry; 16–30°C (60–85°F) in summer.
Moisture Normal humidity; water moderately in summer, sparingly in winter; not needed in funnel.
Feeding Liquid feed after flowering until autumn.
Propagation Remove offsets with roots attached, and pot in summer.
Problems Food shortage results in yellow-green leaves and no flowers; no sun, no flowers; cold plus wet compost rots the base of the rosette.
Special needs Bromeliad compost; regular feeding; deadhead.

BLECHNACEAE
Blechnum

A LARGE AND PRETTY fern from New Caledonia, *B. gibbum* needs a lot of warmth and humidity, but not a great deal of water. The fronds have a maximum length of 90cm (3ft), so a fully grown plant can be nearly 1.8m (6ft) wide; the fronds tend to arch up a little before spreading out. All come from a central crown which develops into a short trunk as the plant matures. Height will eventually be about 90–105cm (3–3½ft). In effect it becomes a miniature tree fern, and is a good plant for creating an "instant jungle" effect.

There is another species from Brazil, *B. brasiliense*, which has fronds 1.2m (4ft) long, and a shorter trunk, and which needs higher temperatures. A variant of this species has crisped and waved edges to the fronds, making it even more attractive, but neither species nor variety is in wide circulation.

Light Light shade or good light.
Temperature Minimum 7°C (45°F) for *B. gibbum*; 13°C (55°F) for *B. brasiliense*; 16–30°C (60–85°F) in summer for both.
Moisture High humidity, with frequent misting in summer as well; water moderately in summer; sparingly in winter.
Feeding Liquid feed little and often while growing.
Propagation Divide, or use spores, in spring.
Problems Scale insect; browning of fronds from dry air; yellowing or pale fronds from too much heat or sun, and insufficient nutrient.
Special needs Does best in loosely packed compost; prefers leafmould to peat in compost mixture.

B. 'Alexandra'

NYCTAGINACEAE
Bougainvillea

THE SPECIES AND varieties in cultivation come from Brazil, *B. glabra* being the commonest, with its rosy purple "flowers". The colourfulness of the bougainvilleas comes, in fact, from the papery bracts which surround the true flowers. Shades of red, purple, pink, and rosy purple are common, but there are also orange-flowered varieties, such as *B.* 'Mrs Helen McLean' (syn. *B.* 'Afterglow' (syn. *B.* 'Orange King'), a yellow one called *B.* 'Albo Ora', and a white one with a pink blush.

Bougainvilleas need plenty of rooting space, so they are ideal plants for a conservatory border. Otherwise 30cm (12in) diameter tubs will be needed. They will also need to be tied in to strong supports, preferably pillars or trellis.

Light As much as possible to flower freely.
Temperature Minimum 7°C (45°F); 16–32°C (60–90°F) in summer.
Moisture Normal humidity, but mist in the hottest part of summer; water freely while flowering, sparingly in winter.
Feeding Liquid feed from early summer until mid-autumn.
Propagation Heel cuttings in summer, with compost heated to 21°C (70°F).
Problems Red spider mite; mealy bug; scale insect; whitefly.
Special needs Light is important at all times; spur prune, or cut back new growth by half any time between early and the end of late winter.

B. longiflora

B. speciosa 'Alba'

RUBIACEAE

Bouvardia

RARELY SEEN AS a houseplant because it needs a lot of light to flower, *B. × domestica* will produce its fragrant flower clusters with abandon in a conservatory so that they cover the whole plant. This is a hybrid, so the flowers vary in colour from plant to plant and may be pale pink, white or light red. Clustered and tubular, they are in season for several months from midsummer until mid-autumn, so they are good value-for-space plants. Height is about 60cm (2ft), and the plant is nearly as wide as it is tall.

There is also a white-flowered species, *B. longiflora* which is very similar, but which blooms in winter.

Light Good, with some daily sun, but avoid midday sun in summer.
Temperature Minimum 10°C (50°F); 16–30°C (60–85°F) in summer.
Moisture Normal humidity, except in summer when it should be high; water freely between spring and the end of flowering; sparingly in winter.
Feeding Occasionally in summer.
Propagation Tip cuttings in early spring in 18°C (65°F).
Problems Red spider mite (if plants are in too hot and too dry an atmosphere); greenfly; mealy bug.
Special needs Plants must be well pinched, otherwise they are sparsely flowered; plenty of winter light; in late winter, cut back last year's new growth to leave about 3cm (1in) of stem; pinch out new shoots until early summer to make plant bushy and well shaped.

SOLANACEAE

Browallia

THE BUSH VIOLET, *B. speciosa*, is an easily grown annual from Colombia that is spectacular in flower, so it can be forgiven for being short-lived. The light blue-violet flowers have open faces at the end of a narrow tube and, although they come singly and die quickly, are produced in such profusion that the plant is constantly covered. Height is about 60cm (2ft). There is also an attractive white form, *B.s.* 'Alba'. Although *Browallia* can be bought in flower, it can easily be grown from seed sown in autumn.

Light Good with some sun daily.
Temperature 16–17°C (60–63°F) while flowering; minimum of 10°C (50°F) for winter seedlings, otherwise 16–24°C (60–75°F).
Moisture Normal humidity; water freely while flowering; moderately in winter.
Feeding Liquid feed from midsummer to mid-autumn.
Propagation Sow seed from mid-winter to early spring in 13°C (55°F), or in early autumn.
Problems Greenfly; bud/flower drop from lack of water or overly high temperatures, or dry air.
Special needs Good winter light for seedlings; for a bushier plant, remove shoot tips occasionally.

B. suaveolens 'Lutea'

SOLANACEAE
Brugmansia

THESE PLANTS (formerly called *Datura*) have very large, trumpet-shaped flowers at least 15cm (6in) long, often much more, making them exceptionally eye-catching and handsome plants. They have correspondingly large leaves and grow rapidly in spring and summer – if you have a border in the conservatory, plant them there, otherwise use a tub 45cm (18in) or more in diameter. Beware though – daturas are poisonous and the seeds in particular should be kept away from children and pets.

Brugmansia suaveolens is the most well-known species, whose 30cm (12in) long white trumpet-shaped flowers open in late summer and early autumn, and are strongly scented. Its leaves are the same length and, in its native habitat of Mexico, the plant makes around 4.6m (15ft); in a container it is more likely to be 1.8m (6ft) tall.

Most of the plants in the genus have white flowers, but in *B. sanguinea* they are orange-red.

Flowering is in mid- to late summer. The softly hairy leaves are evergreen and height is a good deal less than the previous species – 90 or 120cm (3 or 4ft) in a container of 30 or 38cm (12 or 15in) diameter. There is also a yellow form, *B. s.* 'Lutea' which is well scented.

Light Good
Temperature Minimum 4°C (40°F); 16–30°C (60–85°F) in summer.
Moisture Normal humidity; water normally from spring to autumn, sparingly in winter.
Feeding Liquid feed from early summer into autumn.
Propagation Tip stem cuttings 15cm (6in) long in spring in 18–24°C (65–75°F).
Problems Greenfly; whitefly; red spider mite, if atmosphere/soil insufficiently moist; scale insect; capsids.
Special needs Keep cool and provide plenty of light in winter; cut back after flowering or in late winter to leave 5cm (2in) or so of stem.

B. pauciflora 'Macrantha'

SOLANACEAE
Brunfelsia

B RILLIANTLY COLOURED and large-flowered plants grown in containers and under cover, in other words cultivated, they are generally assumed to be hybrids, but many are, in fact, native to their respective countries, where they may be regarded as weeds. *B. pauciflora* (syn. *B. calycina*), an evergreen shrub from Brazil, is no exception. It has beautifully fragrant flowers, produced practically all year round, but most profusely in summer and autumn. One plant will have flowers in three colours – purple, lilac and white – as they open, mature and fade. Each flower is flat and open, 5cm (2in) wide, carried in large clusters. A good form, *B. p.* 'Macrantha' has even larger flowers.

The plant grows slowly to 60cm (2ft) tall.

Light Light shade in summer, good light with some sun in winter.
Temperature Minimum 10°C (50°F), 16–30°C (60–85°F) in summer.
Moisture Normal humidity, but needs misting regularly in temperatures of 21°C (70°F) and above; water freely from mid-spring to mid-autumn; sparingly in winter.
Feeding Liquid feed from midsummer to the end of early autumn.
Propagation Tip cuttings in summer in heated compost.
Problems Scale insect; mealy bug.
Special needs Pot firmly; provide drainage in the pot base; maintain bushiness by light pruning in late winter.

ARACEAE
Caladium

T HE CALADIUMS are members of the aroid family, which also contains the Swiss cheese plant and the calla lily. The varieties of *C. × hortulanum* have huge, tissue-paper-like, arrowhead-shaped leaves that are amongst the most beautiful of any foliage plant, delicately veined or marked with crimson, wine-red, pink, purple or dark green in a fantastic variety of combinations. Inhabitants naturally of the Brazilian jungles, they need high temperatures and a lot of humidity. Spread and height can be 60 to 90cm (2 to 3ft), but is usually less; the leaves die down in autumn, when the tuberous rootstock becomes dormant.

Light Good, not mid-day sun in summer.
Temperature Minimum 16°C (60°F); 21–32°C (70–90°F) in summer.
Moisture High humidity at all times; additional daily misting in summer; water freely in summer, moderately in spring and autumn, sparingly in winter.
Feeding Liquid feed weekly from late spring to midsummer.
Propagation Remove rooted, leaf-bearing offsets when repotting in spring.
Problems Brown leaf edges and/or withering leaves from dry air or compost; yellowing leaves from cold/draughts/overwatering; greenfly; red spider mite.
Special needs Water tubers very sparingly while dormant; pot in spring in mainly peaty (or similar) compost in temperatures of 21°C (70°F) until leaves appear, after which temperatures may be gradually lowered a little; avoid draughts; mist new shoots frequently.

C. × hortulanum hybrids, opposite

M A R A N T A C E A E
Calathea

CALATHEAS ARE AMONGST the most attractive of foliage container plants. *C. insignis* is a multi-coloured foliage plant, its leaves diagonally marked with long and short blotches alternately, chocolate brown on the underside and olive-green on the upper side. It is often called the rattlesnake plant because of this patterning. The leaves are long and narrow, up to 45cm (18in) long and about 7.5cm (3in) wide, and held upright.

Another species, *C. makoyana* (syn. *Maranta makoyana)*, commonly called the peacock plant, has oval leaves handsomely marked with dark green large and small blotches, like *C. lancifolia* (syn. *C. insignis*), and dark green lines, on a silvery green background. On the underside the markings are deep wine-red. The leaves are paper thin, about 30cm (12in) long, held more or less upright, making a plant about 30cm (12in) high and wide.

Light Light shade or good light.
Temperature Minimum 16°C (60°C), 16–30°C (60–85°F) in summer.
Moisture High humidity; water normally from spring to autumn; moderately in winter.
Feeding Liquid feed from midsummer to autumn.
Propagation By division when repotting.
Problems Red spider mite; brown leaf edges/leaf fall from dry air; discoloured leaves from too much light; stems rotting at the base from too much water in winter.
Special needs Plenty of humidity; watering with tepid, soft water; compost moist without being waterlogged; repot in alternate years; keep temperature steady – do not allow to vary.

M Y R T A C E A E
Callistemon

PLANTS GROWING IN very dry places sometimes develop curiously shaped flowers and leaves in an attempt to adapt satisfactorily. These Australian bottle brushes, *C. citrinus*, are no exception, with their cluster of long and colourful stamens at the tip of, and surrounding, a stem, to form a cylinder between 5 and 10cm (2 and 4in) long. As the flower fades, the stem elongates beyond it. The brushes are red, tipped with yellow, and are produced in profusion all over the plant. The genus name, *Callistemon*, is a direct reference to the flower; it comes from the Greek – *kallos* means beauty, *stemon* means stem.

In a container *C. citrinus* will make a shrub with glossy, 9cm (3½in) long leaves all year round, and with red flowers in early summer. Height depends on the size of the container, but 90cm (3ft) can be expected in a 23cm (9in) diameter container, and more when grown in a border.

Light As much as possible except for direct midday sun in summer.
Temperature Minimum 4°C (40°F); 16–27°C (60–80°F) in summer.
Moisture Normal humidity; water freely in spring and summer; sparingly in winter.
Feeding Liquid feed from midsummer to early autumn.
Propagation Heel cuttings in summer.
Problems Scale insect.
Special needs Plenty of ventilation in hot weather; prune only to tidy after flowering, and to prevent crowding of shoots, otherwise flowering growth for next year is removed.

C. 'Adolphe Audusson'

C. 'Barbara Clark'

THEACEAE
Camellia

AMELLIAS – SHRUBS OR small trees from Japan – are ideal plants for conservatories. They are elegant, colourful and well-behaved, flower heavily and keep their leaves all year round. They do not need high temperatures or constant bright light, nor do they need a great deal of attention. It would be difficult to find a better plant, especially as some – the hybrids of *C. reticulata* – flower in winter.

Camellia japonica and its hybrids are the most frequently grown varieties, the flowers of which are in shades of pink, red and crimson, together with white, the shapes varying from peony forms, through formal double and anemone-centred to fimbriated and single.

The whole plant is clothed in glossy evergreen leaves, reminiscent of laurel, but shorter and more rounded, and it grows slowly into a shrub 90–165cm (3–5½ft) tall in tubs. It can be kept at this kind of height by root pruning, and a little shoot pruning. Flowers appear from early to mid-spring, and last for five or six weeks, depending on the conservatory's temperature.

Some good hybrids include: *C. j.* 'Adolphe Audusson': dark red, semi-double; *C. j.* Alba Plena': white, large, formal double; *C. j.* 'Barbara Clark': pink, single; *C. j.* 'Jupiter': red, large, single with large central boss of yellow stamens; *C. j.* 'Lavinia Maggi': pale pink and red splashed, formal double. There are several hundred more from which to choose, but those mentioned supply a basis for a selection of colours and reliable flowering.

Camellia reticulata has large single rose-pink flowers, 7.5cm (3in) wide, between midwinter and early spring. The hybrids can be semi-double or double, and are much larger and more varied in colour: red, mauve-red, striped, white and so on. The growth habit is much more open than that of *C. japonica*.

Camellic sasanqua is even more desirable, as it flowers between autumn and early spring, being white to deep rose pink; it can be double or single, and the flowers are 4–5cm (1½–2in) diameter. The variety *C. s. fragrans* has scented flowers, as have some of the hybrids developed from it.

Light Good to shade.
Temperature Minimum 4°C (40°F) for *C. japonica*, 7°C (45°F) for the other two species and their hybrids; 16–21 °C (60–70°F) in summer, with ventilation.
Moisture Normal humidity; water moderately from spring to autumn; sparingly in winter.
Feeding Provide one dry feed, watered in, of potash-high fertilizer in midsummer.
Propagation Leaf-bud cuttings from summer to early autumn; short – 10cm (4in) – hardwood cuttings in early autumn with heated compost; layering in summer.
Problems Scale insect; yellow leaves from sunlight or alkaline compost.
Special needs Acid compost; use rainwater in alkaline-soil districts; occasional solutions of sequestrated iron; some pruning of mature specimens needed to shape only.

C. isophylla

C. × tagliabuana 'Mme Galen'

CAMPANULACEAE
Campanula

T HE ITALIAN BELLFLOWER, *C. isophylla*, is one of the most charming small plants and among the easiest to grow, adaptable to a wide range of temperatures. Being a trailer, it is ideal for a hanging container, where its waterfall of blue bellflowers can be properly shown off and appreciated, lasting as they do from midsummer until mid-autumn, maybe even longer with suitably warm temperatures.

It grows rapidly from spring to reach a length of 45–50cm (18–20in); as the flowers begin to fade in early autumn, new shoots start to appear from the crown, and may also flower. In general, however, any new growth produced in autumn is short and remains quiescent until spring. There is a variety, *C. i. alba*, with white flowers.

Light Good to light shade.
Temperature Minimum 4°C (40°F), but will take lower for short periods; 16–30°C (60–85°F) in summer.
Moisture Normal humidity; water freely while flowering, moderately in spring and autumn, sparingly in winter.
Feeding Liquid feed from early summer to end of early autumn.
Propagation Divide in early spring.
Problems Greenfly occasionally; yellow leaves from lack of plant food.
Special needs Daily watering in summer; twice a day if temperatures are in the range of 32°C (90°F) plus; remove flowering stems completely after flowering; deadhead regularly.

BIGNONIACEAE
Campsis

C LIMBING FLOWERING plants are excellent subjects for conservatories as they fill space quickly but can easily be kept under control. The Chinese trumpet-flower, *C. grandiflora*, is a particularly strong climber to 6m (20ft) in its native habitat, but nearer 4.5m (15ft) in a container – less if pruned judiciously. In late summer it has clusters of deep orange, 7.5cm (3in) long flowers, lasting into autumn, and opening out into five lobes.

Campsis × tagliabuana 'Mme Galen' has similarly shaped flowers in salmon pink, deepening to red. Both varieties have ornamental feathery leaves, falling in autumn, and need to be tied to their supports.

Light Good with some sun.
Temperature Minimum 7°C (45°F), 16–27°F (60–80°F) in summer.
Moisture Normal humidity; water freely from spring into autumn, sparingly in winter.
Feeding Liquid feed from midsummer to autumn.
Propagation By suckers, root cuttings or hardwood stem cuttings in spring in 21°C (70°F).
Problems Scale insect; greenfly; red spider mite.
Special needs Compost must be well-drained – add one extra part coarse grit and use drainage material in the base of the container; prune by cutting side shoots back to leave two or three buds after leaf fall or in autumn, when the main stems have filled the available space.

C. indica

Cattleya sp.

CANNACEAE
Canna

THE CANNA LILIES, *C. indica* are the epitome of exotic tropical flowers. They are brilliantly coloured, have spikes of large orchid-like blooms, and equally large, handsome leaves, in brilliant green or mixtures of purple and bronze. They need plenty of warmth in summer, but will survive surprisingly low temperatures.

Canna indica is a native of the West Indies and Central America, where it can grow to 1.8m (6ft) tall, and has red or orange flowers. The hybrids derived from this are the cannas commonly grown, either as mixed unnamed colours or as named varieties such as: 'Dazzler': bright red flowers, purple leaves, and 'Lucifer': red with yellow petal edges, green leaves. Height of these in a container is 90–120cm (3–4ft).

Light As much as possible.
Temperature Minimum 13°C (55°F) while growing, preferably in the range 27–36°C (80–95°F) in summer; store rhizomes at 10 °C (50°F).
Moisture Normal humidity, but mist in hottest temperatures; water freely in summer; keep rhizomatous roots just moist in winter.
Feeding Liquid feed from early summer.
Propagation Divide rhizomes at potting time; sow seed soaked in warm water for 24 hours beforehand, singly, 5cm (2in) deep in 7.5cm (3in) pots, at about 24°C (75°F).
Problems Grey mould, basal rot, greenfly – all from too low temperature; red spider mite from air being too dry at high temperatures.
Special needs Plenty of water and food while growing; store rhizomes in pots through winter; start rhizomes in trays of peat or compost at 18°C (65°F) in early spring, transfer to 15–23cm (6–9in) pots when growth well started; disturb roots as little as possible at all times.

ORCHIDACEAE
Cattleya

CATTLEYAS (from Central and South America) are one of the best known groups of orchids, and one of the easiest to grow and flower. The flowers have large, flat, open petals in a wide range of colours, and are produced in a spike carrying up to six blooms in autumn and winter. The base of the plant consists of bulb-like swellings known as pseudobulbs, over which arch the leathery strap-like leaves, and the flowering stem about 30cm (12in) tall emerges from between them.

Cattleya aclandiae is easily grown and flowered; it is fragrant, and has large olive-green petals blotched with deep red-brown, together with a prominent magenta coloured lip. *C. intermedia* has creamy white and purple flowers in clusters of three to five appearing, unusually, in summer, on stems 45cm (18in) tall.

Light Light shade in summer; good light in winter.
Temperature Minimum 10°C (50°F) at night, 18°C (65°F) during the day; in summer, daytime temperature should be in the region of 21°C (70°F) with about 5°C (10°F) less at night.
Moisture High humidity; water moderately from late winter to autumn, allowing to become almost dry between waterings; decrease while flowering to sparing in winter.
Feeding Not required.
Propagation By division.
Problems Mealy bug; red spider mite; thrips; scale insect; slugs; bacterial soft rot; grey mould.
Special needs Use proprietary orchid compost; supply more light and lower temperatures in autumn than in summer – with extra ventilation if necessary – to ensure flowering; high humidity; grow in hanging containers.

ASCLEPIADACEAE
Ceropegia

AN INTERESTING AND unusual hanging plant, *C. woodii* is commonly called hearts' entangled or string-of-hearts. It consists of a curtain of slender purple stems several feet long (if allowed), clothed in pairs of thick, small heart-shaped leaves about 2cm (¾in) wide, marbled white on a dark green surface with a light purple underside. Flowers are produced all summer and into autumn in the axils of the leaves; they, too, are small and tubular, with the mouth of the tube facing upwards. Their colour is lilac with a purple edging to the tip of the tube.

Although flowers are produced in profusion in conservatory conditions, mainly owing to the extra light, the plant is principally grown for the sake of its leaves. With age, the corm can easily become 10cm (4in) wide. There are at least a dozen other ceropegias in cultivation; one or two mimic the flowers of *Stapelia* in the same family, chiefly remarkable for their unpleasant-smelling flowers.

Light Good but not direct sun.
Temperature Minimum 7°C (45°F), 16–27°C (60–80°F) in summer.
Moisture Normal humidity; water moderately in summer, sparingly in winter.
Feeding Not required.
Propagation Use bulbils produced on stems, or tip cuttings in summer.
Problems Corm rotting from overwatering.
Special needs Use half-pot with drainage layer in base; repot every second or third year; place corm with the top level with the surface of the compost; cut back stems as required in early to mid-spring.

PALMAE
Chamaedorea

THE PALMS, LIKE the aspidistra, typify the Victorian age; while the aspidistra was grown as a houseplant, palms were a popular choice for the conservatory, although this particular species, *C. elegans*, from Mexico was also grown as a houseplant, hence its common name of parlour palm. It is a good conservatory plant as well, growing to about 1.2m (4ft) in a container and about 90cm (3ft) wide.

The leaves are frond-like, made up of 12 pairs of leaflets, and it will grow steadily all year, unfurling one leaf at a time. In late winter, in its second or third year, it will produce sprays of tiny, yellow, ball-like "flowers", which usually last for several weeks.

Light Good, but light shade needed when plants are young.
Temperature Minimum 10°C (50°F), 16–30°C (60–85°F) in summer.
Moisture Normal humidity; mist frequently in temperatures over 21°C (70°F); water normally from spring to autumn, sparingly in winter.
Feeding Liquid feed from midsummer to autumn.
Propagation By seed, in temperatures of 27°C (80°F).
Problems Scale insect; greenfly on the inflorescence; brown leaf tips from alkaline water or dry air; yellowing leaves from too much light.
Special needs Stand outdoors in warm summer showers; soft water; provide containers deeper than they are wide – palm pots if they can be obtained; repot only when really potbound, in spring; good drainage; deadhead.

C. comosum 'Variegatum'

Chrysanthemum decorative hybrids

LILIACEAE
Chlorophytum

THE GENERIC NAME of this South African herbaceous perennial, *C. comosum* (syn. *C. elatum*) 'Variegatum', could be applied to any green-leaved plant; the Greek word *chloros* means green, and *phyton* is a plant. The common name, spider plant, is better, though slightly fanciful, referring to its habit of producing plantlets at the end of long stems which arch over from the centre of an upright rosette of narrow, grass-like leaves. They can be up to 30cm (1ft) long, with a central longitudinal white stripe.

Sometimes the plantlets are replaced by a cluster of small white flowers, sometimes they appear together. In time the plantlets develop roots while still attached to the parent plant. The fleshy tuberous roots rapidly fill a container, and can be so packed in that repotting is difficult.

Light Good, with some sun.
Temperature Minimum 4°C (40°F), 16–30°C (60–85°F) in summer.
Moisture Normal humidity; water freely in summer, moderately to sparingly in winter, depending on temperature.
Feeding Midsummer to autumn, but see Special needs (below).
Propagation Detach plantlets when roots are present and pot in 7.5cm (3in) diameter pots.
Problems Greenfly, if short of water/food; pale colouring from shortage of food/light; brown leaf tips from hard water, dry air, or dry compost; brown/yellow leaves from cold.
Special needs Repot in spring and during growing season; if repotted twice, do not bother to liquid feed until autumn; good light to maintain colouring; deadhead.

COMPOSITAE
Chrysanthemum

THE BEAUTIFUL FLORIST'S chrysanthemums (now correctly, though obscurely, known botanically as *Dendranthema*) are not beyond the capacity of the conservatory, particularly if it is a cool one; they do not like high temperatures, and because of this, should be put on a standing-out ground in summer where there is much more air circulating.

There are different forms of flowers: incurved, with all the petals curving into the flower centre, forming a ball; reflexed, in which the petals turn out, away from the centre and back towards the stems; decorative, with a mass of petals with no marked directions, and single, with one row of petals and a centre of stamens, looking like a very large and wide-petalled daisy. Each has its own special charm, and is not difficult to grow, though all need constant small attentions.

Flower colours are mainly bronzes, yellow shades, white and purple, though there are some gorgeous reds and crimsons, as well as orange, apricot and green. Height of these specialist chrysanthemums is about 90–120cm (3–4ft), or a little shorter, depending on the variety.

Most are hybrids, though some are natural sports (where one or more shoots on a plant produce flowers in a completely different colour to the rest, or sometimes a whole plant does so). Cuttings taken from these shoots or plants will carry the differently coloured flowers, but seed taken from them, if available, would certainly be a mixture of colours.

Some named varieties are: *C.* 'Balcombe Perfection': bronze, incurved; *C.* 'Christmas Carol': red and gold, decorative; *C.* 'Green

Chrysanthemum incurved hybrid

C. cruenta hybrids

Chartreuse', green, incurved: *C.* 'My Love': apricot, single; *C.* 'Purple Glow': decorative: *C.* 'Red Glory' (syn *C.* 'Red Woolman's Glory'): single; *C.* 'Snowshine': *C.* 'Yellow Fred Shoe-smith': incurved.

Light Good, with some sun.
Temperature Minimum 4°C (40°F); 10°C (50°F) from late autumn till flowering finishes; outdoor temperatures in summer.
Moisture Normal humidity; water freely in hot summer weather, normally in spring and autumn, sparingly while resting after flowering.
Feeding Liquid feed from the beginning of early summer until colour shows on the buds.
Propagation Soft stem cuttings 7.5–10cm (3–4in) long from base of cut-down crowns in mid-late winter; place singly in 5cm (2in) pots, or in rows in trays, with temperature of 10–13°C (50–55°F). Pot when rooted, successively into larger pots as necessary; use John Innes potting compost, and ram compost firmly in final container. Seed can also be used for singles, to obtain new hybrids, and for doubles, if they are kept short of food so that they revert to singles.
Problems Leaf-miner; greenfly; slugs; mildew; grey mould; eelworm.
Special needs Use a gravel base to stand the containers on in summer outdoors, and supply supports for the stems as they grow; harden off before standing the plants outdoors; bring in in early autumn, and keep well ventilated for first few weeks; cut stems down after flowering to a few cm (in), remove compost, cut back long straggling roots, and place in new compost, allow to rest a few weeks; stop mid- and late autumn-flowering kinds in the middle of mid-spring, and the middle of early summer, but see also specialist chrysanthemum catalogue recommendations; disbud early in late summer, removing all side flower buds, and leaving top flower bud only on each stem – rub buds off while still tiny.

C O M P O S I T A E
Cineraria

THE GROUP OF hybrids derived from *C. cruenta* (now more correctly known as *Pericallis cruenta*) from the Canary Islands make up a collection of brightly coloured, winter-flowering herbaceous perennials with flowers like large daisies. The cinerarias suitable for containers are known collectively as *C.* × *hybrida* (correctly *Pericallis* × *hybrida*), of which there are four groups. *C.* × *h.* 'Multiflora Nana' 23–30cm (9–12in) tall, broad-petalled flowers, colour range pink, crimson, red, white, purple and bright blue; *C.* x *h.* 'Multiflora', 30–38cm (12–15in) tall, similar flowers and colour range with the addition of yellow and bronze; *C.* × *h.* 'Grandiflora'. 38–60cm (15–24in) tall, largest flowers; *C.* × *h.* 'Stellata', 23cm (9in) tall, narrow pointed petals; both this and 'Grandiflora' have the same colour range as 'Multiflora Nana'.

Light Good.
Temperature Minimum 7–13°C (45–55°F) while flowering, 16–21°C (60–70°F) at other times.
Moisture Normal humidity; keep well watered in summer and while flowering, moderately at other times.
Feeding Liquid feed plants from early autumn until flowering.
Propagation Sow seed from mid-spring to early summer for early winter to early spring flowering; sow thinly, cover very thinly, in 16°C (60°F); move seedlings on to successively larger pots; put containers outdoors in early summer, and bring in during early to mid-autumn; put larger plants into bigger pots if necessary.
Problems Greenfly/red spider mite; leafminer.
Special needs Keep cool, well supplied with water, and out of direct sun.

C. limon 'Meyer'

C. mitis

RUTACEAE

Citrus

ORANGES AND LEMONS are varieties of citrus; so, too, are grapefruit, mandarins, tangerines, limes and the calamondin. None is difficult to grow, and the sweet orange is nearly hardy. In ancient times the juice and peel were prescribed as antidotes for poisons; the juice is certainly recommended for good health nowadays, as it has a high vitamin C content.

Citrus sinensis, the sweet orange, comes from China, and has clusters of creamy white, strongly fragrant flowers in spring, glossy evergreen leaves, and round green fruit which either ripen to orange by the autumn, or remain green until the following spring, and then change colour. Height on average is about 1.2m (4ft) in a tub 45–60cm (18–24in) in diameter, with a spread of about 75–90cm (2½–3ft), but size depends very much on the container.

Citrus mitis (correctly but less well known as × *Citrofortunella microcarpa*) is the calamondin, a miniature orange from the Philippines. The tiny fruits, replicas of the sweet orange, are only about 2.5cm (1in) in diameter, edible though bitter (like Seville oranges) and, like them, best used for marmalade. Height is 60cm (2ft) maximum, usually nearer 45cm (1½ft), by 30–38cm (12–15in) wide. It flowers mainly in spring, with occasional flowers in summer and autumn, and has ripe fruit from autumn to spring.

Citrus limon (the lemon tree) has a cultivar, *C. l.* 'Meyer', with long leaves and large pale yellow fruit. *C.* 'Ponderosa' is similar but with even larger fruit, up to 12cm (5in) in diameter.

Light As much as possible; stand outdoors in summer.

Temperature Minimum 4°C (40°F) for sweet orange, 10°C (50°F) for lemon and calamondin, 16–32°C (60–90°F) in summer.

Moisture Normal humidity; spray overhead in temperatures above 24°C (75°F); water moderately in summer, sparingly in winter.

Feeding Liquid feed from midsummer until end of mid autumn.

Pruning Pinch back sweet orange at the tips of shoots in summer to prevent individual branches from becoming too long at the expense of others, and to produce a rounded head. New growth appears in two bursts: immediately after flowering and again in midsummer. Aim is to produce short-jointed shoots capable of bearing the considerable weight of the fruit. Calamondin can be similarly pinched back in late winter. It is advisable to start pruning both when they are young.

Propagation By pips, which germinate easily in 18–21°C (65–70°F), but fruiting is likely to be slow and unreliable; commercially by grafting named varieties on to rootstocks.

Problems Scale insect; red spider mite; greenfly; sooty mould; yellowing of leaves due to alkaline compost.

Special needs Neutral-acid compost; water with solution of sequestrated iron if compost is alkaline or tap-water is hard; ventilate well in spring and autumn.

C. thomsoniae

C. puniceus (foliage detail)

VERBENACEAE
Clerodendrum

THE TWO CLIMBERS described here require warm conservatory temperatures. *C. thomsoniae*, a strong evergreen which flowers all summer, commonly known as the glory bower, is native to tropical West Africa. Its clustered bell-shaped flowers are made up of a swollen cream calyx and starry red flowers, the clusters making a particularly eye-catching display.

Clerodendrum ugandense, the blue glory bower, has bright blue flowers with one violet-coloured lobe and prominent blue stamens. Spring is its main flowering time, though it will flower spasmodically for most of the year. Both species can grow to 3m (10ft) tall, with a good deal of side growth, which can be contained by pruning, if required.

Light Good.
Temperature Minimum 13°C (55°F), 16–30°C (60–85°F) in summer.
Moisture High humidity; mist frequently in temperatures above 24°C (75°F); water freely in summer, sparingly in winter.
Feeding Liquid feed from early summer into early autumn.
Propagation Tip cuttings in mid to late winter and early spring, in 21–24°C (70–75°C) for *C. thomsoniae*, or at the same temperature in summer for *C. ugandense*.
Problems Scale insect; red spider mite; a few leaves will fall in winter as a result of normal leaf shedding.
Special needs Keep compost moist but not waterlogged throughout growing season; enforce rest in winter; cut back flowered shoots to leave about 7.5cm (3in) of their stems immediately after flowering, in either late spring or early autumn, depending on species.

LEGUMINOSAE
Clianthus

OFFICIALLY CLASSIFIED as a shrub, *C. puniceus* is nevertheless a wandering one, and the long, straggling stems can be tied to supports to cover a pillar or wall. Its common name of parrot's-bill could hardly be more apt to describe the shape of the pillarbox-red flower; the lower petal, or keel, is 6.5cm (2 ½in) long, curved and ending in a long point, and the upper petals are similar, but recurved. Carried in clusters of 6 to 12, the flowers open from early summer for two months or more, and are unusual and brilliantly attractive.

The leaves add to the charms of the flowers, as they are feathery with leaflets in pairs, and the whole leaf can be 15cm (6in) long. There is a white cultivar (*C. p. albus*), a lovely pink-flowered one (*C. p.* 'Flamingo'), and also a species notorious for its ability to die off rapidly in cultivation, *C. formosus*, or the glory pea.

Light As much as possible.
Temperature Minimum 4°C (40°F), 16–27°C (60–80°F) in summer.
Moisture Normal humidity; water freely in summer, sparingly in winter.
Feeding Liquid feed occasionally while flowering.
Propagation By seed sown in spring in 21°C (70°F); heel cuttings in summer with heated compost.
Problems Red spider mite.
Special needs Soil-containing compost with one part extra grit; good ventilation in summer; remove flowered stems immediately after flowering is over; cut stems back to fit space as necessary.

C. miniata

A M A R Y L L I D A C E A E

Clivia

THE SOUTH AFRICAN Kaffir lily – *C. miniata* – has a mass of dark green, strap-shaped leathery leaves, from the centre of which extend the 60cm (2ft) flowering stems with a cluster of up to 20 blooms at the end of each. The funnel-shaped orange flowers, with a yellow throat, last into early summer; hybrids can be obtained in yellow and red.

If left in the same container for several years, a plant will produce a number of offsets, each of which can also flower.

Light Good.
Temperature Minimum 4°C (40°F), 16–30°C (60–85°F) in summer.
Moisture Normal humidity; water moderately from spring to autumn, sparingly in winter until flower stems are several inches tall.

Feeding Liquid feed from late winter to midsummer.
Propagation By division at repotting time; by detaching offsets; by seed sown in early spring in 21°C (75°F).
Problems Mealy bug; scale insect; yellow leaves from too much sun or water, or from cold water; no flowers – temperatures not cool enough in winter or not warm enough when flower stems start to appear.
Special needs Keep cool in winter, in the range 4–10°C (40 sF), and give only enough water to prevent being dust-dry; increase temperature to 16°C (60°F) when flower stems appear, and do not allow to drop below this while flowering; repot only when container really crowded; repot after flowering; use soil-based compost containing slow-release fertilizer; deadhead.

C. scandens   *C. hirta*

POLEMONIACEAE
Cobaea

HE COMMON NAME of *C. scandens* is the cup-and-saucer plant, because of its interestingly shaped flowers. The main part consists of a bell 7.5cm (3in) long, cream-coloured at first but then changing to light and deeper purple as it ages. The bell sits in a "saucer" consisting of a light green calyx with broadly toothed edges, and each flower is produced singly on a short stem from the leaf-joints. Flowering starts early in midsummer and continues into autumn; it will go on into winter if the temperature is kept above 7°C (45°F).

Growth is rapid, and it is one of the best climbers for covering a lot of space in a hurry – in the wild it can reach 7.2m (24ft) in a season. It attaches itself to its support by means of tendrils.

Light Good, with some sun.
Temperature Minimum 4°C (40°F), 16–30°C (60–85°F) in summer.
Moisture Normal humidity; water freely in early summer to the end of early autumn, moderately at other times.
Feeding Liquid feed from late summer to early autumn.
Propagation Sow seed in early spring in 16–18°C (60–65°F).
Problems Lack of flower colour from insufficient light; red spider mite; greenfly from lack of water.
Special needs Ventilate well in high temperatures; make sure seed is fresh, to ensure germination; in late autumn or late winter to early spring cut back sideshoots to leave two buds or leaf-joints; remove completely any unwanted side or main shoots.

GESNERIACEAE
Columnea

HE GESNERIAD FAMILY contains some of the most ornamental plants and the columneas are no exception. *C. × banksii* is a hybrid, its parents thought to be *C. oerstediana* and *C. schiedeana*, from Costa Rica and Mexico respectively, so it needs quite warm conditions in winter. As an epiphyte, it does best when positioned as a hanging plant.

One parent is trailing, the other bushy, and the net result is a primarily trailing offspring. It can form a glorious waterfall of bright red, hooded flowers, each about 7.5cm (3in) long, all down the new growth of each 60–75cm (2–2½ft) stem. Flowering time is from late winter to spring. Backing this colour display are dark green, glossy leaves, reddish on the underside.

Columnea hirta is similar but with a covering of reddish-brown hair on stems and leaves, and bright red and orange flowers in winter.

Light Good to shade.
Temperature Minimum 13°C (55°F); 16–30°C (60–85°F) in summer.
Moisture High humidity; particularly in summer; water freely in summer, moderately in winter.
Feeding Liquid feed from midsummer to early autumn.
Propagation By semi-ripe cuttings in spring in heated compost, and air temperatures of 21°C (70°F), with humidity.
Problems Mealy bug; grey mould; leaf-fall from draughts or cold.
Special needs Maintain steady temperature in winter; peat-based compost; cut back most of the stems to leave two or three leaf-joints every few years at repotting time, otherwise much of each stem will be bare of flowers; leave a few stems to clothe the plant while it grows new ones.

C. coccinea

CRASSULACEAE
Crassula

SOMETIMES CALLED the money plant, *C. arborescens* has thick, shiny, spoon-shaped leaves and starry white flowers which last from late spring into summer. It is evergreen, and can take many years to grow to its eventual height of 90–120cm (3–4ft).

Crassula falcata, in complete contrast, has thick, silvery grey, sickle-shaped leaves, setting off perfectly the tiny red spring flowers. It needs support, to prevent it becoming prostrate.

Crassula coccinea is grown for its rosy red fragrant flowers, produced in 12.5cm (5in) wide clusters at the end of 38cm (15in) stems. The triangular leaves are leathery, produced in four ranks to completely clothe the stem.

Light Good with some sun.
Temperature Minimum 4°C (40°F); 16–30°C (60–85°F) in summer.
Moisture Normal humidity; water normally from spring to summer for *C. arborescens* and *C. falcata*; freely for *C. coccinea*; allow to dry between waterings, water all sparingly in winter.
Feeding Liquid feed occasionally in summer.
Propagation Take 7.5cm (3in) stem cuttings in summer; allow to dry a few days before insertion; water a little immediately afterwards; take leaf cuttings for *C. arborescens*, *C. falcata*.
Problems Mealy bug; red spider mite; root aphis; red or brown leaves from too much light.
Special needs Cactus compost (see p. 165); cut *C. coccinea* back hard after flowering.

C. nilotica

C. bromeliodes tricolor, C. zonatus 'Zebrinus', C. bivittatus

ACANTHACEAE
Crossandra

THE CROSSANDRA known as *C. nilotica* is found in what used to be British East Africa and Mozambique – its specific name means "Valley of the Nile". It is part of the same plant family as the acanthus which inspired the classic Greek architects, but is quite different in appearance. It should never be assumed that plants with similar leaves are in the same family, or, conversely, that if the leaves are different the plants must belong to different familes. Plants are classified according to their flower characteristics, and a close look at the flowers of *Crossandra* and *Acanthus* will reveal similarities.

Crossandra nilotica has bright orange flowers with flat open faces, carried in short spikes at the end of the stems in summer. Height is about 60cm (2ft).

Light Good, but important to avoid sun in midsummer.
Temperature Minimum 13°C (55°F), 16–30°C (60–85°F) in summer.
Moisture High humidity at all times, with misting in summer; water freely except in winter, then water moderately.
Feeding Liquid feed from midsummer into autumn.
Propagation Semi-ripe stem cuttings at any time, in warmth of 27°C (80°F) and warmed compost.
Problems Greenfly; leaf and flower drop from dry air/dry compost or too low a temperature in summer.
Special needs Constant humidity; peat-based compost best; deadhead; prune back hard after flowering.

BROMELIACEAE
Cryptanthus

ONE OF THE SMALL species of *Cryptanthus* is known commonly as the earthstar, the rosette of stiff leaves lying flat and spread out. *C. acaulis* is typical of this group, with 7.5–15cm (3–6in) long leaves, light green on the upper surface, white on the underside. *C. bivittatus* grows very slowly to produce leaves about 23cm (9in) long, striped dark and light green, tinged with pink. A particularly attractive variety is *C. bromeliodes tricolor*, but it is rather more difficult to grow.

C. fosterianus is a handsome plant, considerably bigger than these, with 75cm (2 ½ft) long, fleshy leaves, grey-banded in a zigzag pattern on bronze. *C. zonatus* is one of the more imposing cryptanthus and especially well marked, with silvery grey crosswise bands on a brown-green background. The leaves are up to 23cm (9in) long, and about 10cm (4in) wide. All display their best colouring in a good light.

Light Good to light shade.
Temperature Minimum 10°C (50°F), 16–27°C (60–80°F) in summer.
Moisture High humidity from spring to autumn, normal otherwise; keep funnel full of water from spring to autumn, half full in winter; compost just moist at all times.
Feeding Occasionally during growing season.
Propagation By plantlets at the end of short stems or produced from between the leaves.
Problems Mealy bug; scale insect; basal rot from overwatering; brown leaf tips from insufficient humidity; brown patches from too much light.
Special needs Peat-based compost; soft, tepid water for watering (see also p. 164); deadhead.

C. ignea

C. cashmeriana

LYTHRACEAE
Cuphea

THE COMMON NAME of *C. ignea*, an attractive small shrubby plant from Mexico, is the cigar plant. It has tubular scarlet flowers about 2.5cm (1in) long, the mouth of which is tipped purple-black and white. Flowering is in summer, with the blooms scattered all over the plant. An evergreen, it grows to about 30cm (12in) in the wild, and adapts well to a container.

Light Good, with some sun.
Temperature Minimum 4°C (40°F), 16–30°C (60–85°F) in summer.
Moisture Normal humidity; water normally from spring into autumn, moderately in winter.
Feeding Liquid feed from early summer to autumn.
Propagation By tip cuttings in spring or late summer, in 18–24°C (65–75°F); seed sown in early spring in same temperatures.
Problems Red spider mite; greenfly; if old plants become straggly, start new ones.
Special needs Keep compost constantly moist, but not waterlogged, cut back hard in early spring.

CUPRESSACEAE
Cupressus

ONE OF THE MOST beautiful trees, the Kashmir cypress, *C. cashmeriana* (syn. *C. torulosa* 'Cashmeriana') can be grown successfully in a large container. The flat sprays of leaves are blue-grey, hanging from graceful, drooping branchlets, so that the entire tree looks like a misty blue waterfall. Its habit of growth is pyramidal, and height in the wild is about 18m (60ft), but in a container 1.8m (6ft) is more likely, though as usual much depends on the tub size. Direct planting into a border is not advisable, as it will quite quickly need drastic cutting back, and thus be spoilt.

Light Good.
Temperature Minimum 7°C (45°F), 16–27°C (60–80°F) in summer.
Moisture Normal humidity; water freely from spring into autumn, sparingly in winter.
Feeding Liquid feed from midsummer into early autumn.
Propagation Heel cuttings in early summer.
Problems Scale insect; root rot from cold and/or overwatering.
Special needs Ventilate well in temperatures above 27°C (80°F); repot alternate springs, top-dress in between; cut back only to fit space, in early spring; do not cut hard, so start when young.

C. revoluta

C. persicum hybrid

CYCADACEAE
Cycas

PRIMULACEAE
Cyclamen

THE CYCADS ARE one of the few families of plants left over from the fossil age, related to conifers, but instead of cones they have "flowers", albeit the most primitive of any of the flowering plants. *C. revoluta* consists mostly of a large spray of dark green leathery fronds, up to 2.1m (7ft) long in the wild, but nearer 90cm (3ft) in containers, and about 30cm (1ft) wide.

The whole cluster looks much like an inverted shuttlecock, with the feathers arching rather than stiff. The leaves emerge straight out of the ground to start with, but gradually a short fat trunk develops to a final height of about 60cm (2ft), taking many years to do so. It is then reminiscent of a tree fern, but the toughness and dark colouring of the leaves distinguishes it.

Cycads were popular plants for Victorian conservatories, and are easy to grow; they do not need high temperatures.

Light Good to shade.
Temperature Minimum 10°C (50°F), 16–30°C (60–80°F) in summer.
Moisture Normal humidity; but mist in temperatures above 21°C (70°F); water freely from spring into autumn, moderately in winter.
Feeding Liquid feed from early summer into early autumn.
Propagation Use offsets from plant base, in 27–30°C (80–85°F); seed sown in a light, well-drained compost in spring in 30–32°C (85–90°F).
Problems Scale insect; mealy bug; brown leaf tips from not enough humidity or hard water; yellow leaves from not enough water/food.
Special needs Keep compost moist in summer without waterlogging; use tepid soft water; soil-containing compost most suitable.

THE LARGE-FLOWERED cyclamen have been bred from *C. persicum*, a tender species with an inborn tendency to vary in flower colour, from white through deep pink to purple, and in leaf shape and markings. Natural flowering time is in late winter and early spring, but can be advanced with warmth.

Light Needs good light, but not direct sun.
Temperature Minimum 10°C (50°F), normal in summer while resting.
Moisture Good humidity while flowering, with occasional misting; otherwise normal; normal watering with tepid soft water while in leaf, reducing gradually after flowering. Keep dry while resting.
Feeding Liquid feed weekly with half-strength potash-high fertilizer from early winter till flowering finishes.
Propagation Sow seed in early summer, 2.5cm (1in) apart in 16–18°C (60–65°F); allow several weeks for germination. Remove to 5cm (2in) pots when there are three leaves, keep shaded from strong sun and in temperatures of about 10°C (50°F). Pot on the following spring into successively larger pots, then grow as mature plants.
Problems Cyclamen mite – remove and destroy infested plants; vine weevil; yellow leaves, caused by failure to observe Special needs (see below); bacterial soft rot of tuber – discard plant; grey mould.
Special needs Cool temperatures and humidity while flowering. Cyclamen flower best if slightly potbound; repot in midsummer when growth has just restarted, leaving half the tuber above the surface of the compost; use half pots with a drainage layer in the base; avoid splashing the base of stems.

Cymbidium hybrid

ORCHIDACEAE
Cymbidium

YMBIDIUM ORCHIDS are the varieties often used for corsages. The flowers consist of five flat petals and sepals arranged in a semi-circle, with a prominent, variously coloured and spotted "lip". Although some need warm temperatures and expert attention, there are others that will flower relatively easily with only a little heat. Among them are *C. eburneum*, with up to three cream-coloured, fragrant flowers with a yellow-marked lip, on a 25cm (10in) stem, in early to late spring; *C. giganteum*, with up to 15 yellow-green fragrant flowers, marked with purple, and with a yellow lip patched brown-red, 10cm (4in) wide, on 60–90cm (2–3ft) stems, in autumn; *C. lowianum*, from 15 to 40 green flowers with brownish markings, and a creamy lip with crimson border, on 45cm (18in) stems, in spring.

Good varieties include: Babylon 'Castle Hill' (pink) and Swallow 'Exbury' (yellow, light green and reddish spotted) but there are so many that it pays to visit a good orchid grower.

Light Needs shade from hot summer sun, but good at other times.
Temperature Minimum 7°C (45°F), low 20s°C (low 70s°F) in summer.
Moisture High humidity; water moderately from spring to autumn, sparingly in winter.
Feeding Liquid feed occasionally during summer.
Propagation By division when repotting.
Problems Mealy bug; mildew; wilting or lack of flowers from insufficient light.
Special needs Soft tepid water; day-length of 10–15 hours at all times; very moist atmosphere; repotting every other spring. See also p. 166.

83

CYPERACEAE
Cyperus

CYPERUS IS COMMONLY known as the umbrella plant, as each stem is topped by a cluster of narrow, pointed, leaf-like bracts radiating from a central point like the spokes of an umbrella. *C. involucrataus* (syn. *C. alternifolius)* 'Variegatus' has white-striped leaves and stems, which grow to about 1.8m (6ft) at their maximum, but usually less in containers. Clusters of tiny brown flowers appear amongst the leaves in late spring and early summer.

Cyperus papyrus is a much larger plant about 3m (10ft) tall, commonly called the Egyptian reed, or the papyrus plant; it was the one from which the ancient Egyptians made papyrus by cutting the pith from the stems into strips, laying the strips crosswise with overlapping edges, and then putting them in a press.

Light Light shade from spring to summer, good winter light.
Temperature Minimum 10°C (50°F), 16–30°C (60–85°F) in summer.
Moisture Normal humidity; water freely from spring to autumn, moderately in winter.
Feeding Liquid feed from late spring to late summer.
Propagation Divide when repotting.
Problems Greenfly if kept in a dry atmosphere; brown leaf tips for the same reason.
Special needs Repot in early summer as well as in early spring; keep container standing in water – never allow to dry out; remove dead stems occasionally.

CYATHEACEAE
Dicksonia

THE SO-CALLED tree-ferns, as with the more conventional fern species, are left-overs from the fossil age, and are not found growing naturally anywhere other than in the southern hemisphere. Most of the species naturally grow in gorges and deep valleys, and some are nearly hardy. Those described are slow-growing.

D. antarctica is nearly hardy, and its very slow growth makes it ideal for conservatory cultivation; final height can be 10.5m (35ft), but it would be many years before it reached this, even in a border. The feathery fronds have yellowish veins, and are up to 1.8m (6ft) long when mature, with a width of 90cm (3ft), but again for much of its life in a conservatory, this fern's fronds will be considerably smaller, of the order of 60–90cm (2–3ft) long. *Dicksonia fibrosa* is the golden tree-fern, so-called from the colour of the fibrous rootlets covering the trunk. Height can be 4.6m (15ft), and the fronds produced in a cluster at the top of the trunk are 90–180cm (3–6ft) long.

Light Shade from spring into early autumn, good light at other times.
Temperature Minimum 7°C (45°F), 16–27°C (60–80°F) in summer.
Moisture Good humidity; water freely in summer, moderately in winter.
Feeding Liquid feed occasionally during summer.
Propagation Use suckers in spring; spores at same time.
Problems Scale insect; brown fronds from dry air/compost.
Special needs Trunks must be sprayed thoroughly with water twice a day during summer, and also keep just moist in winter; ventilate well in summer.

D. marginata 'Tricolor'

LILIACEAE
Dracaena

MUCH GROWN AS houseplants, the dracaenas are evergreen tropical foliage plants with considerable variation in their leaf shape and colouring, which tends to be variegated.

Dracaena marginata 'Tricolor' is an elegant and attractive species with a long thin trunk, crowned with a rosette of narrow 45cm (18in) long leaves striped in dark and light green and cream, with rosy pink edges. Its height in a container is about 1.5m (5ft). *D. sanderiana* has grey-green leaves, striped with cream, 4cm (1½in) wide.

A further variation is found in *D. surculosa* (syn. *D. godseffiana*), whose leaves are smaller and heavily spotted; its habit is shrubby, and height will only be about 60cm (24in).

Light Good.

Temperature Minimum 4°C (40°F) for *D. sander-*

iana; minimum 10°C (50°F) for the other two; 16–30°C (60–85°F) in summer.

Moisture Normal humidity; water normally from spring to autumn, sparingly in winter.

Feeding Liquid feed from early summer to autumn if not repotted in spring.

Propagation By suckers, potted in warmed compost during summer; by short lengths of cane cut off with a bud or two on each, inserted upright in warmed compost; in both cases keep humid and shaded until rooted.

Problems Scale insect; red spider mite; brown leaf tips from dry air or insufficient water, too much feeding or draughts; brown spots on leaves from lack of water.

Special needs Spray overhead in summer in temperatures above 24°C (75°F); repot in alternate springs; care with winter watering and minimum temperatures.

E. scaber

E. glauca

B I G N O N I A C E A E

Eccremocarpus

THE CHILEAN GLORY flower, as *E. scaber* is commonly known, is easily grown, and will survive outdoors against a sheltered sunny wall or fence. But when grown under cover in cool climates it flowers much more profusely. Its evergreen leaves are feathery, and clusters of orange-red, tubular flowers 2.5cm (1in) long appear from mid-spring until autumn all the way up the 3m (10ft) stems. It climbs using tendrils. There are varieties with red or yellow flowers, and also a mixture called *E.* 'Anglia Hybrids' whose flowers are red, orange, yellow, carmine and bicoloured.

Light Good, with some sun.
Temperature Minimum 4°C (40°F), 16–30°C (60–85°F) in summer.
Moisture Normal humidity; water normally in summer, sparingly in winter.
Feeding Liquid feed from midsummer into early autumn.
Propagation By seed sown in late winter in 18°C (65°F) for flowering the same year.
Problems Greenfly from lack of water; dead growth from low temperatures.
Special needs Remove dead growth in late winter, and cut back by about half or more so that new growth fits the space available.

C R A S S U L A C E A E

Echeveria

THE COLOURING OF the leaves of *E. glauca*, a succulent from Mexico, is so outstanding that it is sometimes known as the blue echeveria. It consists of a rosette about 10cm (4in) wide, made up of spoon-shaped leaves about 4–5cm (1½–2in) long, with rounded tips, and 2cm (¾in) wide at the base, coloured blue-grey with a narrow rosy pink margin. If kept short of water and/or plant food, the whole rosette becomes flushed rosy pink as well.

With time, it very slowly develops a stem and a cluster of flowers, when it will need support; it also produces miniature rosettes at the base of the stem.

Light As much as possible.
Temperature Minimum 4°C (40°F) for short periods if compost dry; 16–30°C (60–85°F) in summer.
Moisture Low humidity; water normally in summer, very sparingly in winter.
Feeding Liquid feed occasionally in summer.
Propagation Detach rooted offsets in summer.
Problems Mealy bug; sudden leaf drop from insufficient water in summer or from cold water; basal rot/discoloured leaves from too much water in winter.
Special needs Well-drained compost, see cactus compost, p. 165; tepid water; water every 4–8 weeks in winter; allow compost to become just dry in summer between waterings.

E. sylvestrii

E. 'London Glory'

CACTACEAE
Echinopsis

A DELIGHTFUL SMALL cactus, the peanut cactus (*E. sylvestrii*) has fat little stems rounded at the tips and seldom more than 7.5cm (3in) long, often less. They lie flat along the soil and each is covered in short, white hair-like spines. The funnel-shaped flowers are orangey-red, about 5cm (2in) long, produced in late spring and summer, short-lived but continuously replaced by others.

Echinopsis eyriesii has much larger, open-mouthed white flowers at the end of a long tube carried on a round-bodied plant about 15cm (6in) wide, covered in short brown spines when mature. Beautiful in flower, they will not bloom until the body is 7.5cm (3in) wide.

Light Good with some sun, but shade from midday summer sun; as much as possible in winter.
Temperature Minimum 2°C (34°F), 16–32°C (60–90°F) in summer.
Moisture Low to dry humidity; water moderately in spring and summer; keep almost dry in winter.
Feeding Liquid feed *E. eyriesii* while flowering, *E. sylvestrii* from midsummer to autumn.
Propagation By fallen stems or rooted offsets.
Problems Mealy bug and root mealy bug; rot at base from too much winter water; leaf discolouration in summer from too much light.
Special needs Use cactus compost (see p.165); allow to just dry between waterings; expose to short period of frost to induce flowering for *E. eyriesii*; handle *E. sylvestrii* carefully when repotting as stems are very loosely attached.

CACTACEAE
Epiphyllum

T HE WATERLILY CACTUS is easy to grow successfully, so that one plant has 20 or 25 of its magnificent funnel- or cup-shaped flowers several inches wide. Flowering time is usually spring, and in some years it will repeat in autumn; sometimes it produces a few flowers in late winter, and flowers fully in late spring.

Flower colour can be pink, white, red, cream, salmon, yellow, purple and sometimes striped in these colours, and some flowers are fragrant. There are many named hybrids, and a particularly good series has the prefix 'London'.

The stems are flattened, and quite wide, up to 5cm (2in), and need to be supported by tying to split canes. Height is about 30–38cm (12–15in), width can be 45cm (18in). Sometimes rounded, reddish purple fruits form after the flowers.

Light Good, or light shade.
Temperature Minimum 10°C (50°F), 16–30°C (60–85°F) in summer.
Moisture High humidity in hot weather; otherwise normal; water normally in summer, sparingly in winter, and for a few weeks immediately after flowering.
Feeding Liquid feed occasionally in summer.
Propagation By division after flowering; by cutting a branching stem off at a convenient joint in early summer and leaving cut surface for a day or two to callus over before potting.
Problems Shrivelling from cold/lack of water; red-brown spotting from cold/lack of/too much water; mealy bug.
Special needs Allow to just dry between summer waterings; use soft tepid water; repot every third or fourth year; use clay pots as plants become top-heavy; for compost, see p. 165; cut some of the oldest stems down to soil level in early autumn.

E. cupreata

E. comosa

GESNERIACEAE
Episcia

I N A WARM conservatory *E. cupreata* is a pretty running plant which provides good ground cover between plants in a border, or grown amongst a group of them in a large container. It will also trail over the edge of staging or a shelf, or hang from a hanging pot or basket, but in all cases, it needs plenty of humidity to do well.

The toothed oval leaves have a broad band of light silvery green down the main central vein, extending along the secondary veins, on a dark green, copper-tinted background. Tubular scarlet flowers with a yellow eye are produced throughout the summer and, as the season progresses, runners extend and root into the compost from the leaf-joints; height is never more than about 15cm (6in).

Light Good, but not direct sun in summer.
Temperature Minimum 13°C (55°F), 16–30°C (60–85°F) in summer.
Moisture High humidity; water normally while growing, moderately to sparingly in winter.
Feeding Liquid feed from midsummer into early autumn.
Propagation Detach rooted runners between spring and autumn.
Problems Brown leaf edges from insufficient humidity; red spider mite; falling leaves, flowers and buds from draughts, sudden temperature drop or cold.
Special needs Drainage layer in base of container, or one part additional grit in compost; keep compost moist at all times, but never soggy.

LILIACEAE
Eucomis

T HE PINEAPPLE FLOWER *E. comosa*, gets its common name from the tuft of narrow leaves perched on top of the flower spike, similar to the tuft on top of the delicious fruit. Rather unusually for a South African plant, it flowers in midsummer instead of winter (summer in South Africa), producing small greenish white flowers in a loose spike up to about 30cm (12in) long. Its narrow, 7.5cm (3in) wide leaves are purple-spotted on the underside, and can grow as much as 60cm (2ft) long; they die down in autumn. The flower spike is handsome and unusual, and lasts for several weeks.

Light Good, with some sun.
Temperature Minimum 7°C (45°F), 16–30°C (60–85°F) in summer.
Moisture Normal humidity; water normally in summer, keep almost dry in winter; water sparingly from early spring until growth is well under way.
Feeding Liquid feed from end of flowering until leaves begin to yellow.
Propagation By offsets in autumn.
Problems Mealy bug; root mealy bug or root aphis.
Special needs Pot bulb 7.5cm (3in) deep; use 12.5cm (5in) diameter container; pot in spring.

E. pulcherrima vars

EUPHORBIACEAE

Euphorbia

THE EUPHORBIAS ARE a very curious group of plants with an extraordinarily varied range of growth habits. There are over 1000 species in the genus, found throughout the world in cool, warm and tropical climates, and ranging from hardy annuals to cacti-like succulents.

Euphorbia fulgens is mostly only seen as a cut flower at the florist, but it is not difficult to grow. In its native Mexico it grows into a 1.8m (6ft) high shrub, flowering at almost any time of the year, producing long arching sprays of bright orange-red "flowers". Its leaves are long and narrow, much like those of the willow.

One of the cactus-like species, *E. horrida*, is technically a shrub; it has succulent, deeply ridged stems with many spines along the edge of the ridges. It comes from South Africa where it grows to about 90cm (3ft) tall, but will make around 45cm (18in) in a container. Its flowers, in a circle at the end of the stems in late summer and autumn, are white to pale purple.

Mostly the euphorbias are referred to as spurges; however, *E. milii splendens* is commonly called the crown of thorns. Its grey stems are fleshy, its ovate leaves thin and bright green, mostly at the end of the shoots, and its 2cm (¾in) wide flowers are scarlet, consisting of a pair of rounded bracts, on and at the end of the stems in spring and summer. With plenty of light, it too will flower almost all year.

The best-known of the indoor euphorbias is *E. pulcherrima*, the poinsettia, which produces an

89

eye-catching display at Christmas. It does particularly well in a warm conservatory and its showy red "petals" are of course the bracts, the true flowers making up the yellow centre. With modern hybridizing and selection, pink and white cultivars have been produced, on shorter stems, and these new varieties are easier to manage, too, being less likely to drop their leaves and flowers. Height is 30–45cm (12–18in), and spread about 30–38cm (12–15in).

Light Good with some sun, shade from midday summer sun.
Temperature Minimum 13°C (55°F), 16–30°C (60–85°F) in summer.
Moisture High humidity for poinsettia, mist in summer on hot days for *E. fulgens*, otherwise normal; poinsettia needs watering well, but allow compost to dry (almost) before watering in winter; water freely in summer; other species; water moderately spring to summer, sparingly in winter.
Propagation By tip cuttings in spring or early summer in 18–21°C (65–70°F), allow sap to dry before inserting in sandy compost.
Problems Greenfly; red spider mite; whitefly; mealy bug; wilting from over/under-watering; leaf and/or flower fall from draughts, cold, bad light, dry air or faulty watering.
Special needs Repot all but poinsettia in alternate years; leave four to five stems on cut-down poinsettias, and repot in fresh compost when new growth starts in spring; to obtain well-coloured flowers keep in complete darkness for 14 hours every day through early and mid-autumn, then return to prevailing day-lengths; when poinsettias have finished flowering reduce the temperature to the minimum, and reduce the watering to sparing until growth re-starts; cut poinsettia down to leave 7.5cm (3in) stem immediately after flowering or in early spring; use peat or sawdust to mop up the sap; cut back some of the flowered shoots of *E. fulgens* after flowering.

GENTIANACEAE

Exacum

THE PERSIAN VIOLET, *E. affine*, sometimes also called the Arabian violet, is a small neat plant about 20cm (8in) tall and nearly as wide, forming a rounded mass of leaves covered with star-like purple, yellow-centred fragrant flowers for a long season, from midsummer into mid-autumn. Recently lavender-pink and white-flowered varieties have been produced.

Although in the same family as the gentians, its flowers have no resemblance to the dazzling blue trumpets of the familiar alpines. Nevertheless botanically the plants are similar.

Light Good with some sun, but shade from summer sun.
Temperature Minimum 16°C (60°F), 16–32°C (60–90°F) in summer.
Moisture High humidity; water moderately.
Feeding Liquid feed from midsummer to early autumn.
Propagation Grow from seed sown in autumn in 21–24°C (70–75°F), and supply a final container size of 9cm (3½in), or sow in late winter/early spring – plants will not be so good and will start flowering later.
Problems Greenfly.
Special needs Care with watering – allow to almost dry between waterings, the compost should never be soggy and surplus water must drain off; deadhead.

F. japonica 'Variegata'

F. sellowiana

ARALIACEAE
Fatsia

A HANDSOME SPREADING evergreen which can be grown outdoors in the sheltered gardens of cool climates, *F. japonica* will be seen at its best under the protection of a conservatory. The large, deeply lobed, palm-shaped leaves are dark glossy green, at least 30cm (12in) wide, and cover a plant which grows to about 3m (10ft) at maturity. In mid-autumn rounded heads of tiny creamy-white flowers start to appear, in large, stalked clusters, lasting until early winter. These are sometimes followed by round black berries.

There is an unexpectedly striking variety *F. j.* 'Variegata', whose leaves are white-tipped at the end of the lobes; it grows less tall, to about 1.2m (4ft), whereas the species will grow to about 1.8m (6ft) in a container.

Light Good, or light shade; good light for the variegated form.
Temperature Minimum 4°C (40°F), 16–27°C (60–80°F) in summer, but see Special needs.
Moisture High humidity; water normally while growing, sparingly in winter.
Feeding Liquid feed from early summer to mid-autumn.
Propagation Suckers or root cuttings taken in early to mid-spring.
Problems Shrivelled leaves from hot sun/dry air or too high temperatures; yellow, wilted, falling leaves from overwatering; brown-edged leaves, or pale and spotted ones, from underwatering.
Special needs Ventilate well in hot weather, or stand outdoors; spray overhead regularly in high temperatures; supply as good a light as possible in winter, and keep cool – around 10 °C (50°F); cut back to fit the space available, if necessary, in early spring.

MYRTACEAE
Feijoa

G REAT FUN TO GROW; *F. sellowiana* (now more correctly *Acca sellowiana*) has edible flowers (eaten in salads or fried in batter), and egg-shaped fruit. Its common name is pineapple guava or fruit salad plant, and it has glossy evergreen leaves, like those of camellia, with a white underside. Height and spread are normally around 120 by 75–90cm (4 by 2½–3ft).

Feijoa flowers in midsummer, producing pairs of axillary, 4cm (1½in) wide flowers, which consist of outer petals, red in the centre, paling to white at the edges, and a central brush of prominent red stamens, tipped with yellow.

Plenty of warmth well into autumn is needed for certain fruit production. Two specimens are also needed in most cases, grown from seed, as the flowers are self-sterile. There are cultivars available such as *F. s.* 'Mammoth' with large fruit, and *F. s.* 'Apollo' which is self-fertile and less vigorous, so it is suitable where space is limited and there is room for only one plant.

Light Good with some sun, not hot midday sun in summer.
Temperature Minimum 4°C (40°F), 16–30°C (60–85°F) in summer.
Moisture High humidity; water normally from spring to early autumn, moderately in winter.
Feeding Liquid feed from midsummer to early autumn.
Propagation Semi-hardwood cuttings in mid-to late summer, with heated compost.
Problems Scale insect; grey mould on flowers; falling buds from cold or overwatering.
Special needs Hand pollinate; ventilate well in temperatures above 21°C (70°F); prune in late winter, if control of size is necessary.

91

F. benjamina 'Variegata', *F. deltoidea*, *F. elastica*, *F. e.* 'Variegata'

MORACEAE
Ficus

THE TREE WHICH carries the delicious fruits and the rubber tree both belong to this genus; the fig tree is *F. carica*, and the rubber tree is *F. elastica*, much grown in India as a shade tree. It was in fact the earliest source of rubber, hence the name India rubber, but rubber is nowadays obtained from a different plant, *Hevea brasiliensis*.

Species of ficus are grown for their decorative foliage, and there are many available which have leaves considerably varied in shape and size. For the conservatory there are four which are especially suitable.

Ficus benjamina grows into a delightful small tree with graceful drooping shoots and glossy, pointed leaves, light to dark green depending on age. Height and spread will be as much as the container and the conservatory will allow; it tends to be tall rather than wide. Some leaves will

inevitably turn yellow and fall with age, but will be replaced by new ones. A variegated form, *F. b.* 'Variegata', has white-splashed leaves.

The rubber plant has some handsome improved forms, such as *F. elastica* 'Doescheri', with grey-green and dark green patches on the upper side and an irregular creamy white edging to the leaves, which are longer and narrower than in the species. *F. e.* 'Variegata' has pale yellow leaf margins and grey-green blotches on a rounded leaf. *F. e.* 'Black Prince' has leaves which are such a dark wine colour as to be almost black, though this tends to be lost as the leaves mature; the growing point is crimson.

You could be forgiven for not recognizing the mistletoe fig, *F. deltoidea*, as a ficus; it has small rounded triangular leaves about 5cm (2in) long, covering a twiggy plant up to 90cm (3ft) tall. Dull-yellow round berries, about the size of a

F. deltoidea

F. verschaffeltii

large pea, appear suddenly in the leaf-joints, without apparently any need for preliminaries in the form of flowers or pollination. But they grow in the same way that figs do; the minute flowers are produced inside a structure which will eventually be the fruit, and pollination occurs inside it, after which it swells into the berry.

Ficus sagittata (syn. *F. radicans*) 'Variegata' crawls over the ground rooting where its stems touch and so making good groundcover; it can also be used as a trailer, or attached to a support such as a moss stick. The narrow, pointed leaves are 5cm (2in) long and broadly and irregularly edged with cream.

Light Good or light shade; variegated kinds need good light and some sun.
Temperature Minimum 10°C (50°F), 16–27°C (60–80°F) in summer.
Moisture High humidity; mist creeping species daily in temperatures above 24°C (75°F); water normally to moderately while growing; sparingly in winter.
Feeding Liquid feed from midsummer to early autumn.
Propagation Tip or semi-hardwood stem cuttings in summer in heated compost and humidity.
Problems Scale insect, particularly on *F. benjamina*; red spider mite, particularly on *F. sagittata* in dry air; leaf-fall of small-leaved types from dry air; rubber plant: yellowing lower leaves from cold, overwatering or age; falling without discolouring from shade or overwatering.
Special needs Care with watering, use tepid water on all; repot in alternate years, slightly underpot; prune only to fit space available, in winter; use cottonwool, peat or cocofibre to absorb white latex from cut.

ACANTHACEAE
Fittonia

THE FITTONIAS commonly grown in cultivation are small creeping and trailing plants, the foliage of which makes decorative ground cover. As they originate from the rain forests, they need a lot of humidity.

Fittonia verschaffeltii has rose-pink veining, so that the overall tone of the leaf is pink-flushed. The variety *F. verschaffeltii argyroneura* has 10cm (4in) long, spoon-shaped leaves and white veins forming an intricate network on the leaf surface. There is a small version, *F. v. a.* 'Nana', commonly called the snakeskin plant, with 2.5cm (1in) long leaves, which is much easier to grow.

Light Good, but avoid sun.
Temperature Minimum 16°C (60°F), 16–30°C (60–85°F) in summer.
Moisture High humidity; but can be normal for *F. v. a.* 'Nana'; water freely from spring to autumn, sparingly in winter.
Feeding Liquid feed at half-strength from early summer to autumn.
Propagation Use rooted portions of creeping stems.
Problems Yellow leaves from overwatering; shrivelled leaves from too much light or dry air.
Special needs Frequent misting in summer; warmth in winter without draughts; tepid water.

Freesia hybrids

F. 'Thalia'

IRIDACEAE
Freesia

THE FREESIAS WHICH form the cut flowers provided by florists in winter are quite easy to grow, and only need a little artificial warmth in winter to ensure that they flower. They are all hybrids, mainly from *F. refracta*, *F. armstrongii* and the fragrant *F. corymbosa*, which has provided their unique fragrance. This is most marked in the pale colours; virtually all the colours of the rainbow are included, though the blue does have a tendency towards purple. Pink and lilac are also found.

The funnel-shaped flowers, 4cm (2¼in) long, form a one-sided spray on stems 30–45cm (1–1½ft) long, between mid-autumn and early spring, depending on the method of propagation.

Light Good, with some sun from autumn to spring.
Temperature Minimum 4°C (40°F) at night, 16°C (60°F) in the day, while flowering; when corms are resting in early to mid-summer, 19–30°C (68–85°F) is ideal; 16–21°C (60–70°F) at other times.
Moisture Normal humidity; water normally except when leaves are dying down, then decrease gradually until none when corm is fully dormant.
Feeding Liquid feed after flowering.
Propagation Can be propagated from seed for mid-autumn to early winter flowering, but most easily done from bought corms or offsets planted in midsummer and put outside in shade until mid-autumn, placing corms with 2cm (¾in) compost above "nose"; keep watered. Flowering will be from midwinter to early spring.
Problems Greenfly on flowers from too warm, dry atmosphere or not enough ventilation.
Special needs Support stems with split canes; rest dry corms in the dark from time leaves die to midsummer; keep cool in summer while growing.

ONAGRACEAE
Fuchsia

MUCH-LOVED GREENHOUSE plants in this century, fuchsias were equally popular as conservatory plants in the previous one, when their stems were trained into many different shapes, pyramids and standards being the most popular. The bell-like flowers of the modern hybrids come in a range of colours, deep purple and carmine red being the most common combination, but hybridization has added pink, blue-purple, white and white flushed pink to these, and there are endless variations and combinations as a result. Size of flower varies, too, from 2.5 to 7.5cm (1 to 3in) long (not counting the length of the stamens).

The plants flower profusely, dangling from the shoots. To appreciate them properly, put them above eye level, so that the centre of the flowers can be seen. If allowed to, they will flower all winter as well as in summer; they never seem to have a close season, and will bloom while the temperature is above 10°C (50°F).

There are trailing kinds as well as bushy ones, for hanging baskets or shelves, varieties with cream-variegated or flushed leaves, and species which are also worth growing, albeit a little different. Fuchsias were named after Leonard Fuchs, a German botanist who lived from 1501 to 1566; most of them were introduced to cultivation in the 1800s.

There are many hybrids and cultivars to choose from. Here is a selection: (where two colours are given, the first is the outer sepals, the second the inner corolla): *F. boliviana* 'Luxurians': deep crimson, narrow-tubular, in many-flowered drooping clusters; 'Caroline': single pink; 'Golden Marinka': red to deep red, leaves yellow-

F. 'Pink Profusion'

variegated on top, flushed beneath, trailing; 'Kon Tiki': double, white and deep purple-blue; 'Koralle': deep coral pink, tubular; 'Lye's Unique': single, white and salmon; 'Marine Glow': single, white and purple; 'Pink Profusion': double, pink; 'Sierra Blue': double, white and purple-blue to lilac; 'Snowcap': double, white and bright red; 'Thalia': single, orange scarlet; 'White Fairy': double, white.

Light Good or light shade, but never sun.
Temperature Minimum 2–4°C (35–40°F) provided the compost is almost dry; maximum 24°C (75°F), but preferably in range 16–24°C (60–75°F) in summer.
Moisture High humidity, with frequent misting of the bark of the stems and trunk; water freely from spring to mid-autumn, then gradually decrease to sparingly in early winter, and induce resting by virtually stopping watering in winter.
Feeding Liquid feed from early summer to early autumn.
Propagation Tip or semi-ripe cuttings in summer; seed sown in spring in 13°C (55°F).
Problems Whitefly; red spider mite; greenfly; grey mould.
Special needs Keep cool in summer and water well; induce resting in winter by lowering temperature and reducing watering. In late autumn cut back shoots to leave three leaf-joints, remove weak and damaged shoots completely; pinch back tips of new shoots in spring to leave two pairs of leaves, and repeat on subsequent shoots as required to encourage bushiness; this will delay flowering.

95

G. jasminoides

G. superba rothschildiana

RUBIACEAE
Gardenia

THE MAGNOLIA-WHITE double flowers of *G. jasminoides* are heavily and luxuriously scented, and will saturate the conservatory with their fragrance in spring. Each flower is about 10cm (4in) wide, carried singly, on a shrub which can grow to 1.8m (6ft), and half as much wide, but usually much less in a container. The glossy oval leaves are evergreen, much like camellia foliage, but less rounded and more pointed at the tip and stalk end. Although gardenias are usually thought to be difficult and expensive plants to grow, they are no more difficult than foliage houseplants that require as they do, a good deal of warmth in winter and humidity all year round. They do, of course, need good light, especially in winter.

Light Good with some sun in winter, but avoid hot summer sun.
Temperature Minimum 16°C (60°F), 16–30°C (60–85°F) in summer.
Moisture High humidity; water normally from spring to autumn, moderately in winter.
Feeding Liquid feed from mid-spring to end of midsummer.
Propagation Short ripe sideshoots 7.5cm (3in) long in spring, in warmed compost and 24–27°C (75–80°F).
Problems Scale insect; red spider mite; mealy bug; yellow patches on leaves from cold or soggy compost; bud drop from faulty watering or irregular temperatures.
Special needs Use soft tepid water; do not let compost dry, but avoid waterlogging; repot every two to three years; use acid compost; ensure day temperature of about 21°C (70°F) and night temperature 5°C (10°F) less when flower buds forming; prune to shape, if needed, in late winter.

LILIACEAE
Gloriosa

A TUBER WHICH can climb is unlikely enough; a lily which does so is on a par with unicorns, but the glory lily – *G. superba rothschildiana* – combines all three characteristics. Its flowers are brilliantly coloured, the petals being mostly scarlet with a golden base and golden margins, and each of the six is reflexed in a semi-circle back to the stem, like a Turk's-cap lily. Additionally they have eye-catching long stamens emerging at right angles to the petals. The flowers are produced from the leaf-joints, from early summer until autumn.

Height is about 1.8m (6ft), with sideshoots produced high up on the stems, which attach themselves to their support by leaves modified to tendrils. Although exotic-looking plants are often difficult to grow, the glory lily is an exception. Young plants, however, take some years to flower.

Light Good with some sun, but shade from hot summer sun.
Temperature Minimum 13°C (55°F); 16–30°C (60–85°F) in summer.
Moisture Normal humidity; water sparingly when first potted, freely while in full growth; reduce gradually to dry in autumn.
Feeding Liquid feed from late spring until early autumn.
Propagation By offsets in spring; by seed sown in early spring in 24°C (75°F).
Problems Greenfly in low temperature; tuber rot from cold and/or wet compost.
Special needs Good compost drainage, with drainage layer in container base; keep tuberous roots dry and warm until early spring, then plant one to a 15cm (6in) diameter container, placing it upright with the top about 2.5cm (1in) below the compost surface; deadhead.

G. robusta

G. lingulata

P R O T E A C E A E

Grevillea

T HE AUSTRALIAN silk oak, *G. robusta*, comes from New South Wales, where it can grow to 30m (100ft) or more, and has clusters of yellow flowers. Under cover, it grows well in containers and is a handsome foliage plant with graceful feathery leaves, dark green on top and silvery beneath, much divided and held out horizontally from the trunk, often more than 30cm (12in) long. It grows rapidly when young, 45–60cm (18–24in) in a season in a good light and good summer temperatures, but it can become lanky and get out of hand quickly unless the growing point is nipped out. Sideshoots will then extend and they, too, will need stopping in due course. Height can be whatever suits the space available and spread about 90cm (3ft).

Light Good with some sun.
Temperature Minimum 4°C (40°F), 16–30°C (60–85°F) in summer.
Moisture Normal humidity; water freely in summer, sparingly in winter.
Feeding Liquid feed from midsummer to early autumn if not repotted in early to midsummer.
Propagation Tip cuttings in late summer in warmed compost; seed sown in spring in 16–21°C (60–70°F).
Problems Red spider mite; yellow leaves and lack of growth from cold, too much water or badly drained compost; lower leaves falling from lack of water.
Special needs Care with water and compost drainage; cut back top and sideshoots to fit space available in growing season.

B R O M E L I A C E A E

Guzmania

T HE GUZAMANIAS ARE a very colourful group of bromeliads grown both for their ornamental leaves and showy flowerheads. They mainly originate in the rain forests of the Andes and from the West Indies, and need more warmth and humidity than most of the family.

Guzmania lingulata is one of the most decorative and easily grown; about 45cm (18in) wide, the leaves form a rosette from the centre of which a 30cm (12in) high flowerhead emerges, the brilliantly red bracts centred with a cluster of white flowers. These last only a few days, but the star-like bracts remain for many weeks. There is a small form, *G. l. minor*, with shorter leaves.

Guzmania musaica is even larger, having leaves 60cm (24in) long in a mature specimen. Their bright green colour is marked with dark green in irregular bands, and with purple on the underside. It does have a flowerhead, in similar colours to *G. lingulata*, but is much less striking. Flowering for both species occurs in late spring and summer.

Light Good.
Temperature Minimum 16°C (60°F); 18–30°C (65–85°F) in summer.
Moisture High humidity; keep funnel full of water from late spring to autumn, otherwise half-full; keep compost just moist.
Feeding Occasionally liquid feed in summer and spring.
Propagation By offsets removed when several months old.
Problems Scale insect; mealy bug; leaves with brown tips from hard water or dry air or insufficient water.
Special needs Keep out of sun in summer; mist in temperatures above 24°C (75°F).

G. sarmentosa

H. gaertneri

C O M P O S I T A E
Gynura

A SMALLISH PLANT, *G. sarmentosa* often has a tendency to trail as it matures. Its chief claim to fame is the intensely purple, velvety fur which covers the leaves and stems, themselves a dark bottle-green colour. Although its natural habitat is amongst lightly wooded terrain, it will need plenty of light in a conservatory. In spring it has pale orange daisy-like flowers.

It can be grown as a trailer, or trained up a support, reaching about 38–45cm (15–18in), and its foliage will be at its most showy if the flowers are removed. Another species called *G. aurantiaca*, which is definitely a shrub, to 90cm (3ft), has the same furry leaves, but with yellow flowers, opening in winter. It originates from Java whereas *G. sarmentosa* comes from India.

Light Good with some sun, especially in winter to ensure intense colouring.
Temperature Minimum 10°C (50°F), 16–30°C (60–85°F) in summer.
Moisture Normal humidity; water freely in summer, sparingly in winter.
Feeding Liquid feed from midsummer to autumn.
Propagation Tip cuttings in summer.
Problems Greenfly.
Special needs Good light to maintain colour; nip back the tips of shoots as they grow to maintain a bushy and well-clothed habit.

C A C T A C E A E
Hatiora

A MUCH easier name for *H. gaertneri* (syn. *Rhipsalidopsis gaertneri*) is the Easter cactus; it looks much like the Christmas cactus (see p.131) but naturally flowers several months later. Previously called by the generic names of rhipsalidopsis, schlumbergera and zygocactus, it is sometimes still sold under one of these names.

It has the same flat, notched stems as the Christmas cactus, arching over with age, but may have pointed-toothed edges to the stems, instead of rounded serrations, in which case it is likely to be a hybrid form. Its flowers are produced from the end of the stems and are pillar-box scarlet.

Light Good.
Temperature Minimum 10°C (50°F), 16–30°C (60–85°F) in summer.
Moisture High humidity in summer, normal at other times; water normally from mid-winter until after flowering, sparingly from mid-autumn to the end of early winter; see also Special needs.
Feeding Liquid feed from the appearance of the flowerbuds until after flowering.
Propagation Stem cuttings of end two "pads".
Problems Mealy bug and root mealy bug; shrivelling from lack of water; brown spots, cold; pale stems, few flowers indicates need for new compost, or insufficient feeding; reddening of stems from too much light; bud drop from draughts, cold, sudden change in temperature or moving plant.
Special needs Plunge pot outdoors in shady place and leave to be watered naturally, but water during drought; indoors in summer, water moderately; rest from autumn into early winter; keep out of artificial light in evenings; in autumn to early winter as this affects flowering; supply temperature of 16–18°C (60–65°F) while flowering.

H. algeriensis 'Gloire de Marengo'

H. 'Golden Ingot', *H.* 'California Gold'

ARALIACEAE

Hedera

EDERA IS THE botanic name for a much-loved climber and groundcover plant, the ivy. Common, or English, ivy (*H. helix*), found abundantly in broad-leaved woodland, has large, deep green three-lobed leaves, but there are varieties and cultivars of this with smaller and variegated leaves, and there are also large-leaved ivies, variegated and somewhat differently shaped to the common species. There are now so many altogether that there is a specialist society devoted entirely to the genus.

Although ivies grow naturally as climbers, and attach themselves to supports by short aerial roots on the stems, they can also grow as trailers or hangers, and can be trained to a variety of shapes such as circles, triangles and pillars, with the help of canes and moss poles (see p. 163). The small-leaved varieties tend to grow slowly, but some of them produce sideshoots with great freedom.

Varieties of *Hedera helix* include *H. h.* 'Butter-cup': small yellow leaves, very slow-growing; *H. h.* 'Cristata': leaves up to 5cm (2in long) with edges much crinkled and enfolded, like parsley; *H. h.* 'Glacier': silvery grey-green leaves with cream edges; *H. h.* 'Goldheart': dark green leaves that are 2.5cm (1in wide) and 4cm (1½in) long with an irregular bright golden centre and reddish stems in winter; *H. h.* 'Sagittifolia': arrow-shaped leaves 5cm (2in long) and 4cm (1 ½in) wide with centre lobe long and narrow; *H. h.* 'Tricolor': grey-green, white edged, pink flushed in winter, large-leaved.

Another good ivy for the conservatory is *H. algeriensis* 'Gloire de Marengo' (syn. *H. canariensis* 'Variegata').

It has very large leaves, up to 10cm (5in) long and 8cm (3in) wide with dark green or grey-green patches merging into the creamy white margins and red stems. It is slightly tender. *Hedera canariensis* 'Ravensholst' has red leaf stalks.

Hedera colchica, Persian ivy, has heart-shaped deep green leaves up to 25cm (10in) long and 20cm (8in) wide.

Light Good, not summer sun.
Temperature Minimum 2–4°C (36–40°F), but 7°C (45°F) for *H. algeriensis* 'Gloire de Marengo'; 13–21°C (55–70°F) in summer, especially at night.
Moisture High humidity in summer, otherwise good; water normally, but sparingly in winter.
Feeding Not required except for *H. algeriensis*, which should be given liquid food occasionally in summer.
Propagation Remove lengths of stem with aerial roots during growing season, lay on surface of compost, and pin down; alternatively, put 10cm (4in) long cuttings in a glass of water in normal room temperatures in bright indirect light until roots are 4cm (1½) long. Pot in 7.5cm (3in) pot with standard potting mix.
Problems Red spider mite in hot, dry conditions; brown patches from sun; greenfly occasionally.
Special needs Ventilate well in temperatures above 21°C (70°F) and mist frequently; prune to restrict growth if necessary.

Hippeastrum hybrid

MALVACEAE
Hibiscus

IN ITS NATIVE HABITAT, *H. rosa-sinensis* grows to at least 1.8m (6ft) tall, with beautiful funnel-shaped flowers in summer and autumn. Grown under cover, in containers, it will not be so large, more like 90 or 120cm (3 or 4ft), but will still be decorated with flowers, even when quite small – only 30cm (1ft) or so tall. Commonly called the rose of China, after its country of origin, its deep red single flowers are a good 12cm (5in) wide, with the characteristic long column of fused stamens protruding from the centre beyond the edge of the petals. There are now a good many cultivars of this species in various colours, in pinks, oranges, yellows and whites.

Hibiscus rosa-sinensis has plain green, evergreen leaves except for the cultivar *H. s.* 'Cooperi', whose leaves are variegated cream and red, with the red flowers of the species. *H. s.* 'Holiday' is a magnificent red variety, *H. s.* 'Nairobi' is golden, and *H. s.* 'Rose' is pink.

A particularly pretty species from east Africa, *H. schizopetalus*, is a startling orange-red, somewhat drooping, and with deeply cut backward-curving petals. Its slender stems usually need some support.

Light Good with some sun; avoid hot midday sun.
Temperature Minimum 13°F (55°F), 16–30°C (60–85°F) in summer.
Moisture Normal humidity, spray overhead in temperatures higher than 24°C (75°F); water freely in summer, sparingly in winter.
Feeding Liquid feed from early summer into early autumn.
Propagation Layer in midsummer, short ripe sideshoots in autumn with warmed compost, or tip cuttings in spring in 24°C (75°F) and warmed compost.
Problems Red spider mite; greenfly; whitefly; leaf and bud drop from lack of or too much water or sudden drop in temperature.
Special needs Plenty of warmth and light in late summer and autumn; cut back in late winter, either removing only the tips of shoots, or cutting back by half the previous year's growth, if space is lacking.

H. rosa-sinensis hybrid, opposite

AMARYLLIDACEAE
Hippeastrum

HIPPEASTRUM HYBRIDS ARE those bulbs with superb, funnel-shaped flowers in winter or spring, often called, wrongly, amaryllis. Hippeastrum hybrids grow about 60cm (2ft) tall from a bulb 10cm (4in) in diameter; their leaves are strap-shaped, 30cm (1ft) long, and the flowers 15cm (6in) wide, in a range of colours. 'Candy Cane' is bright red with a white stripe; 'President Johnson' is white with a narrow red edge to the petals. Some are heavily scented.

Light Good light but not sun.
Temperature Minimum 4°C (40°F), 16–30°C (60–85°F) in summer.
Moisture High humidity; water sparingly until growth is well under way, then normally; dry off as leaves die down and keep dry while resting.
Feeding Liquid feed from flowering time until end of early autumn.
Propagation Offsets, at repotting time.
Problems Mealy bug; red spider mite; thrips; non-flowering from lack of feeding.
Special needs Pot in 15cm (6in) diameter containers, with half of bulb exposed, in autumn if "prepared" for early flowering, or in midwinter for spring flowering; support flower stem; minimum temperature while flowering 13°C (55°F), preferably higher; soft water; encourage resting by reducing water and lowering temperature; deadhead; remove flower stem when completely withered.

H. forsteriana

H. bella

P A L M A E
Howeia

SOMETIMES called the Kentia palm – Kentia is the capital of Lord Howe island in the Pacific – *H. forsteriana* grows quickly to about 2.4m (8ft) tall though in the wild it can grow to 18m (60ft). It is the palm of Palm Court orchestra fame.

Howeia belmoreana is similar, but grows less tall in the wild, to about 10.5m (35ft), and has narrow leaflets.

Light Good or light shade.
Temperature Minimum 10°C (50°F), 16–27°C (60–80°F) in summer.
Moisture Normal humidity; water moderately in summer, sparingly in winter.
Feeding Liquid feed occasionally in summer.
Propagation Difficult – by seed in 27°C (80°F).
Problems Scale insect; red spider mite; mealy bug; brown tips to leaves from dry air, hard water, or alkaline compost; discoloration of lowest leaves occurs naturally – remove them.
Special needs Deep containers; repot when plant is rootbound, in spring; good compost drainage; never allow compost to dry; wash leaves occasionally; keep night temperature in winter below 16°C (60°F).

A S C L E P I A D E A C E A E
Hoya

THE HOYAS ARE evergreen, with thick, pointed-oval leaves and flowers in clusters. Excellent climbing plants, they are easily grown, and flower when only two years old.

Hoya bella is a small shrubby plant to about 45cm (18in) tall, with white, wax-like flowers with a red centre; it comes from India. *H. carnosa*, from Australia, is the more commonly grown species, know as the wax flower, also with clustered flowers, but pink, and strongly fragrant in the evening and at night. It flowers more easily, and has long stems, to as much as 4.5m (15ft), from which aerial roots extend, making it a good plant for a moss pole. Both species flower between spring and autumn, mainly in late spring and early summer.

Light Good, but not direct summer sun.
Temperature Minimum 7°C (45°F), 16–30°C (60–85°F) in summer.
Moisture High humidity, with occasional misting; water moderately but thoroughly in summer, sparingly in winter.
Feeding Liquid feed if not repotted, from early spring to early summer.
Propagation Layer in spring or summer.
Problems Scale insect; mealy bug; greenfly; mildew; yellow leaves from too much water, alkaline water or compost; no flowers from shortage of plant food/lack of light; buds falling from movement of plant,
Special needs Soft water; acid compost or water with sequestrated iron compound; repot every few years, top-dress otherwise; train stems of *H. carnosa* on to supports, cut back to fit space available in late winter; allow flowers to fall naturally as next year's buds are immediately adjacent to them.

H. phyllostachya 'Splash'

I. 'New Guinea' hybrid

ACANTHACEAE
Hypoestes

FRECKLE FACE, OR the polka dot plant, to give it its common names, has coloured foliage covered with bright pink spots and blotches.

Hypoestes phyllostachya (usually sold as *H. sanguinolenta*) is a small plant to between 30 and 60cm (12 and 24in) tall, with wiry black stems and pointed leaves, heart-shaped at the stalk end. In the cultivar *H. p.* 'Splash', there is so much pink marking that the green is hardly visible; it grows more slowly than the species. It is a pretty plant, and its soft leaf colouring, which lasts all season, gives it the edge on equally attractive but often fleeting flowers.

Light Good with some daily sun but avoid midday summer sun.
Temperature Minimum 10°C (50°F), 16–30°C (60–85°F) in summer.
Moisture Good humidity; mist frequently in high temperatures; water normally while growing, sparingly in winter.
Feeding Liquid feed from midsummer to autumn.
Propagation Take cuttings in spring in warmed compost.
Problems Scale insect; greenfly, if short of moisture.
Special needs Good light required to maintain vividness of colouring; pinch back the stems to encourage bushiness early in growing season and prevent flowering.

BALSAMINACEAE
Impatiens

There are two kinds of this impatiens, better known as busy Lizzie or patient Lucy, that are commonly grown: the bedding varieties, which are used for outdoor planting, and the container kind.

The container plants are much taller, to 30–45cm (12–18in), branching, and with coloured leaves as well. Colourful, succulent-stemmed plants, they are easily grown, and willing to flower heavily all year if given a chance. The colour range is red, pink, orange, salmon and white. Practically all the named plants available are varieties of *I. walleriana*.

There are also the fairly recently introduced hybrids of *I. linearifolia* from New Guinea, the height of which is up to 90cm (3ft), and whose long, narrow leaves are many coloured, often with a deep yellow centre; its flowers are larger.

Light Good, with some sun in winter, but avoid sun in summer.
Temperature Minimum 13°C (55°F), 16–30°C (60–85°F) in summer.
Moisture High humidity in summer, normal in winter; water freely while growing, especially in high temperatures, moderately in winter.
Feeding Liquid feed from early summer to end of early autumn.
Propagation Tip cuttings in spring and summer, in water.
Problems Red spider mite; whitefly; greenfly; leaf/bud drop from lack of water, humidity or draughts.
Special needs Moisture in air/compost in summer, otherwise red spider mite is a great problem; plenty of light for good flowering; pinch back tips early in growing season to keep bushy and floriferous, and repeat if necessary.

I. tessellatus

J. polyanthum

GRAMINEAE
Indocalamus

THE MAJORITY OF bamboos would be too vigorous and too large to attempt to confine them to a container, and in a border they would get out of hand, but some are small enough to be controllable in a container such as a tub. One of the most attractive of these is *I. tessellatus* also sometimes listed as *Arundinaria ragamowskii*, or *Sasa tessellata*.

It will grow rapidly to about 90–120cm (3–4ft) in a container (to 1.8m (6ft) in the wild) and has much the largest leaves of all the bamboos that are capable of withstanding frost; up to 60cm (24in) long and 10cm (4in) wide. It forms a mound-shaped plant, with drooping leaves, and is a good plant for providing an instant jungle effect.

Light Good or light shade.
Temperature Minimum –20°C (–4°F), 13–24°C (55–75°F) in summer.
Moisture Normal humidity; water moderately while growing, sparingly in winter.
Feeding Liquid feed from late spring to early autumn.
Propagation Remove suckers in spring.
Problems Brown leaf edges occur naturally in winter.
Special needs Repot every two to three years, top-dress other years; remove unwanted shoots to fit space available at any time.

OLEACEAE
Jasminum

THERE ARE MANY jasmines, mostly with a powerful fragrance, especially in the evening *J. azoricum* is less rampant than most. The white tubular flowers, with five petal-like lobes, open in midsummer and continue to appear well into autumn, scenting the conservatory continuously. With its shrubby tendency, height may only be a few feet or so.

Jasminum officinale, the common jasmine, which grow outdoors in sheltered cool-temperate gardens, is extremely vigorous, and could be difficult to deal with within two years; *J. polyanthum* has the merit of flowering from late autumn until spring, but needs much more warmth and plenty of light; its average height is about 2.4m (8ft). *J. × stephanense* is attractive, with pink, fragrant flowers in summer, but is a rampant grower, to 4.5m (15ft) or more, like common jasmine.

Light Good, with some sun.
Temperature Minimum 7°C (45°F), 16–32°C (60–90°F) in summer; *J. polyanthum*, minimum 13°C (55°F), preferably higher to induce and maintain flowering.
Moisture Normal humidity; water normally in summer, moderately in winter.
Feeding Liquid feed from late spring into early autumn.
Propagation Layer in summer; detach suckers; hardwood cuttings from spring to summer in 18–24°C (65–75°F).
Problems Greenfly; red spider mite; scale insect; lack of flowers from insufficient light or wrong pruning; yellow leaves from lack of nutrients.
Special needs Keep compost moist. Cut back after flowering; it flowers on growth made the previous season, so some new shoots should be left uncut.

J. carnea

J. brandigeana

Justicia

THE SHRIMP PLANT, *J. brandigeana* (syn. *Beloperone guttata*), commonly grown as a houseplant, is transformed in a conservatory, where it grows much larger and flowers profusely. Its flowerheads consist of flat, overlapping, pinky orange bracts forming a drooping cylinder, decorated with tubular white, purple-spotted flowers protruding from between the bracts. In conservatories these flowerheads can be 10cm (4in) or more long, and flowering can continue for most of the year, unless the plant is deliberately rested.

In its native Mexico it is a shrubby plant, where it grows to 90cm (3ft), but in a pot it will be nearer 60cm (2ft).

Another justicia species, *J. carnea* (syn. *Jacobinia carnea*), was once much grown in warm greenhouses. It lost its popularity when fuel became expensive and, unfortunately, it does not grow well in the home. However, it is regaining popularity now that conservatories are back in fashion. Its rose-pink flowers unfold in late summer and early autumn, at the end of the shoots on a plant which can be 1.5m (5ft) tall, but in a container is usually nearer 1.2m (4ft). Each flower is tubular in a rather mop-headed cluster 15cm (6in) long; the leaves are evergreen.

Light For *J. brandigeana*, good with some sun; for *J. carnea*, good, with some sun in winter.

Temperature For *J. brandigeana*, minimum 10°C (50°F), but will take 5°F lower for short periods; 16–30°C (60–85°F) in summer; for *J. carnea*, minimum 13°C (55°F), 16–30°C (60–85°F) in summer.

Moisture For *J. brandigeana*, normal humidity; water freely from late spring to mid autumn, moderately in winter; for *J. carnea*, high humidity, water normally in summer, moderate to sparingly in winter.

Feeding Liquid feed from early summer to early autumn.

Propagation Tip cuttings in spring in warmed compost and 21°C (75°F).

Problems For both, red spider mite in high temperatures and too much sun; for *J. carnea*, whitefly; greenfly; reddish leaves from too much water.

Special needs For *J. brandigeana*, encourage resting in winter by reducing water and temperatures, otherwise constant flowering results in a short-lived plant; for *J. carnea* do not let compost dry out between waterings in summer; mist in temperatures above 27°C (80°F); repot every other year; cut back new growth by about half after flowering; pinch back tips in late spring to encourage bushiness.

K. blossfeldiana

CRASSULACEAE
Kalanchoe

FAMILIAR AS A winter-flowering houseplant, *K. blossfeldiana* has clusters of tiny red flowers on 30cm (12in) stems, surrounded by a rosette of toothed, succulent, dark green leaves. With hybridization, there are now other colours such as orange, yellow, cream and lilac, and also dwarf varieties only 15cm (6in) tall, usually red or yellow flowered. Blooming can continue for many weeks, and flowering plants can be obtained at almost any time of year.

Kalanchoe daigremontiana (syn. *Bryophyllum daigremontianum*) is a succulent grown for its decorative leaves. It is particularly interesting because the fleshy triangular leaves carry plantlets on the toothed margins. Each leaf is about 15cm (6in) long when fully grown, grey-green with chocolate markings on the underside, and the whole plant is about 60–90cm (2–3ft) tall.

Light Good with some sun; as much light as possible in winter.

Temperature Minimum 10°C (50°F); 16–30°C (60–85°F) in summer.

Moisture Normal humidity; water freely in summer, allowing it to become just dry between waterings; moderately in autumn, sparingly in winter.

Feeding Liquid feed occasionally from mid-spring to late summer.

Propagation Use plantlets; by seed for *K. blossfeldiana*, sown late winter in 16–21°C (60–70°F).

Problems With leaves, from cold, dryness or nutrient shortage; with flowers, from lack of summer light.

Special needs Rest for four to six weeks after flowering; use cactus compost (see p. 165) for *K. daigremontianum*.

L. camara

L. rosea

VERBENACEAE
Lantana

THE MOST distinctive feature of the flowers of *L. camara* is the way that they change colour as they mature. Each rounded cluster of flowers opens from the centre outwards and each flower opens white, pale yellow or pink, and becomes deep orange or red. The colouring is peculiarly clean and clear-cut, so a plant in flower is a real eye-catcher, even though the actual flowers are small. There are also white and golden forms.

Blooming can start in late spring, though early summer is more usual, and continue until mid-autumn, making it good value for money, and compensating for its rather dull appearance out of flower; average height is 1.5–1.8m (5–6ft) in a container, width 60–75cm (2–2½ft). The whole plant is aromatic and often prickly. Because of its long flowering season, lantana is often used as a bedding plant in cool climates.

Light As much as possible at all times with the exception of midday summer sun.
Temperature Minimum 13°C (55°C), 16–30°C (60–85°F) in summer.
Moisture Normal humidity; water normally in summer, sparingly in winter.
Feeding Liquid feed from early summer into early autumn.
Propagation Tip cuttings in spring in 16–21°C (60–70°F) and warmed compost.
Problems Whitefly; greenfly; red spider mite.
Special needs Repot alternate years, top-dress in between; prune in late winter to shape and fit space available.

LILIACEAE
Lapageria

THE CHILEAN BELL FLOWER, *L. rosea*, has six-petalled flowers, coloured deep rose-pink on the outside, and paler pink within, from midsummer to mid-autumn. It is best appreciated if the twining stems are trained along the underside of the conservatory roof so that the flowers can hang down.

The long pointed evergreen leaves clothe the stems which can reach 4.5m (15ft), but may only be 3m (10ft). There is also a pure white form. In Chile many colour variants are grown, but only this pink one is widely available elsewhere.

Light Good with some sun, but no midday summer sun.
Temperature Minimum 7°C (45°F), cool in summer, maximum 21°C (70°F).
Moisture High humidity; water freely in summer, moderately in winter.
Feeding Liquid feed from late spring to late summer.
Propagation Layer in spring or autumn; sow seed as soon as ripe in 13–18°C (55–65°F).
Problems Greenfly; slugs; mealy bug; scale insect; thrips.
Special needs Ventilate well in high temperatures; essential to provide well-drained soil-containing compost, with one extra part grit and three extra parts peat; high humidity is particularly important until flowering starts; cut out weak shoots and cut remainder back to fit space available in early spring.

L. scoparium

L. muscaensis, L. berthelotii

MYRTACEAE
Leptospermum

LEPTOSPERMUMS ARE very prettily flowered evergreen shrubs or small trees, almost hardy and certainly capable of being grown outdoors in milder climates.

One of the best is the manuka, or tea tree, from New Zealand; although it is a small tree 6m (20ft) tall in the wild, its varieties are much smaller and easy to manage. *L. scoparium* has white, open, five-petalled flowers in clusters which almost cover the plant from late spring to early summer. Height in a container will be 2 or 3m (several feet), and 60 or 90cm (2 or 3ft) wide, and it will need to be planted in a tub or a border.

Leptospermum scoparium 'Sunraysii', one of its cultivars, has apple-blossom pink and white flowers in massive quantities; *L. s.* 'Leonard Wilson' has double white flowers. The wild variety *L. s. nanum* is only 30cm (12in) tall, but smothered in pale pink flowers with a crimson centre, and there are several cultivars of this available.

Light Good with some sun, but avoid midday summer sun.
Temperature Minimum 4°C (40°F), 16–24°C (60–75°F) in summer, but see Special needs.
Moisture Normal humidity; water normally from spring to autumn, moderately in winter.
Feeding Liquid feed from early summer to early autumn.
Propagation Semi-hardwood stem cuttings in summer.
Problems Scale insect; greenfly; red spider mite.
Special needs Ventilate well in temperatures above 21°C (70°F); well-drained compost with one extra part grit if soil-containing, and drainage layer for tubs; tip shoots after flowering to increase bushiness of plant.

LEGUMINOSAE
Lotus

ALTHOUGH *L. berthelotii* has been in cultivation for over a century, it is only now being grown to any degree, largely as a bedding plant, but it is a very good conservatory plant as well, both in flower and out. It has trailing stems to about 60cm (2ft), covered in a mass of silvery-grey needle-like leaves all year round. In late spring large scarlet flowers, rather like sweet peas in shape and size, are produced from about half-way down the stems, making a vivid display against the silvery background of foliage. Another species, *L. muscaensis* (syn. *L. musquensis*) is similar but with bright yellow flowers.

Light Good with some sun.
Temperature Minimum 10°C (50°F), 16–30°C (60–85°F) in summer.
Moisture Normal humidity; some misting in hot weather; water normally in spring and autumn, freely in hot weather, sparingly in winter.
Feeding Liquid feed from early summer to early autumn.
Propagation Heel cuttings in summer in sandy compost; sow seed in spring in 18°C (65°F).
Problems Lack of flowers from insufficient food/light; leaf fall from not enough water or from cold.
Special needs Plenty of light to ripen shoots in summer; care with winter watering; cut back flowering stems by about half immediately after flowering.

M. rhodantha

M. 'Cerise'

C A C T A C E A E

Mammillaria

MAMMILLARIAS, NATIVE TO Mexico, are those round fat little cacti, crowned with a ring of flowers, and occasionally with a ring of rounded fruits below them as well.

Mammillarias grow in clusters, becoming shortly cylindrical with age, and have spines and sometimes hairs as well. Flowering starts in late spring or early summer; height is seldom more than about 20cm (8in).

There is enormous variation within the genus. Some defy even the most experienced professional's care, others are easily grown and particularly attractive, for instance: *M. bocasana*: cream to pink flowers, 15cm (6in) tall, long white silky hairs instead of spines; *M. gracilis*: white or yellow flowers and spines, cylindrical, 10cm (4in); *M. rhodantha*: magenta to pink, spines red-brown or yellow, cylindrical, 20cm (8in); *M. zeilmanniana*: purple and yellow, white spines, rounded to cylindrical, 10cm (4in), flowers when very small.

Light As much as possible.
Temperature Minimum 7°C (45°F), 16–32°C (60–90°F) in summer.
Moisture Humidity low to dry; water normally from spring to mid-autumn, keep dry from late autumn and winter in minimum temperatures; but water sparingly on mild days if shrivelling occurs.
Feeding Liquid feed from midsummer into early autumn.
Propagation Use rooted offsets or seed sown in spring in sandy compost in 21–24°C (70–75°F).
Problems Mealy bug; root aphis; shrivelling from lack of water; spotting from cold; no flowers from lack of food/light; basal rotting from too much water or poorly drained compost.
Special needs Use cactus compost (see p. 165); care with winter watering.

A P O C Y N A C E A E

Mandevilla

KNOWN AS THE Chilean jasmine (although it hails from Argentina), *M. laxa* (syn. *M. suaveolens*) has a profusion of fragrant white flowers all summer on climbing stems that will reach at least 4.5m (15ft) if allowed to, but which can easily be kept under control. In full flower it is most attractive, with its tubular blooms opening out into a trumpet about 5cm (2in) wide, hanging in clusters along the stems.

Mandevilla splendens (syn. *Dipladenia splendens*) from Brazil has glossy evergreen leaves like *M. laxa*, but its funnel-shaped flowers are rose-pink with a yellow throat on the inside. It flowers well into the autumn, and will flower when young. Height can eventually be 4.5cm (15ft).

Light Good.
Temperature Minimum 4°C (40°F), late winter to midsummer 13–18°C (55–65°F), otherwise prevailing temperature for *M. laxa*; minimum 13°C (55°F); 16–30°C (60–85°F) in summer for *M. splendens*.
Moisture High humidity; water freely from late winter to early autumn, moderately in autumn and early winter, not at all in mid-winter for *M. laxa*; normally from spring to autumn, sparingly in winter for *M. splendens*.
Feeding Liquid feed from early summer into early autumn.
Propagation Ripe sideshoots 7.5cm (3in) long in summer in warmed compost and 24–30°C (75–85°F).
Problems Scale insect; mealy bug; greenfly; red spider mite; lack of flower from lack of food.
Special needs Encourage winter rest; *M. laxa* needs a border or very large trough; cut back in autumn to remove flowered shoots and fit space.

M. leuconeura erythroneura   *M. magnifica*

MARANTACEAE
Maranta

MARANTAS ARE familiar, ornamental foliage plants for the home, but they are not particularly easy to grow in such surroundings, mainly because there is insufficient humidity.

Maranta leuoconeura has elliptic leaves up to 15cm (6in) long, with dark brown blotches; *M. l. kerchoviana* has grey-green, rather than light green, leaves, dark brown patches changing to dark green, and a purple underside to each leaf. *M. l. erythroneura* is even more attractive, since all its main veins are carmine-red, accounting for its common name of the herring-bone plant, and *M. l. massangeana* has silvery white veins and midrib on a velvety olive-green background.

All these are handsome and well worth growing; height is about 20cm (8in), but the spread of mature plants can be considerably more, up to double the height when grown in conservatories.

Light Shade in summer, shade from sun in winter, otherwise good light then.
Temperature Minimum 13°C (55°F), 16–24°C (60–75°F) in summer.
Moisture High humidity with frequent misting in temperatures above 24°C (75°F), water freely from spring to autumn, sparingly in winter.
Feeding Liquid feed from early summer into early autumn.
Propagation Divide when repotting.
Problems Brown leaf edges from dry air or lack of water; curling up or discoloured leaves from too much light; rotting stems from cold and/or too much water or poor compost drainage.
Special needs Good humidity at all times, especially when increasing by division; repot during first growing season; maintain even temperature; repot every other year; use soft tepid water.

MELASTOMATACEAE
Medinilla

IF GIVEN THE right care, *M. magnifica* makes a highly attractive shrub; a conservatory kept warm in winter provides the ideal environment, and should result in a spectacular flower display.

Medinilla can grow to 1.5m (5ft) high in the wild, but in containers it will be nearer 90cm (3ft) and about 60cm (2ft) wide. Its evergreen leaves are large, up to 25cm (10in) long, and the bright pink flowers are produced in long hanging clusters in late spring. Their stalks are pinkish, as are the petal-like bracts carried in tiers; the anthers are conspicuously purple.

Light Good.
Temperature Minimum 16°C (60°F), 16–32°C (60–90°F) in summer, but see Special needs.
Moisture High humidity, with misting; water moderately from spring to autumn, sparingly in winter.
Feeding Liquid feed from late spring into early autumn.
Propagation Semi-hardwood cuttings in spring in warmed compost, high humidity and 24–27°C (75–80°F).
Problems Red spider mite.
Special needs Humidity is important at all times, together with warmth in winter; ventilate in temperatures above 32°C (90°F); maintain steady temperature; prune to shape only, immediately after flowering.

M. jalapa

M. deliciosa borsigiana

NYCTAGINACEAE
Mirabilis

COMMONLY CALLED MARVEL of Peru, *M. jalapa* is also known as the four o'clock plant, from its habit of opening its flowers late in the day. It is a delightful plant, as it is strongly scented, and has a mass of flowers.

The commonest colour is crimson-purple, but yellow and white are nearly as frequently found in the wild. All these colours can be found not only on one plant, but in one cluster on one plant, and often a flower may combine two of them, one spotted with another, or a flower can be divided equally between two colours. The variation is extensive, and the flowers on a plant can be differently coloured. Orange-red and pink are also frequently seen.

Flowering starts in midsummer, sometimes earlier, depending on planting time, and height is 60–90cm (2–3ft), with a spread of 45–60cm (1½–2ft). The stems usually need supports.

Light As much as possible.
Temperature Minimum 4°C (40°F), 16–32°C (60–90°F) in summer.
Moisture Normal humidity; mist in temperatures above 27 °C (80°F); water freely from late spring to early autumn, sparingly until dormant, then keep dry until repotting.
Feeding Liquid feed from early summer into early autumn.
Propagation Seed sown in mid-spring 21–24°C (70–75°F).
Problems Greenfly; tuber rot in store from frost; yellow leaves from lack of nutrient.
Special needs Pot tubers each spring in fresh compost and 23cm (9in) diameter containers; store dry in pots from end of growing season; pinch back tips when two pairs of leaves are formed, to make it bushier.

ARACEAE
Monstera

THE MONSTERAS HAVE such distinctive foliage that they are quite outstanding, and make dramatically handsome plants. Their common names are the Swiss cheese plant or the Mexican bread plant.

Monstera adansonii, sometimes sold under the name of *M. pertusa*, will grow to 3m (10ft), and has 45cm (18in) long leaves, given the space and a suitable container. There is a much larger one, *M. deliciosa borsigiana* (often sold as *M. deliciosa*), whose height can be 6m (20ft), and leaves 1.2m (4ft) long. Both have slashed and perforated leaves and both grow thick aerial roots, best trained into a moss pole. They have white flowers and fruit when mature, the fruit being cone-shaped and 15–23cm (6–9in) long with a pineapple scent (in the case of *M. d. borsigiana*).

Light Light shade, good light in winter.
Temperature Minimum 10°C (50°F), 16–32°C (60–90°F) in summer.
Moisture High humidity; water freely in summer, allow the compost to become just dry between waterings; sparingly in winter.
Feeding Liquid feed when not repotted in spring.
Propagation Cut off top with aerial root attached and pot.
Problems Red spider mite; no holes in adult leaves from cold, lack of food/water or not enough light; yellow leaves from over/under watering or lack of food; pale leaves from too much light; brown edges from dry air.
Special needs Use moss pole and aerial roots for support; repot alternate years; wash adult leaves or put plant out in summer showers; watering needs care.

M. acuminata

MUSACEAE
Musa

THIS GENUS CONTAINS the banana, *M.* × *paradisiaca*, which grows much too big for the average conservatory, but the flowering banana, *M. coccinea*, develops into a reasonably sized plant 90–120cm (3–4ft) tall, with leaves only 90cm (3ft) long. Its red bracts are tipped with yellow and the flowers themselves are yellow also, followed by small red bananas, which turn orange-yellow when ripe, but are not edible.

For an edible fruiting variety, grow *M. acuminata* 'Dwarf Cavendish', a commercial crop in the Canary Islands, though it is actually of Chinese origin. Height is 1.8m (6ft), and the leaves 90cm (3ft) long. The tubular flowers have reddish purple bracts, from which the fruit curve upwards.

Light Good, with some sun.
Temperature Minimum 13°C (55°F), 16–32°C (60–90°F) in summer.
Moisture High humidity at all times; water freely in summer, normally in winter.
Feeding Liquid feed from late spring to mid-autumn.
Propagation Detach rooted suckers in summer and plant in 24–27°C (75–80°F).
Problems Red spider mite; root and stem rot.
Special needs High temperatures (not less than 18°C/65 °F at night in summer) if fruits required; grow in 38cm (15in) diameter (or larger) tubs or in border; good drainage.

M. communis

N. domestica

MYRTACEAE
Myrtus

ALTHOUGH *M. communis*, the common myrtle from southern Europe, is hardy in milder gardens, in the majority of cases it will only grow satisfactorily in a conservatory. However, it is well worth growing for its fragrant white flowers with a prominent cluster of golden stamens, produced in mid- to late summer. The bush itself is densely covered in glossy, aromatic, dark green leaves.

In open ground it can grow to 3m (10ft), but is more likely to make 2m (6ft plus) in a tub; a smaller variety (around 90cm/3ft high) is *M. c. tarentina*, which has smaller leaves.

One of the oldest plants in cultivation, it is still customary to include it in a wedding bouquet, where its aromatic leaves and scented flowers make it a charming addition.

Light Good, with some sun.
Temperature Minimum 4°C (40°F), 16–30°C (60–85°F) in summer, but see Special needs.
Moisture Normal humidity; water normally in summer, sparingly in winter.
Feeding Liquid feed from midsummer until mid-autumn.
Propagation Cuttings in summer in warmed compost.
Problems Scale insect.
Special needs Ventilate well in high temperatures above 30°C (85°F); prune (to shape only) after flowering.

BERBERIDACEAE
Nandina

THE HEAVENLY BAMBOO, *N. domestica*, from eastern Asia is another of those strange classifications, as it so closely resembles a bamboo as to make no difference.

Nandina grows 1.8m (6ft) tall in the wild, rather less in the container, and its delicate stems and pointed, narrow leaflets lend a distinctly oriental air to its surroundings. In autumn the light green colour of the leaves changes to crimson though, as they are evergreen, few of them will fall. Small white flowers in large, airy clusters at least 30cm (12in) wide appear from early to midsummer, followed by red berries. There is a much smaller cultivar called *N. d.* 'Nana Purpurea', whose leaves are purple-tinted all summer.

It is not difficult to grow, needing only cool conservatory conditions, and will not get out of hand, unlike many of the true bamboos.

Light Good, or light shade.
Temperature Minimum 4°C (40°F), 16–30°C (60–85°F) in summer.
Moisture Normal humidity; water normally in summer, moderately to sparingly in winter.
Feeding Liquid feed from midsummer to autumn.
Propagation Heel cuttings in late summer in warmed compost.
Problems Red spider mite; scale insect.
Special needs Ventilate well in high temperatures above 30°C (85°F); deadhead; remove oldest stems occasionally.

N. 'Tête à Tête'

N. × *coccinea* (pitcher detail)

A M A R Y L L I D A C E A E

Narcissus

DAFFODILS and jonquils are good bulbs for a conservatory, as they need little extra heat to flower several weeks early; the jonquils can provide an almost overpowering fragrance.

To bring narcissi on early, plant two large-flowered daffodils or five jonquils/narcissi in a 12.5cm (5in) pot in early autumn, with the tips just showing (there should be a drainage layer in the base) and keep in a cool, completely dark place for eight weeks.

Light After eight weeks bring containers into light shade for two to three weeks, then give good light.
Temperature In light gradually increase over range 10–16°C (50–60°F).
Moisture Normal humidity; water normally in dark and in light until leaves start to die, then gradually decrease till barely moist.
Feeding Liquid feed weekly after flowering until leaves start to yellow.
Propagation By offsets at potting time.
Problems Rotting of base, discard; very long leaves from too much warmth and/or light; short growth from too short a rooting period or dry compost while rooting; brown buds from not enough or irregular watering while rooting; roots showing at top of container from bulb planted too firmly or from compacted compost.
Special needs Wait until buds are 2.5cm (1in) tall before bringing into light; keep cool and moist in dark; increase warmth/light slowly. After flowering keep bulbs barely moist and cool, leave in containers until autumn.

N E P E N T H A C E A E

Nepenthes

THE NEPENTHES, carnivorous perennials from Malaysia, belong to the group of plants commonly called pitcher plants, with curiously modified leaves in which the midrib lengthens into a long tendril, at the end of which the "pitcher" develops. It has a ring of honey glands just inside, which are attractive to insects; once caught, the insect slides into the pepsin liquid at the base of the pitcher.

Nepenthes × *coccinea* has deep red pitchers – about 15cm (6in) long – with a little yellow spotting, and a green lid with red streaks and patches. The leaves are long and narrow, and the plant has a tendency to climb, so needs support. Cultivation is specialized, as the plants grow in boggy soil short of nutrient, obtaining the minerals they need by digesting the trapped insects.

Light Shade with some sun.
Temperature Minimum 16°C (60°F), 18–32°C (65–90°F) in summer.
Moisture High humidity; water freely from early spring into early autumn, moderately otherwise.
Feeding Liquid feed every few weeks from the time pitchers start to form until autumn; occasionally introduce flies and other insects.
Propagation Tip cuttings in living sphagnum moss, in 27 °C (80°F), in spring.
Problems Lack of pitchers from lack of light; slow or no growth from low temperatures.
Special needs Soft tepid water; compost of living sphagnum moss, or sphagnum moss and peat in equal parts; provide drainage layer, and do not allow to stand in water; grow on rafts, bark or in hanging baskets.

N. exaltata 'Bostoniensis'

N. bowdenii

OLEANDRACEAE

Nephrolepis

THE TROPICAL NEPHROLEPIS ferns are amongst some of the easiest and most attractive to grow in the conservatory. In the case of *N. exaltata* 'Bostoniensis' they quickly develop into graceful specimens with arching fronds at least 60cm (2ft) long; in mature plants, they will be 1.2m (4ft) long and 15cm (6in) wide. Their slightly pendulous habit is particularly suitable for hanging baskets, in which they will push new growth through the base and make a complete ball of greenery.

There are many varieties; the one shown here is one of the best, with *N. e.* 'Whitmanii' a close second because of its feathery frond edges. All grow rapidly, and a small plant a few centimetres tall will be at least 30cm (12in) tall and as much wide by the second growing season.

Light Good to shade.
Temperature Minimum 10°C (50°F), a little lower if kept dryish, maximum 24°C (75°F).
Moisture High humidity, mist in temperatures above 24°C (75°F); water moderately in summer, sparingly in winter, but keep compost moist at all times.
Feeding Liquid feed every few weeks when not repotted, from spring to autumn.
Propagation By plantlets produced from runners, in spring or summer.
Problems Scale insect; red spider mite; brown fronds from dry air, lack of water or cold; yellowish or pale fronds from too much light.
Special needs Soft water; peat-based, acid compost; repot every two to three years when adult; ventilate well in high temperatures; remove fronds as they mature and wither.

AMARYLLIDACEAE

Nerine

THE NERINES, natives of South Africa, have spidery petals in shades of pink, the most common colour, plus red, salmon and white, and long stamens protrude from the centre of the flower. Their resting or ripening time is after flowering, either mid-autumn to spring or mid-spring to late summer, depending on species.

Two species are commonly grown: *N. bowdenii*: pale pink flowers carried six to twelve in a cluster on 30cm (12in) stems; and *N. b.* 'Pink Triumph': rose-pink and slightly taller. Leaves are present from late spring to mid-autumn. *N. sarniensis*, the Guernsey lily, to 45cm (18in), has colours varying through orange-red, red and pale pink and the foliage lasts from late autumn to spring.

Light Good with plenty of sun.
Temperature Minimum 4°C (40°F) for *N. bowdenii*; 10°C (50°F) for *N. sarniensis*; 16–27°C (60–80°F) in summer for both.
Moisture Normal humidity; water sparingly in late summer when first planted, normally while flowering; for *N. bowdenii*, decrease watering until kept dry from late autumn to early spring, then soak well once, and water normally; for *N. sarniensis*, water moderately after flowering until late spring, then decrease and keep dry until late summer; soak well at the end of late summer.
Feeding Liquid feed occasionally after the second year when foliage is present.
Propagation By offsets at potting time.
Problems Mealy bug; greenfly.
Special needs For *N. bowdenii* keep cool and dry from autumn to spring; for *N. sarniensis*, rest from late spring to late summer; repot every four to five years in late summer; place bulbs with tips just showing above compost, three to a 15cm (6in) pot, early in late summer.

A P O C Y N A C E A E

Nerium

KNOWN MORE FAMILIARLY as the olean-der, *N. oleander* is a decorative and large evergreen shrub, with narrow dark green, leathery leaves, and pink or white, funnel-shaped flowers 5–7.5cm (2–3in) wide. There are rose-pink, purple or crimson, and double-, as well as single-flowered kinds.

Nerium oleander 'Variegatum' has creamy yellow edges to the leaves, and pink flowers. The flowering season is a long one, from early summer into mid-autumn, so they are good value for space. Height in the open can be 4.5m (15ft), but in tubs is likely to be only 1–2m (3–6ft), and 60–75cm (2–2½ft) wide.

☐ Oleanders need to be handled carefully, since the whole plant is poisonous, especially the flowers and seeds, which can be fatal if eaten.

Light Good with some sun.
Temperature Minimum 7°C (45°F), 16–30°C (60–85°F) in summer, but see Special needs.
Moisture Normal humidity; water freely from early spring to early autumn, moderately to late autumn, sparingly in winter.
Feeding Liquid feed from late spring to early autumn.
Propagation Heel cuttings in summer, hardwood stem cuttings 15cm (6in) long in summer in warmed compost.
Problems Scale insect; mealy bug; red spider mite.
Special needs Ventilate well in temperatures above 30 °C (90°F); care with watering while resting; cut back the season's new growth to within 10cm (4in) of its origin in mid-autumn.

O R C H I D A C E A E

Odontoglossum

THESE SOUTH AMERICAN orchids are am-ongst some of the most beautiful there are; the flowers are in clusters of three or four, carried in an arching spray, each flower consisting of flat, wide sepals and petals and being as much as 17.5cm (7in) wide. They flower in autumn and winter, in a wide range of colours. One of the most popular species is the tiger orchid, *O. grande*, with yellow, brown-banded petals and sepals, and a creamy white lip with an orange crest.

Another extremely popular one is *O. crispum*. Each spike has 6 to 12 flowers, each about 10cm (4in) wide, usually white flushed pink, with a yellowish lip. Season of blooming is mainly winter and early spring and there are many named variants.

Light Good, with some sun in autumn.
Temperature Minimum 10–13°C (50–55°F), but ideal all year is 16°C (60°F), with 2–3°C (4–5°F) drop at night.
Moisture High humidity; water moderately from spring to autumn, sparingly in winter, but never let compost dry out completely.
Feeding Liquid feed occasionally in summer.
Propagation Divide when repotting, ensuring three stems on each division.
Problems Scale insect; red spider mite; thrips; mealy bug; slugs; black leaf spot; rot; virus.
Special needs Compost should consist of two parts osmunda fibre/one part sphagnum moss; repot alternate years (see also p. 167); keep *O. grande* almost dry in winter; keep temperature as steady as possible at all times; ventilate similarly; deadhead.

O. microdasys 'Albispina'

CACTACEAE

Opuntia

O PUNTIA STEMS consist of a chain of pads carrying spines or hairs; on the edge of these pads flowers open out from a long tube, followed by oval fruits in various colours. The prickly pear, *O. ficus-indica*, is a large plant (with edible fruit) which needs to be planted in a conservatory border where it will grow 1.5m (5ft) tall; when covered in its yellow flowers, it is a handsome and striking plant.

A much smaller species grown in containers is *O. microdasys*, whose pads are 12.5–15cm (5–6in) long, to 30 or 45cm (1 or 1½ft) tall, with yellow flowers and pale yellow bristles. *O. m.* 'Albispina' has pale yellow flowers and white bristles.

Light As much as possible, but shade from hottest summer sun.

Temperature Minimum 4°C (40°F), but 10°C (50°F) is better, 16–32°C (60–90°F) in summer.

Moisture Low to dry humidity; water normally from spring to autumn, sparingly to almost dry in winter.

Feeding Liquid feed from midsummer into early autumn.

Propagation By stem cuttings of two to three pads, allowed to dry for a few days before potting.

Problems Mealy bug; root mealy bug and root aphis; red spider mite; scale insect; brown spots from cold; shrivelling from lack of water; no flowers from lack of nutrient and/or light.

Special needs Cactus compost, see p. 165; increase watering gradually from winter to spring, decrease gradually from early autumn until winter. Water least in winter; remove oldest stems occasionally.

117

Paphiopedilum sp.

ORCHIDACEAE
Paphiopedilum

MORE recognizable under the common name of the slipper orchid, these orchids have a lip that has been modified into a pronounced pouch. The flower colouring is extremely varied from species to species, green, yellow and white being some of the commonest colours. Each flower can be as much as 15cm (6in) wide, and lasts for two months in some varieties.

Whereas most orchids form pseudobulbs, this genus produces rhizomes instead, from which a cluster of strap-shaped leaves develops, and from the centre of which the flower stem emerges.

Some species and a variety which do not need high temperatures are: *P. fairrieanum*: 25cm (10in), red-striped white petals, green pouch with deep red-brown lines, late summer to mid-autumn; *P. insigne*: 35cm (14in), yellow-green, white-tipped petals, deep coppery yellow pouch, whole flower 1.25cm (5in) wide, winter; *P.i. sanderae*: pale yellow with brown spots and large white patch on vertical petal.

Light Requires shade.
Temperature Minimum 10°C (50°F) at night for those described here; for best flowering 16–18°C (60–65°F) all year.
Moisture High humidity; water moderately from spring to autumn, sparingly in winter.
Feeding Liquid feed occasionally in summer.
Propagation Divide at repotting time.
Problems Mealy bug; scale insect; red spider mite; greenfly; basal rot from too much water or too low temperatures.
Special needs Use compost of equal parts good loam, sphagnum moss and osmunda fibre; repot alternate years in early spring; ventilate at all times; keep compost moist, supply plenty of drainage material; deadhead; see also p. 166.

P. chrysocanthion

P. caerulea

C A C T A C E A E
Parodia

MANY OF THE parodias are fairly new to cultivation, and are mostly small, round cacti, though some become more cylindrical with age, and grow 15cm (6in) or more wide and correspondingly taller. Their colourful spines are a particular attraction.

Parodia chrysocanthion is covered in bright golden spines. The flowers are yellow and tubular, opening out into a funnel and generally found singly on top of the plant in early summer. There are other species with salmon flowers (*P. mairana-na*), or with red ones (*P. sanguiniflora*).

Light As good as possible.
Temperature Minimum to almost freezing; 16–30°C (60–85°F) in summer.
Moisture Low to dry humidity; water normally from spring to autumn, sparingly in winter.
Feeding Liquid feed in years when not repotted, from mid-spring to autumn.
Propagation Seed, with slow germination and slow growth in first year.
Problems Mealy bug; root aphis and root mealy bug; scale insect; red spider mite; shrivelling from lack of water; no flowers from lack of sun or nutrient or from too much nitrogen.
Special needs Keep almost dry in lowest temperatures; repot in 2nd or 3rd years; use cactus compost (see p.164).

P A S S I F L O R A C E A E
Passiflora

THE BLUE PASSIONFLOWER, *P. caerulea*, will survive outdoors in sheltered cool-temperate gardens, but is well suited to conservatory cultivation, where plants will be evergreen. The passionflower can, however, be a rampant climber, and therefore does best in a border; it can also be grown in a large tub.

The leaves are palmate and narrowly five-to-seven lobed, and the curious flowers, 10cm (4in) wide, are produced singly from early midsummer until mid-autumn. Colouring is a combination of blue, purple, white, green and orange.

Passiflora caerulea bears egg-shaped, pale orange fruits, which are prolifically set in warmth; they are edible but insipid. For really delicious fruit, it would be necessary to grow *P. edulis*, whose flowers are white, green and purple, and whose fruit are pale yellow or purple, or *P. quadrangularis* with fragrant flowers, and purple fruit at least 20cm (8in) long; both these need higher temperatures, and the last named is even more rampant.

Light Good with some sun.
Temperature Minimum 4°C (40°F) for *P. caerulea*, minimum 13°C (55°F) for the others; 16–27°C (60–80°F) in summer.
Moisture Normal humidity; water freely from spring into early autumn, moderately in winter.
Feeding Liquid feed from late spring to autumn.
Propagation Layer in summer; sow seed in mid-spring in 21 °C (70°F).
Problems Greenfly; red spider mite; brown tips to stems from cold.
Special needs Keep compost moist without waterlogging; repot young plants during growing season; cut back by half or more in late winter to fit space available.

P. 'L'Elegante' with ivy-leaved pelargoniums

GERANIACEAE
Pelargonium

COMMONLY CALLED geraniums, these plants are deservedly popular. Among the easiest plants to grow, they have a great deal of variation in flower shape, flower colour, aroma, size, habit and leaf colouring. One of their outstanding attributes is their ability to flower for many months, even when the temperatures drop in winter.

Pelargoniums are divided into different groups:

Zonal pelargoniums

These are mostly seen as bedding or outdoor container plants. This group contains the bright scarlet geranium, of which *P.* 'Paul Crampel' and *P.* 'Gustav Emich' are the most familiar. Its members have a fairly tightly packed cluster of smallish flowers, each about 3cm (2½in) wide, on a short stem originating from a leaf joint. They can be as tall as 1.8m (6ft) and more, with a wall to provide support. Good varieties include: *P.* 'Fiat',

salmon-red; *P.* 'Orangesonne', orange; *P.* 'Queen of Denmark', salmon-pink.

Irene pelargoniums

This group of hybrids have semi-double flowers on a compact plant – they are particularly free- and long-flowering. Some of the most ornamental are: *P.* 'Apache', deep crimson; *P.* 'Lollipop', orange-scarlet; *P.* 'Modesty', large and white; *P.* 'Rose Irene', rose-pink with a white centre.

Regal pelargoniums

These form another group and are less free-flowering and with a shorter season. Their individual flowers are much larger and more attractive, being funnel-shaped with waved and frilled edges to the petals. Three or four grow in a cluster on short stems attached to the top of a single stem. They flower in the main from mid- to late summer, but the season may be longer. Some

Ivy-leaved pelargoniums

Zonal pelargoniums

attractive hybrids include: *P.* 'Aztec', pink with brown blotches; *P.* 'Brown's Butterfly', (syn. *P.* 'Black Butterfly'), black-red marked deep brown; *P.* 'Carisbrooke', rose-pink with maroon blotches; *P.* 'Golden Princess', with gold-variegated leaves; *P.* 'Grand Slam', crimson with red blotches; *P.* 'La Paloma', white with purple markings, and *P.* 'Lavender Grand Slam', lavender-purple.

Scented-leaved pelargoniums

These each smell differently when lightly rubbed. Most of these are species, and have much cut and divided leaves; their flowers are small and brightly coloured and their stems are thinner and tougher, woody rather than herbaceous. Amongst them are: *P.* 'Attar of Roses', lilac flowers, rose-scented leaves; *P. crispum* 'Variegatum', pink flowers, and lemon-scented curled leaves; *P. graveolens*, rose-pink flowers, orange-scented leaves; *P. odoratissimum*, white flowers, apple-scented leaves; *P. tomentosum*, white flowers, peppermint-scented leaves.

Ivy-leaved pelargoniums

These have a trailing habit – ideal for hanging containers or for trailing down from shelves or other flat surfaces; *P.* 'L'Elegante' is one of the best. As well as being remarkably easy to grow, it has large, narrow-petalled white flowers with purple lines, and grey-green leaves edged with white and pink. *P.* 'Rouletta' has white flowers, whose petals have a bright red edging.

Fancy-leaved pelargoniums

These grow on average to 15cm (6in) tall. Among them are: *P.* 'Red Black Vesuvius', with scarlet flowers, and dark red-brown, almost black flowers; *P.* 'Golden Harry Hieover' with red flowers and gold-green leaves with red-brown markings;

P. 'Mr Henry Cox', pale pink flowers, green-centred leaves with a golden edge and red and black band; *P.* 'Princess Alexandra', pink flowers and silvery green leaf; *P.* 'Robert Fish', with red flowers and golden leaves.

Light Good with some sun.

Temperature Minimum 4°C (40°F), 16–27°C (60–80°F) in summer; miniatures: minimum 7°C (45°F).

Moisture Normal to low humidity; water freely at each watering, but allow to just dry out between waterings; sparingly in winter to almost dry.

Feeding Liquid feed from midsummer to mid-autumn.

Propagation Semi-ripe cuttings 5–10cm (2–4in) long, from midsummer to early autumn; do not allow second leaf-joint to touch the compost, to avoid rot; sow seed late winter to mid-spring in 18°C (65°F) – will flower same season if sown late winter.

Problems Whitefly; red spider mite; greenfly; rust; black stem rot on cuttings; yellow lower leaves (still firm) from overwatering; yellow lower leaves (wilting) from underwatering; red or brown leaf edges from cold.

Special needs Do not overwater; use well-drained compost; repot in mid- to late winter into pots 2.5cm (1in) diameter smaller, cut root-ball back as necessary; water well to encourage new growth, and then repot as required; scented leaved pelargoniums are slower growing and do not need repotting every year, and some need more pinching otherwise they become leggy; ivy-leaved ones are repotted early spring, and pinching back is not required unless they get too long; keep *P.* 'L'Elegante' on the dry side for best leaf colouring; remove plain-green leaved shoots as soon as seen. Miniatures need not be pinched back, and pot size should be 7.5–11.5cm (3–4½in); cut hard back in late autumn to 5–10cm (2–4in) long, or to fit the space available; pinch out shoot tips in spring to make bushier.

ADIANTACEAE
Pellaea

THE NEW ZEALAND button fern, *P. rotundi-folia*, has 30cm (12in) long unfern-like fronds. Instead of feathery leaflets, it has round shiny ones in pairs all along the rough, wiry leaf stem, which arches over. The rootstock is creeping and, unusually for a fern, does not require a great deal of moisture or generally damp surroundings. It will exist quite happily in dry air and with little moisture in the compost.
with little moisture in the compost.

Light Good or light shade.
Temperature Minimum 7°C (45°F), 16–27°C (60–80°F) in summer.
Moisture Normal humidity; water moderately while growing, sparingly in winter.
Feeding Liquid feed at half-strength from early summer to autumn.
Propagation Divide rootstock at potting time.
Problems Scale insect; pale colouring from too much light or lack of nutrient.
Special needs Use soft, tepid water; acid compost.

PIPERACEAE
Peperomia

PEPEROMIAS ARE A large group of fleshy plants, grown for their foliage, which inhabit, in the main, the tropical rain forests of America. Some are bushy, some are trailing, and all provide decoration all year round.

The most well known is the rat-tail plant, *P. caperata*, whose heart-shaped, corrugated, dark green leaves are topped by long white spikes of flowers on pink stems in summer; there is a form *P. c.* 'Variegata' with creamy white leaf edges.

Peperomia obtusifolia (syn. *P. magnoliifolia*) is 15cm (6in) taller, at 30cm (12in), much more upright with thick shiny leaves 12.5cm (5in) long, marked with creamy white, sometimes almost completely white. In contrast, there is the trailing *P. scandens* 'Variegata', a cultivar with yellow-marked shiny leaves and pink stems. All these are rather slow growing.

Light Good or light shade.
Temperature Minimum 10°C (50°F); 16–30°C (60–85°F) in summer.
Moisture Normal humidity; water moderately while growing, sparingly in winter.
Feeding Liquid feed occasionally while growing.
Propagation Use tip cuttings in summer at prevailing summer temperatures.
Problems Leaf drop in winter from cold; brown tips and edges to leaves from sudden falls in temperature at any time; wilting leaves; stem rot or brown swellings on undersurface of leaves from overwatering.
Special needs Care with watering at all times; use tepid water; repot every three to four years.

P. erubescens 'Imperial Red'

ARACEAE
Philodendron

THERE ARE MANY philodendrons in cultivation, mostly grown in the home (with some difficulty) in cool-temperate climates, and all grown for their foliage. Some are climbers, some shrubs; the species *P. scandens* is a climber, commonly called the sweetheart plant.

It has fleshy stems, clothed with heart-shaped leaves which mature to a length of 30cm (12in), though in containers they may only be half this length. It grows quickly and can be trained up a moss pole, or the aerial roots can be directed down into the compost, and the height varies according to the space available. There is a variegated version, with attractively marbled white leaves. *P. erubescens* has 20cm (12in) long, arrow-shaped leaves which are tinted deep-red in the form, *P. e.* 'Imperial Red'.

Light Good to shade.
Temperature Minimum 10°C (50°F), but preferably a little higher; 16–32°C (60–90°F) in summer.
Moisture Normal humidity; water freely from late spring into autumn, sparingly in winter.
Feeding Liquid feed from early summer to autumn.
Propagation Tip stem cuttings in summer; offsets if available.
Problems Lower leaves yellow from too much or not enough water; all leaves a sickly yellow from too much light; rotting stems from cold or too much water; red spider mite.
Special needs Variegated type needs good light to retain variegation; soft tepid water; repot every two to three years when adult; cut back in late winter as required; pinch back tips in growing season to make bushy instead of climbing.

POLYPODIACEAE
Platycerium

LIKE THE BUTTON FERN (*Pellaea*), *P. bifurcatum* is a most uncharacteristic fern in its leaf shape. Its common name, the stag's-horn fern, describes its main fronds exactly. They have a leathery texture, and are covered in a thin, felt-like covering of white hairs. If this is rubbed off, the fronds tend to brown and shrivel, so great care should be taken not to damage it.

These forked fronds, which are fertile, emerge from one point low down on a cylinder which is made up of the barren fronds, green when they first develop, but later becoming brown and papery. These are produced in successive layers, like onion skins, and may wrap themselves round the support if it is flat, otherwise they form the cylinder, hollow and upright. The forked fronds will normally be at least 60cm (2ft) long.

Platycerium grows naturally in the forks of forest trees, and on their branches. Consequently their roots are few and small, and containers need only be shallow.

Light Good to shade.
Temperature Minimum 10°C (50°F), 16–30°C (60–85°F) in summer.
Moisture High humidity; water moderately from spring to autumn, sparingly in winter.
Feeding Liquid feed occasionally from midsummer to autumn.
Propagation Plantlets, which sometimes grow at soil level; spores.
Problems Scale insect; brown patches on fronds from sun scorch or loss of down covering; yellowing from cold and/or too much water.
Special needs Care in handling; use peat-based compost, or mixture of peat and sphagnum moss; grow hanging in air, or on high shelves.

GRAMINEAE
Pleioblastus

PREVIOUSLY KNOWN AS *Arundinaria auricoma*, *P. auricomus* (syn. *P. viridistriatus*) is one of the smaller bamboos, whose growth does not get out of hand because of runners, as so many other bamboos do. Maximum height is about 1.2m (4ft) and width about 45cm (18in); the stems are purplish green, while the leaves are striped deep gold on dark green. Their length varies between 7.5 and 20cm (3 and 8in) long, and width is about 2cm (¾in) and, oddly for a bamboo, they are furry to the touch. It is a brightly coloured and interesting bamboo, which does well in a tub, supplying an authentically Oriental atmosphere.

Light Good light with some sun.
Temperature Minimum 4°C (40°F), but will survive below freezing for short periods, 16–30°C (60–85°F) in summer.
Moisture Normal humidity; water normally in summer, moderately to sparingly in winter.
Feeding Liquid feed from early summer into autumn.
Propagation By division in early spring.
Problems Scale insect; lack of colour from low light intensity.
Special needs Repot in spring every two to three years; do not let compost ever dry out; cut down hard in late autumn or late winter to produce entirely new growth for the coming season.

P. auriculata

P. rubra

PLUMBAGINACEAE
Plumbago

THE CAPE LEADWORT *P. auriculata* (syn. *P. capensis*) is a beautiful evergreen climber with a long flowering season from late spring until autumn. The sky-blue flowers are phlox-shaped, carried in clusters all over the plant. If they are removed immediately they have faded, the plant will quickly start to bloom all over again.

Height can be between 3 and 4.5m (10 and 15ft), depending on whether it is planted in a border or in a large tub; even in a 23cm (9in) container it will make a 1m (3ft) tall plant. Trained up a pillar and associated with jasmine, it will form a delightful feature in a cool conservatory over an extended period.

Light Good, with some sun.
Temperature Minimum 4°C (40°F), 16–30°C (60–85°F) in summer, but see Special needs.
Moisture Normal humidity; water freely from spring to autumn, moderately in winter.
Feeding Liquid feed from early summer to autumn.
Propagation By sideshoots 7.5cm (3in) long in summer in 16–21°C (60–70°F); natural layers.
Problems Greenfly; red spider mite; rarely scale insect; brown tips to leaves from lack of water in summer/too much sun.
Special needs Keep well fed and watered while growing; ventilate well in temperatures above 21°C (70°F); directly after flowering, cut flowering stems back to about 23cm (9in); prune again in late winter to 7.5cm (3in) if space is at a premium; encourage winter rest.

APOCYNACEAE
Plumeria

SOMETIMES CALLED West Indian jasmine, *P. rubra* is better known as frangipani, because the perfume of its flowers is like that invented by an Italian nobleman of that name during the Renaissance in Europe.

Plumeria has fleshy leaves in clusters at the end of the branches, and the funnel-shaped flowers end in five segments like petals. Their colouring is variable, usually pink, but can also be creamy or white, with a heavy perfume which is retained long after they have withered, making them good for inclusion in potpourri. Flowering time is from early summer into early autumn.

In its native country it is a small tree, but in containers it is a shrubby plant about 1.8m (6ft) tall, depending on the container size, and in a border it will grow larger still.

Light Good.
Temperature Minimum 18°C (65°F); 21–30°C (70–85°F) in summer.
Moisture High humidity until flowering, then normal; water freely while growing, moderately in winter.
Feeding Liquid feed from late spring until the end of late summer.
Propagation Ripe cuttings 7.5–30cm (3–12in) long in spring or summer, in warmed compost, with high humidity.
Problems Scale insect; mealy bug.
Special needs Prune immediately after flowering; peat-based compost preferable; moisture and warmth important at all times.

P. obconica hybrid

P R I M U L A C E A E

Primula

T HE PRIMROSE IS a species of primula, and the primulas grown in containers have flowers of the same shape, but variously coloured, depending on species. Another difference is that they flower during mid- and late winter and those named here are slightly tender.

Primula obconica has the largest flowers, up to 4cm (1½in) wide, in pink, red, magenta, lilac and white, and rounded leaves; *P. sinensis* (syn. *P. praenitens*) has smaller but fringed flowers, in the same colour range, and toothed leaves, and the third, *P. malacoides*, is usually lilac, occasionally rose-pink, with small delicate flowers 1.5cm (½in) wide, and frilly edged leaves.

Light Good, but avoid sun.

Temperature Minimum 10°C (50°F) while flowering, a little higher for *P. sinensis*; otherwise minimum 7°C (45 °F), cool in summer.

Moisture High humidity in temperatures above 21°C (70 °F), otherwise normal; water freely while flowering, normally until flowers faded, then sparingly until early autumn, normally again until flowering.

Feeding Liquid feed from time buds show to end of flowering.

Propagation Sow seed in early midsummer, pot on seedlings as they grow into final container diameter of 12.5cm (5in); divide after flowering.

Problems Red spider mite; greenfly; brown patches on leaves from sun scorch; nibbled leaf edges from vine weevil.

Special needs Repot after flowering; plunge outdoors in shady place from late spring until early autumn or keep shaded and well ventilated in conservatory; cool while flowering to avoid leggy plants and short flowering period; deadhead.

P. granatum

R. fiebrigii

PUNICACEAE
Punica

A SMALL TREE from the eastern Mediterranean region, the pomegranate, *P. granatum*, bears its pink or red round fruit in autumn. The species grows to at least 4.5m (15ft) in its native habitat, but in a tub is more likely to be an evergreen shrub about 2.4m (8ft) tall. It grows slowly and has decorative bright red flowers, tubular but opening out at the mouth and about 5cm (2in) long, in summer. The variety *P. g. nana* is much smaller, to 60–90cm (2–3ft), with proportionately smaller flowers, but otherwise the same. It may set fruit and retain them to maturity, but needs plenty of late summer and autumn warmth and light to do so. The large form does not flower until six to eight years old.

Light Good with some sun.
Temperature Minimum 7°C (45°F), 16–32°C (60–90°F) in summer.
Moisture Normal humidity; water freely from spring to autumn, sparingly in winter.
Feeding Liquid feed from early summer to early autumn.
Propagation Heel cuttings in mid- to late summer, in warmed compost.
Problems Scale insect (rarely); leaf fall in low temperatures.
Special needs Ventilate well in summer; tip back in late winter.

CACTACEAE
Rebutia

THE REBUTIAS ARE good starter cacti as they flower easily, and are pretty plants, blooming profusely in many colours. They are short-lived, but easily increased and will flower when only a year old.

The funnel-shaped flowers with long tubes come from near the base of the plant, which has a round body, produced singly or in clusters. Rebutias are terrestrial and are found in the mountains; others are found growing in grass in their native Andes. *R. minuscula* is 4cm (1½in) tall, with red flowers in summer; *R. fiebrigii* (syn. *R. muscula*) is covered in soft white spines, and produces light orange-red flowers in early summer; *R. xanthocarpa* is 5cm (2in) tall and double the width and has red flowers from late spring to late summer; its variety, *R. × salmonea*, has salmon-pink flowers.

Light As much as possible.
Temperature Minimum 4°C (40°F), 16–24°C (60–75°F) in summer.
Moisture Low to dry humidity; water normally from spring to autumn, sparingly in winter.
Feeding Liquid feed from midsummer to autumn.
Propagation Offsets from spring to summer; seed which may germinate where it falls after the fruit splits open.
Problems Mealy bug and root mealy bug; red spider mite; brown spots from cold; rotting base from cold and/or overwatering or poor drainage; shrivelling from lack of water or overwatering in winter.
Special needs Care with winter watering.

R. simsii hybrids

ERICACEAE
Rhododendron

THE RHODODENDRONS ARE a vast genus of evergreen shrubs mostly occurring in the Himalayas and China. *R. simsii*, the Indian azalea, has flowers which vary in colour between rose-pink and dark red; its normal flowering time is late spring and its height is about 1.5m (5ft).

Spontaneously arising variants (sports) and flower doubling have further widened the choice of colour and form. There are now many which flower heavily, remain in bloom for several weeks, and do well in a conservatory. Height of these hybrids in containers is around 30cm (12in); spread up to 45cm (18in).

Light Good or light shade.
Temperature Minimum 7°C (45°F); while flowering 10–16 °C (50–60°F); 16–21°C (60–70°F) at other times.

Moisture High humidity while flowering, normal at other times; water freely while flowering, moderately at other times.
Feeding Liquid feed from early summer to early autumn.
Propagation Heel cuttings in summer in warmed sandy compost.
Problems Whitefly; leafminer; red spider mite; scale insect; azalea gall fungus disease – thickened leaves with white-grey covering, discoloured flowers and dead buds: remove as soon as seen; yellow leaves from iron deficiency; bud drop from dry air/drop in temperature/lack of water.
Special needs Acid compost; tepid soft water; cool, humid environment; rest when new growth stops elongating until autumn, and plunge outdoors in shaded, cool place and keep watered.

R. makoyana

Saintpaulia hybrids

ACANTHACEAE
Ruellia

THE TWO species of this genus that are commonly grown have prettily coloured trumpet-shaped flowers, not unlike those of achimenes. Both come from the warmer parts of South America.

Ruellia macrantha is the larger – a shrubby plant to about 90cm (3ft), larger where there is space, with rose-pink trumpets 9cm (3½in) long veined purplish in the throat. *R. makoyana* has similarly coloured but smaller flowers, and beautifully coloured leaves, dark green tinted with purple and veined white, purple on the underside, and velvety to the touch. Height is about 60cm (2ft), but it needs to be tied to supports; flowering time of both species is in winter and early spring.

Light Good with some sun but not midday summer sun.
Temperature Minimum 13°C (55°F); 18–27°C (65–80°F) in summer.
Moisture High humidity; water freely spring into autumn, moderately in winter.
Feeding Liquid feed from early summer to early autumn and occasionally while flowering.
Propagation Tip cuttings in spring to summer in 21–30°C (75–85°F) and warmed compost.
Problems Red spider mite; greenfly occasionally; leaf drop from cold.
Special needs Mist daily in temperatures above 21°C (70 °F); pinch back tips of shoots in late spring to early summer to increase flowering; keep warm in winter.

GESNERIACEAE
Saintpaulia

THE AFRICAN VIOLET *S. ionantha* is a familiar and much-loved houseplant but it grows even more successfully in a conservatory where the air is more moist than in the average room.

Flower colours are delightful, and include pink, white, magenta, crimson, almost blue and shades of all these; some flowers are bicoloured, with whole petals in one or other colour. Some have a picotee edging and some have fimbriated petals. The leaves, too, vary in the shade of green, or may be variegated creamy white or yellow, and finally there are creeping kinds, which root at the leaf-joints.

The Diana and Rhapsodie strains are particularly good – the latter are easier to grow and their flowers do not fall until they are completely withered.

Light Good in winter, light shade in summer.
Temperature Range through year: 16–24°C (60–75°F).
Moisture High to very high humidity; water moderately, but if in doubt, don't.
Feeding Liquid feed from spring to autumn.
Propagation Leaf cuttings with stem attached from spring to autumn.
Problems Cyclamen mite; whitefly; mealy bug; vine weevil larvae; white patches on leaves from cold water; yellow leaf patches or pale leaves from too much sun; crown rot from too much water; no flowers from lack of light/food/cold/disturbance/ sideshoots not removed or wrong nutrient.
Special needs Humidity, but do not mist leaves; steady temperature; repot only when pot-bound, use peaty compost and pan up to 10cm (4in) diameter; tepid water; deadhead and remove whole flower stem.

S. stolonifera　　　　　　　　　　　　　　　　　　　　　　　　　　　*S. arboricola* 'Variegata'

SAXIFRAGACEAE
Saxifraga

APTLY CALLED mother-of-thousands, *S. stolonifera* is a neat small evergreen, whose rounded hairy leaves are dark green, marbled with white on the upper surface, and red-purple beneath.

The creeping stems emerging from the crown are the same reddish colour, and will root at each leaf-joint (if lying along the ground), from which plantlets grow. If they are allowed to trail, however, the plantlets will still form, and the stems can grow to 60cm (2ft) long. In addition, it has pretty flowers in white and yellow forming airy clusters on stems 23–30cm (9–12in) tall in late spring and early summer.

There is a cultivar, which is even more attractive, called *S. s.* 'Tricolor', whose leaves are white-variegated on light green, flushed with pink, and with pink edges. It grows more slowly, is less likely to flower, and has fewer runners, but in the right conditions will grow satisfactorily.

Light Light shade, but good light for *S. s* 'Tricolor'.
Temperature Minimum 4°C (40°F), and 16–21°C (60–70°F) in summer; minimum 10°C (50°F) and 16–27°C (60–80°F) in summer for *S. s.* 'Tricolor'.
Moisture Normal humidity; water moderately in summer, sparingly in winter.
Feeding Not necessary.
Propagation Detach plantlets when roots are present and pot.
Problems Greenfly; red spider mite; crown rot from overwatering or poor drainage; yellowish leaves from too much light.
Special needs Use half-pot, with good drainage layer; keep *S. s.* 'Tricolor' on dryish side for best colouring; remove flower heads to encourage leaf and runner growth; care with watering.

ARALIACEAE
Schefflera

THE PARASOL TREE, *S. arboricola* (syn. *Heptapleurum arboricola*) 'Variegata', is grown for its foliage, much blotched and splashed with yellow in this form, and formed of long, narrow leaflets radiating out from a central point and arching over the top of the stem. It grows quickly and can be tree-like in form with a single stem, which needs a little support. Height is about 1.8m (6ft), spread about 45cm (18in), or it can be induced to be bushy by removing the growing tip at whatever height is preferred. Large plants which grow quickly and are easy to care for are not too common, and this is one of the more ornamental space-fillers.

Light Good, but no sun.
Temperature Minimum 16°C (60°F), 16–30°C (60–85°F) in summer.
Moisture Good humidity; water freely in summer, sparingly in winter.
Feeding Liquid feed from early summer to autumn.
Propagation Tip cuttings from late spring to early summer in 21°C (70°F).
Problems Scale insect; leaf drop from draughts, drops in temperature or dry air.
Special needs Care with watering; mist in temperatures above 24°C (75°F), and wash leaves occasionally; prune while growing to fit space available.

S. × buckleyi

CACTACEAE
Schlumbergera

THE CHRISTMAS CACTUS, *S. × buckleyi*, can easily be grown and flowered in a cool conservatory; with a little heat the flowers will appear on time for the mid-winter festival. The flattened stems consist of thickened segments in chains, with the flower-buds unfolding from the end of each chain. The flowers are magenta pink and fuchsia-like, having long stamens protruding far beyond the petals. Plants can be up to 23cm (9in) tall, and the spread is a good deal more than this, up to 60cm (2ft).

Light Good.
Temperature Minimum 7°C (45°F), 16–27°C (60–80°F) in summer.
Moisture Normal humidity, but mist occasionally in temperatures above 24°C (75°F); water moderately from early autumn to end of flowering, sparingly after flowering; keep compost moist.
Feeding Liquid feed while budding and flowering in years when not repotted.
Propagation Use cuttings of two segments, and allow to dry for a few days before potting.
Problems Mealy bug and root mealy bug; root aphis; lack of flowers from insufficient water in summer/worn-out compost/cold/lack of light or lack of feeding; buds dropping from moving the plant or dry atmosphere.
Special needs Rest after flowering until mid-spring, then repot if necessary. Keep shaded and watered until autumn; repot every second or third year; keep out of artificial light in the evenings in mid- and late autumn, and keep cool, near 13°C (55 °F) until near the time flowers are required, then raise the temperature to 16–21°C (60–70°F); remove one or two of the oldest stems after flowering on older plants.

S. speciosa 'Tiger' strain

GESNERIACEAE
Sinningia

MUCH BETTER KNOWN and loved as gloxinias, these are superb display plants during summer and autumn, flowering for two months or more. The modern varieties have been developed from a single species, *S. speciosa*, with pale lavender flowers on 15cm (6in) stems. It is, however variable in the wild – white-flowered varieties, tall stems up to 30cm (12in) and white-veined leaves have all been found. Most of the species that are familiar to conservatory owners today were introduced in the last century.

Today's hybrids carry flowers which are velvety and bell-shaped, flaring out into five lobes, 5–7.5cm (2–3in) wide across the mouth, and about the same length. Colours are rich and jewel-like: ruby, purple, blue-purple, white and pink, and some varieties have a white edge to the trumpet, while some have differently coloured throats, and the Tiger strain is magnificently spotted. *S. s.* 'Red Tiger' has cream-coloured throats to the flowers, heavily spotted in red, and *S. s.* 'Royal Tiger' is similar but with deep purple spotting. They are surprisingly big plants, as they

S. spciosa hybrid

S. scutellarioides

can carry 10–20 flowers each, the leaves may be 30cm (12in) long and 12–5cm (5in) wide, and the total height may be up to 45cm (18in).

A few named kinds include: *S. s.* 'Duchess of York', deep purple with white edge; *S. s.* 'Duke of York', deep red with white edges; *S. s.* 'Kaiser Friedrich' (syn. *S. s.* 'Emperor Frederick'), light red with picotee edge to frilly trumpet; *S. s.* 'Royal Pink', rose with creamy yellow throat.

If you can track it down, there is a species which is heavily scented: *S. tubiflora*, about 30cm (12in) tall, with white or creamy white flowers. It comes from Buenos Aires and has round tubers.

Light Light shade.
Temperature Minimum 10°C (50°F), 16–30°C (60–80°F) in summer.
Moisture High humidity; water moderately from spring to midsummer, freely until flowering finishes, gradually decreasing to dry.
Feeding Liquid feed from late summer to early in mid-autumn.
Propagation Young leaves with stems used as cuttings from spring to early summer in 18–24°C (65–75°F); division of larger tubers spring; seed sown with silver sand, left uncovered in fine, peaty, moist compost in dark and humid atmosphere and temperature of 18°C (65°F) in midsummer or late winter will flower 5 to 6 months later.
Problems Vine weevil larvae; grey mould; rotting tuber from badly drained compost or overwatering; brown leaf edges or unopened buds from dry air.
Special needs Start tubers in peat in late winter or mid-spring and 18°C (65°F), put hollow side uppermost or look for last year's roots on the underside; if started very late in spring they will still be in flower in autumn when artificial heat will be required to keep them going; pot when shoots are 1.5cm (½in) high into 15cm (6in) containers with base drainage; deadhead.

LABIATAE
Solenostemon

THE FLAME NETTLE, *S. scutellarioides* (syn. *Coleus blumei*), more than justifies its common name as regards its leaf colouring, which is very much more spectacular than that of many flowers.

Not only that, the leaves, which are deeply toothed, can be bizarrely shaped into variations described as antlered, parsley-leaved, fringed, fingered and fern-leaved. A packet of the seed strain *S. s.* 'Fantasia' will produce a range of all these colours and shapes, which last all summer and autumn.

If allowed to flower, the flame nettle has either spikes of blue flowers, or purple and white ones in mid to late summer; the plants may by then be 75cm (2½ft) tall and 45cm (1½ft) wide. The leaf colour gradually fades with the loss of light in autumn and, though they can be kept through the winter, they are not then ornamental.

Light Good with some sun.
Temperature Minimum 10°C (50°F), 16–30°C (60–80°F) in summer.
Moisture Normal humidity; but mist in temperatures above 30°C (85°F); water freely in summer.
Feeding Liquid feed from midsummer into autumn.
Propagation Sow seed in 18°C (65°F) in early spring; transfer seedlings to tray where they will be slow to grow to start with, even with warmth, but catch up after a few weeks; pot into successively larger diameter pots; tip cuttings in late summer and overwintered.
Problems Greenfly if watered insufficiently; lack of colour, not enough light.
Special needs Plenty of water in summer, pinch out tip of shoots once or twice to keep bushy at about 45cm (18in); if tall, support with canes.

S. wallisii

TILIACEAE
Sparmannia

THE AFRICAN HEMP or indoor linden, as *S. africana* is sometimes called, is a tall-growing, tree-like plant with large, evergreen, softly hairy leaves up to 17.5cm (7in) long, pale green in colour, and clusters of fragrant white flowers in late winter and spring. The flower buds are pendent but straighten as they open, and each flower is centred with a powder puff of red and yellow stamens, rarely seen when it is grown as a houseplant, as it usually is, but a regular occurrence in the good light conditions provided by a conservatory.

In its native habitat *S. africana* can be a shrub 6m (20ft) tall, but in a container the height is more likely to be 1.2 or 1.5m (4 or 5ft), depending on the root-room available. It grows quickly, and often becomes starved, as it rapidly absorbs all the nutrient in the compost. A dwarf form, *S.a.* 'Nana', flowers more readily than the species.

Sparmannias are at their most attractive when about two years old, so take cuttings (which root easily) every other year, and discard older parent plants.

Light Good, with some sun; avoid direct sunlight.
Temperature Minimum 7°C (45°F); 16–30°C (60–85°F) in summer.
Moisture High humidity; mist overhead in high temperatures; water freely from late spring to autumn, moderately otherwise.
Feeding Liquid feed from midsummer to mid-autumn.
Propagation Tip cuttings in spring/summer (it is easily rooted, even in water); cuttings rooted in spring will often produce flowers by late winter.
Problems Greenfly; whitefly; red spider mite; yellow lower leaves falling from lack of plant food/draughts/dry air/dry roots.
Special needs Repot during growing season; ventilate in high temperatures; prune after flowering to maintain shape; encourage young rooted cuttings to branch by pinching out main shoot in spring.

S. africana, opposite

ARACEAE
Spathiphyllum

THE PEACE LILY, *S. wallisii*, is a member of the same family as the calla lily, and has the same curious flower formation as that genus (*Zantedeschia*) and anthuriums. The main part of the flower is a single, large, white "petal" or spathe, and from the base of this comes a yellow spike, or spadix, which carries the pollen. The spathe lasts several months and has given the plant its other common name of "white sails".

Height is about 25cm (10in), and the narrow evergreen leaves form an attractive background to the flowers just above them. Flowering is in spring and sometimes also again in autumn. There is a larger version, *S.* 'Mauna Loa', named after a resort in Hawaii, which remains in flower nearly all year, but it needs more warmth in winter. The genus of *Spathiphyllum* comes from South America.

Light Good in summer; good with some sun in winter.
Temperature For the species: minimum 13°C (55°F), 16–27°C (60–80°F) in summer; for *S.* 'Mauna Loa': minimum 16°C (60°F), 18–30°C (65–85°F) in summer.
Moisture Very high humidity; water normally in spring and summer, moderately in autumn and winter.
Feeding Liquid feed weekly while growing.
Propagation By division when repotting.
Problems Brown tips and leaf edges from dry air or cold; pale leaf patches from too much sun; basal rot from cold or overwatering.
Special needs Plenty of humidity, and sponge the foliage occasionally; remove faded flowers and flower stems; keep away from draughts.

135

S. floribunda

ASCLEPIADACEAE
Stephanotis

H EAVILY FRAGRANT, the waxy white flowers of *S. floribunda* are much used in
wedding bouquets and corsages. Although
it has a common name, the Madagascar jasmine, it
is generally known as stephanotis. Its tubular
flowers open out into a star shape of five
segments, and are carried in clusters directly from
the axils of the leaves. Flowering starts in late
spring and can continue until early autumn,
though sometimes it may not start until later
summer and then goes on until late autumn.

As a climber, it is fairly vigorous, making a
height of between 3 and 4.5m (10 and 15ft). It
produces flowers on second-season and older
growth. Its evergreen leaves are thick and oval,
about 9cm (3½in) long; the flowers are followed,
in its native habitat, by plum-like fruit.

Light Good, or light shade.
Temperature Minimum 10°C (50°F), though
slightly higher is better, 16–32°C (60–90°F), in
summer.
Moisture Normal humidity; water normally in
summer, sparingly in winter.
Feeding Liquid feed from mid-spring to early
autumn if not repotted.
Propagation Cuttings from previous year's
sideshoots in warmed compost, in spring and
18–24°C (65–75°F).
Problems Scale insect; mealy bug; yellowing
leaves from iron deficiency – supply sequestrated
iron; no flowers from lack of light/food; falling
flowers from movement of plant.
Special needs Mist in temperatures above 27°C
(80°F); avoid hot sun and draughts; top-dress in
spring; repot every fourth year. Cut back during
the winter to remove weak growth and to fit the
space available.

MUSACEAE
Strelitzia

T HESE LARGE PLANTS (*S. reginae*) are
native to the Cape of Good Hope where
they grow to about 1.5m (5ft) tall. Their
strikingly handsome flowers are spectacularly
shaped and exotically coloured, and do indeed
resemble a bird which has just landed on the plant
and whose wings are still outstretched. The
spring-blooming flowers are blue and orange,
consisting of several vertical, flame-coloured,
pointed petals and bracts, together with two or
three dark blue ones. These all emerge from a
large, light green, horizontal bract, the whole
being carried on a stem between 90cm and 1.5m
(3 and 5ft) tall. Flowers will be produced successively for several weeks, but only after plants are
at least four years old. The leaves are in
proportion and are somewhat like those of the
banana, which is a member of a related plant
family; the stalk and the blade together measure
about 90cm (3ft), and the leaf-blade is narrow and
rounded at the tip.

Light Good with some sun, but avoid hot summer
sun.
Temperature Minimum 13°C (55°F), 16–30°C
(60–80°F) in summer.
Moisture Normal humidity; water freely in
summer, sparingly in winter.
Feeding Liquid feed from late spring into early
autumn.
Propagation Detached rooted suckers when
repotting; sow seed in warmed compost spring, in
18–24°C (65–75°F). New Hybrid strains will
flower in two to three years and plants are not as
large.
Problems Mealy bug; scale insect; lack of flowers
from too large a container/too frequent repotting of
young plants; crown rot from poor drainage/too
much water, especially in winter.
Special needs Use tubs at least 25cm (10in)
diameter; John Innes No 3 compost with one extra
part grit, and drainage layer; plant firmly and water
moderately until plant is obviously growing; repot
adult plants every third or fourth year, and
top-dress otherwise; deadhead.

S. reginae, opposite

S. × hybridus

GESNERIACEAE
Streptocarpus

THE CAPE PRIMROSES, from South Africa, flower from midsummer to mid- or late autumn, and do best in cool temperatures – they are ideal for a north-facing conservatory. The group known as *S. × hybridus* supplies various named hybrids and strains. The plants consist of a rosette of long, strap-shaped leaves, from the centre of which come the 15–20cm (6–8in) flower stems carrying tubular, trumpet-shaped flowers.

Amongst the best varieties are: 'Constant Nymph', with blue, white-throated flowers, pencilled in a darker shade; the Concorde strain of F_1 hybrids in a delightful range of pastel shades, heavily pencilled in the mouth; the Royal strain, deep-coloured large flowers in red, violet and magenta, as well as white, with deep red-purple pencilling; 'Baby Blue', light blue and white-throated, early flowering, only 10cm (4in) tall.

Light Light shade.
Temperature Minimum 4°C (40°F), 13–21°C (55–70°F) in summer.
Moisture Normal humidity; water moderately in summer, sparingly in winter.
Feeding Liquid feed from early summer to mid-autumn.
Propagation Divide carefully when repotting; leaf-cuttings of bottom half of leaf pushed upright into warmed compost to quarter its length, in summer; seed sown with silver sand in spring, in 13–18°C (55–65°F), will flower four months later.
Problems Mealy bug; greenfly; crown rot from too much water/poor drainage; no flowers from shortage of light/nutrient.
Special needs Mist frequently and ventilate well in temperatures above 21°C (70°F); be careful with watering in high temperatures.

S. jamesonii

S. dyerianus

SOLANACEAE

Streptosolen

THIS SOUTH AMERICAN shrub, *S. jamesonii*, is a brilliantly flowered evergreen plant that will flower for most of the growing season, but especially from early to midsummer. Height can be at least 1.8m (6ft). Its somewhat straggling growth needs support, but if pinched back a couple of times in mid and late spring, it becomes much more bush-like.

Its funnel-shaped flowers start in a mixture of yellow and pink, then change to orange, and finally an eye-catching orange-red; they come in clusters at the end of the shoots. The leaves are softly hairy and somewhat wrinkled, carried alternately on the arching stems. It is one of the best plants for a border.

Light Good.
Temperature Minimum 10°C (50°F), 16–30°C (60–85°F) in summer.
Moisture Normal humidity; water freely from late spring to mid-autumn, sparingly in winter.
Feeding Liquid feed from early summer into early autumn.
Propagation Cuttings of sideshoots in summer; heel cuttings in spring in warmed compost and 18°C (65°F).
Problems Greenfly; whitefly; scale insect.
Special needs Increase humidity in spring before flowering; keep out of summer sun; do not allow compost ever to become dry; use large pots or tubs; cut back hard after flowering; pinch back shoot tips to make bushy.

ACANTHACEAE

Strobilanthes

ONE OF THE MORE outstanding amongst the purple-leaved conservatory plants, *S. dyerianus* from Malaysia is grown for its unique shades of this colour. The pointed 15cm (6in) long leaves are purple beneath, and a beautiful violet colour on the surface on an olive green background, which is really only apparent along the leaf veins. As the leaves mature, the colour lightens almost to lilac, giving a silvery effect, and a plant in full growth thus has an overall colouring of purple, with silver, lilac and dark green blended in.

It will also flower in summer; colour is pale blue and the shape of the flowers is tubular opening to a funnel, and carried in short spikes. With maturity it can become straggly, but quickly produces sideshoots if the main-stem tips are pinched back.

Light Good.
Temperature Minimum 10°C (50°F), 16–32°C (60–90°F) in summer.
Moisture Normal humidity; water freely from late spring into mid-autumn, sparingly in winter.
Feeding Liquid feed from midsummer to autumn.
Propagation Heel cuttings 7.5cm (3in) long in spring in warmed compost and 24–27°C (75–80°F).
Problems Greenfly; pale colouring from lack of winter light/nutrient.
Special needs Spray overhead in temperatures above 27°C (80°F), and increase watering; pinch back tips from late spring to midsummer to prevent straggling.

T. capensis

T. grandiflora

B I G N O N I A C E A E
Tecomaria

THE SOUTH AFRICAN Cape honeysuckle, *T. capensis*, will certainly climb, but it is not over-enthusiastic about doing so and tends to sprawl sideways. Height is ultimately between 1.8 and 2.4m (6 and 8ft) in a container, and spread can be 90cm (3ft), depending on the amount of root room it is given.

Its glossy evergreen leaves are pinnate, and about 10–15cm (4–6in) long. They provide a good backdrop for the clusters of bright orange-red, tubular flowers. *T. capensis* has one of the longest flowering times of any of the conservatory plants, since it can start to flower in spring and still be in bloom in early winter, though its main flowering period is summer. A variety called *T. c.* 'Aurea' has yellow flowers.

Light Good with some sun.
Temperature Minimum 4°C (40°F), 16–30°C (60–80°F) in summer.
Moisture Normal humidity; water freely from mid-spring to mid autumn, sparingly otherwise.
Feeding Liquid feed from early summer into early autumn.
Propagation Layer or take heel cuttings in summer.
Problems Greenfly; red spider mite; no flowers from lack of light.
Special needs Ventilate well and spray overhead in temperatures above 27°C (80°F); plenty of light in winter; prune from late winter to early spring, cut out weak and dying shoots, and some side-shoots by half their length, others to leave a stub, depending on the space available; the plant can be spur-pruned (see p. 164).

A C A N T H A C E A E
Thunbergia

THUNBERGIAS ARE MORE familiar in the South African species *T. alata*, known as black-eyed Susan, an annual climber with yellow-orange flowers centred with black, and this also makes a perfectly good conservatory plant. But *T. grandiflora* from India is especially exotic, and has pale blue flowers, with flat, open faces up to 7.5cm (3in) wide, carried singly or in clusters for the three summer months. It is an evergreen, and its leaves are up to 15cm (6in) long.

If you have a large conservatory, then this will do well on a wall, or trained up a pillar and under the roof – it needs a good deal of space. For a less rampant plant, *T. alata* is a better choice at 1.2–1.8m (4–6ft), and can be trained upwards, or allowed to trail; it, too, flowers prolifically, well into autumn.

Light Good with some sun but shade from midday summer sun.
Temperature Minimum 13°C (55°F) 16–32°C (60–90°F) in summer.
Moisture High humidity in summer, normal in winter; water freely while growing, sparingly otherwise.
Feeding Liquid feed from late spring to early autumn.
Propagation Semi-hardwood stem cuttings 7.5cm (3in) long spring in 24–30°C (75–85°F); seed for *T. alata*, sown early spring in 18–24°C (65–75°F), and flowered in 12.5cm (5in) containers.
Problems Scale insect; whitefly; red spider mite; greenfly.
Special needs *T. grandiflora* requires a border or as large a tub as possible. To keep within space available, prune in late winter.

T. urvilleana

T. ionantha

MELASTOMATACEAE
Tibouchina

ONE OF THE PRETTIEST and most rewarding of flowering shrubs to grow in a conservatory, *T. urvilleana* (syn. *T. semidecandra*) from Brazil will flower almost throughout the year, its best period being the autumn. However, it is advisable to persuade it to rest in winter, otherwise it will be shortlived. In spite of its origins, it does not need great winter warmth and survives quite well in cool temperatures.

The whole plant is stiffly haired, except for the flowers, and even these look velvety; the evergreen oval leaves are 7.5–15cm (3–6in) long and cover a bushy plant 2 or 3m (several feet) tall and a metre (3ft) wide in the border or a large tub 45cm (18in) diameter. Flowering may start at any time from early to midsummer, when its deep purple, 10cm (4in) wide flowers will be produced singly or in clusters all over the plant.

Light Good with some sun.
Temperature Minimum 10°C (50°F) 16–27°C (60–80°F) in summer.
Moisture High humidity while growing, normal in winter; water freely from spring to end autumn, sparingly in winter.
Feeding Liquid feed from early summer to mid-autumn.
Propagation Heel cuttings in spring and summer in warmed compost and 24°C (75°F).
Problems Red spider mite; greenfly; lack of flowers from not enough light.
Special needs Maintain humidity in summer; encourage winter rest by lowering temperature and reducing watering; do not allow to become root-bound; prune to shape in late winter.

BROMELIACEAE
Tillandsia

THERE ARE TWO completely different types of tillandsia: one has the familiar bromeliad growth habit of a rosette of stiff, leathery leaves from the centre of which comes an equally stiff flower spike, and the other has clusters of grass-like, or twisted leaves, or consists simply of trails of beard-like stems.

Tillandsia lindenii (syn. *T. lindeniana*) is the conventionally shaped species, which has a beautiful flowerhead about 30cm (12in) long consisting of flattened, bright pink bracts from which come deep blue flowers, white-marked in the throat, in summer.

In complete contrast to this, *T. ionantha* (syn. *T. erubescens*) is only about 5cm (2in) tall and not as wide, and consists of a silvery grey cluster of leaves, rosy coloured at the tip when young. When the violet flowers appear in the centre in spring, the inner leaves change to red. There are several other species of these air plants in cultivation and, although small, they will provide a good display if grown in a group on driftwood.

For *T. lindenii*, see p. 164 for general bromeliad care. For *T. ionantha* and other air plants:

Light Good with some sun.
Temperature Minimum 13°C (55°F), 16–27°C (60–80°F) in summer.
Moisture High humidity but no watering needed.
Feeding Not needed.
Propagation Divide in late summer.
Problems Basal rotting from cold; lack of flower from not enough warmth/humidity/light.
Special needs Grow on bark, driftwood or coral and attach with wire; compost not required; humidity essential; deadhead.

T. fortunei

P A L M A E
Trachycarpus

THE WINDMILL PALM from China, *T. fortunei*, is one of the fan palms whose leaves are made up of a series of pleats radiating out in a semi-circle from one point at the end of the leaf stem. Its height in the open depends on the temperature; in cool conditions it grows only 3.6m (12ft) tall, but where the climate is tropical it will reach 12m (40ft).

In a container 2 or 3m (6 or 9ft) is more likely, with a spread of 1.2 or 1.5m (4 or 5ft) – the leaves can be more than 60cm (2ft) long, with stalks the same length, and 90cm (3ft) wide. The leaves unfold one at a time, in constant succession if provided with steady warmth, and tiny yellow flowers may appear in long clusters in spring.

Light Light shade.
Temperature Minimum 4°C (40°F), 16–30°C (60–80°F) in summer.
Moisture Normal humidity; mist in temperatures above 24°C (75°C); water moderately from spring to autumn, sparingly in winter.
Feeding Liquid feed from late spring to mid-autumn when not repotted.
Propagation Detach rooted suckers in spring.
Problems Scale insect; red spider mite; greenfly on flowers; brown leaflet tips from hard water/alkaline compost/dry air; yellow lower leaves from cold or too much water.
Special needs Deep container; extra part grit in compost; drainage layer; do not repot unless root-bound; ventilate well in high temperatures.

T. f. 'Quicksilver'

T. zebrina T. z. 'Purpusii'

COMMELINACEAE

Tradescantia

THERE ARE THREE species in this genus which are good conservatory plants, all grown for their foliage. *T. fluminensis* 'Quicksilver' is the wandering Jew, with fleshy stems trailing to 60cm (2ft) in one season and 6.5cm (2½in) long leaves, striped with white. There is another version with yellow stripes, less often seen, but just as effective. Both are stout-stemmed vigorous plants.

There is another group of tradescantia cultivars whose stems are much thinner, and whose leaves are much smaller, about 2.5cm (1in) long; amongst these *T. f.* 'Variegata' is narrowly striped white, and *T. f.* 'Laekenensis' is purple-flushed at the leaf edges as well as being marked with white.

Tradescantia zebrina (syn. *Zebrina pendula*) also has the common name of wandering Jew, but is quite different in colouring. It, too, has trailing stems, slowly growing to 30–45cm (1–1½ft) in a season, and leaves broadly striped silvery green and purple on the upper side and all purple on the underside; the stems are purple. *T. z.* 'Purpusii' is completely wine-purple, and *T. z.* 'Quadricolor' has leaves striped purple and grey-white on green, and deep purple undersides.

The purple heart, *T. pallida* 'Purpurea' (syn. *Setcreasea purpurea*) resembles the previous two species only in its trailing growth habit, which will root as it grows, making it a good plant for providing groundcover. The stems and leaves are fleshy, but the leaves are narrow and pointed, like those of willow, and sheathe the stem, and the whole plant is deep purple. It is the most likely of the three to have flowers, coloured purplish rose in late summer, enclosed in two purple bracts at the tip of the stem.

Light Good; if kept through the winter as much as possible.

Temperature Minimum 4°C (40°F), but 10°C (50°F) for *T. pallida* 'Purpurea'; 16–30°C (60–85°F) in summer.

Moisture Humidity normal; water *T. fluminensis* 'Quicksilver' normally, *T. zebrina* moderately, and *T. pallida* 'Purpurea' freely; water all sparingly in winter.

Feeding Liquid feed from midsummer to mid-autumn.

Propagation By tip cuttings between late spring and late summer, or by cuttings removed in late winter when repotting and discarding the parent plant.

Problems Greenfly; red spider mite; pale or yellowing leaves from lack of light/nutrient; lack of variegation from not enough light; leaves brown-tipped or completely withered from cold/dry air; whole shoots plain green on variegated plant indicates reversion – remove completely as soon as seen.

Special needs Mist heavily in temperatures above 27°C (80°F); keep *T. f.* 'Tricolor' on the dry side for best colouring; take care with watering *T. zebrina* and *T. pallida* 'Purpurea'; pinch back the tips if stems are outgrowing their space.

143

A S C L E P I A D A C E A E

Tweedia

O NE OF THE MOST fascinating aspects
about the Argentinian climber, *T. caerulea*
(syn. *Oxypetalum caeruleum*) is the way in
which the flowers change colour as they mature.
They open pale blue, become tinted with green
and change to purplish, finally fading to lilac as
they finish, so a plant in full flower during the
summer and autumn is a kaleidoscope of colour.
Each flower consists of a tube opening out into
five narrow petals like a star and all are fragrant;
the heart-shaped leaves are hairy on both sides. It
is a twining plant which climbs modestly to 60 or
90cm (2 or 3ft) with a spread of 30–45cm
(1–1½ft).

Light Good.
Temperature Minimum 7°C (45°F), 16–27°C
(60–80°F) in summer.
Moisture High humidity in spring, normal at
other times; water freely from spring to autumn,
moderately in winter.
Feeding Liquid feed from early summer into early
autumn.
Propagation From seed in spring in 24°C (75°F);
basal cuttings in warmed compost in spring in
same temperature.
Problems Greenfly.
Special needs Good drainage in compost and
drainage layer in container base.

A R A C E A E

Zantedeschia

A N ITALIAN BOTANIST of the late
eighteenth century, Giovanni Zantedeschi,
is the namesake of this handsomely
flowered lily-like genus, commonly called calla
lily. *Z. aethiopica* is the one most often grown, its
large white trumpets consisting of a single "petal"
or spathe, turning back to reveal the central
yellow spike. Each flower can be as much as 23cm
(9in) long, carried on 90cm (3ft) stems in spring,
lasting until early summer.

Zantedeschia elliottiana is slightly less tall, and
with deep golden-yellow flowers in early summer.

The leaves of both species are arrow-shaped,
and in their natural habitat both plants grow in
marshes in South Africa.

Light Good with some sun, but not midday
summer sun.
Temperature Minimum 4°C (40°F), outdoors in
summer in 16–32°C (60–90°F).
Moisture Humidity normal; water freely in
spring, and in dry weather outdoors, moderately in
autumn and winter.
Feeding Liquid feed weekly while flowering.
Propagation By division at potting time in late
winter.
Problems Brown leaf tips and flowers from root
rot; brown spots on leaves from minor fungus
disease – remove when seen; light brown leaf
patches from too much sun; white lines and spots
on leaves, white patches on stems from virus –
there is no cure.
Special needs Repot in mid-autumn each year,
preferably in peat-based or similar compost; *Z.
elliottiana* should be kept indoors all year and
repotted in mid-winter.

CONSERVATORY MANAGEMENT

Creating the right environment for plants is an essential part of successful conservatory management. This section is divided into four chapters. The first explains how to deal with temperature, light, and humidity throughout the seasons. The second discusses in detail watering and feeding, planting, repotting and pruning, with special sections on cacti, bromeliads and orchids. The third chapter analyses the common ailments affecting conservatory plants, how to spot them and how to deal with them. The final, and fourth, chapter explains how to propagate plants from cuttings and seed.

MANAGING THE ENVIRONMENT

ALTHOUGH A conservatory can be run without taking much notice of the day-to-day environment and the changes that occur in it as a result of the state of the weather outside it on any particular day, such an approach will not make the best of the plants. In the home, there is little to do regarding the environment beyond regulating the temperature and maintaining it at a level which ensures that the people in it are at ease. Even less has to be done as far as the light is concerned; the humidity of the atmosphere is seldom noticed and wind has no effect.

If you have a few houseplants, you are probably accustomed to making minor modifications to the atmosphere in winter, to make it more humid. Otherwise your work will have been limited to moving the plants about so that they are in the positions which suit them best. However, in a conservatory the transparent roof and walls increase the vulnerability of the plants to shifts in the weather; temperature and light changes are much more extreme from hour to hour, the humidity varies constantly, and protection from draughts will be required.

One also has to take into account the fact that there will be many more plants to deal with, and that these needs have to be balanced with those of the humans who use the conservatory. Many conservatories are effectively extra living-rooms in which there are plants, but, in a conservatory, the plants have a habit of quietly increasing in numbers. Not only that, they grow large quickly and take up much more room, so that their needs gradually become paramount. But there is consolation in the fact that a good environment can be summed up neatly: if you feel comfortable, so will the plants.

However, this does still mean that adjustments to the environment have to be made at intervals to ensure that both humans and plants are happy in it.

Seasonal treatment

A primary reason for a conservatory is to grow plants that would otherwise be damaged by rain, wind, sun, frost and so on, particularly frost, since many of the plants are tender, coming from tropical countries where frost and snow are unknown. On the other hand, too much warmth can be just as much of a problem. So modification of the temperature inside a conservatory is one of the main requirements.

In cool-temperate climates, the temperature rises more or less steadily from spring into summer until it reaches a peak where it remains, with minor deviations, for some weeks or even months in a good summer. With the onset of autumn, it gradually drops, and continues to drop as winter sets in, until it once more steadies, at a low which is constant until the equinox is passed and the sun's strength increases.

Thermometers for the conservatory
The conventional models of maximum and minimum thermometers have a glass tube shaped like a "U", with a tiny index just above the top of each column of mercury. As the temperature rises, so the mercury expands up the right-hand side of the tube, pushing up the index, and thus showing the maximum temperature. With a drop in temperature, the mercury contracts down the tube, leaving the index behind, but rises up the left-hand, or minimum, side. The indices are magnetized and can be re-set with a magnet supplied with the thermometer.

Spring

In spring it may be necessary to supply artificial heat although this is usually not required in daytime unless the weather is particularly bad. Most plants will survive a minimum winter temperature of 4°C (40°F), so that any extra heating should maintain it at, or preferably above, this – for example, at 7°C (45°F). With this minimum the plants are undoubtedly in much better condition by the time spring comes again. If you are growing plants from the South American rain forests or from tropical Asia, 10°C or even 16°C (50°F or 60°F) will be the minimum temperature that they can tolerate.

During the day, high temperatures in spring can be reduced simply by opening windows, doors and/or ventilators. In general, if you have ventilators in the roof, open these first, then windows or side ventilators, and finally doors. The object is to get the air circulating, so that the hot air, being lighter, will rise and go out through the roof, and the cooler air will come in low down and rise up in its turn, reducing the temperature throughout.

But plants should never be subjected to draughts; some of them (noted in the Plant Lists, pp. 182–185) particularly hate sudden drops in temperature. So it is better to allow air in gradually, and to start doing this before the temperature races up to 27°C or 32°C (80°F or 90°F). As evening comes, the temperature will start to drop, but it is advisable to close up the conservatory well before then, to avoid unnecessary heating costs. With experience, you will get a feel for when doors and windows should be shut to conserve the day's warmth; the time to do so is *before* you start to feel chilly, which is why experience is needed!

Summer

In summer you will be relieved of the necessity of heating the conservatory at night. Instead, the main problem is to keep the temperature down during the day to a level around 21°C or 27°C (70–80°F). Even a tropical plant does not grow as well in high temperatures as it does when in the middle range – around 18–20°C (the high 60°sF); if temperatures are high, the plants will still grow, but more slowly.

There are four ways of reducing the temperature: ventilation, shading, spraying and fanning. Ventilation will mean opening everything as much as possible from early in the morning, depending on the aspect, until late in the day. If it faces west, maximum ventilation will not be needed until midday; if it faces north, it may need only to be partial.

Shading You will probably decide that shading is essential, especially for a south-facing conservatory, if only to cut down on the sun's glare. The main area that needs to be shaded is the roof. If you can shade the south- or east-facing sides as well, so much the better; the west-facing side is less important as the sun starts to lose strength as it sets.

There are various types of shading available. Some conservatory manufacturers will supply made-to-measure curtains or blinds and, if you are having a non-standard conservatory

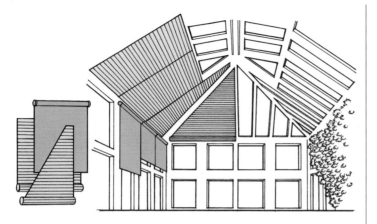

Blinds
Various forms of shading can be used successfully in the conservatory, including the spring-loaded roller blinds shown here, which can be tailor-made to suit the occasionally awkward shapes created by the pitched roof. They can be fixed with the spring mechanism at the head or foot of the blind, but with the latter will need tracks to keep them in place.

built, it is worth thinking in advance about shading and finding a manufacturer who will supply this service, otherwise it can be very difficult to find any ready-made shades that will fit the particular shapes of the glassed area.

Shading can take the form of blinds on spring-loaded rollers, or the shades can run on wires and rings and be drawn back manually or with a hooked pole. Materials can vary and they include polyester fabric, pleated plastic, plastic reeds held together with woven thread, and rattan or wooden slats that filter the light. External roller blinds can be fitted, if this is preferred, and there is a useful shading paint for external use which is opaque when dry, but becomes translucent when wet, thus allowing more light in on dull, rainy days.

Shading will, of course, be necessary for only part of the year, from sometime in spring until the end of late summer, but if curtains are used, they will help to keep warmth in at night in winter. Whatever type of shading is employed, it should be made of lightweight materials, otherwise the atmosphere can become stifling, even when good ventilation is provided.

Spraying The inside of the conservatory can be cooled down quickly, but only temporarily, by using water as a spray or a mist. In a greenhouse one way of doing this is to damp down the paths and ground beneath the benches by spraying them with water from a can or hosepipe. In a conservatory this is rarely practicable, but water sprayed from a can over the top growth of the plants is a good substitute, or the plants can be misted with the special misting sprayers now available; this needs to be done frequently to be effective. However, some plants can take high temperatures and need not be so treated, thus cutting down the time required to deal with them.

If there is no-one available to look after the conservatory during the day, there is a further method of applying water to reduce the temperature: by setting up a unit used in mist propagation, which automatically supplies a fine mist of water droplets during a specified time at pre-set intervals.

Fanning This is self-explanatory, and has the advantage over spraying that it does not impinge on your use of the conservatory. There are various types of electrical fans: ceiling fans, and portable fans, and also fan-heaters, which can be set merely to blow unheated air round the conservatory without the heating element functioning, until a pre-set minimum is reached. Time-switches can be used to turn fans and heaters on and off automatically.

Humidity All the foregoing methods of reducing heat are important, and one of the most important in the equation is the presence – or absence – of moisture in the atmosphere. Practically every plant requires moist, or humid air, and one of the most obvious symptoms of its lack is brown leaf tips and leaf margins, followed by withering of the entire leaf, if the air continues to be dry for long enough. Another common symptom is the falling of flower buds before they open, or the premature falling of open flowers.

Plants give off moisture from their leaves as water vapour through openings called stomata and, while this is being constantly transpired, it forms a shield just above the leaf surface. This prevents the leaf tissues (and the rest of the plant) from drying up, and keeps the leaf relatively cool.

There is a great need to keep up the humidity in hot weather, so that plants transpire moisture less rapidly, and therefore keep their own temperature at such a level that they can develop at their maximum rate. Humidity is clearly important for plants that come from the tropical rain-forests, though not for plants that grow naturally in deserts, and in other dry regions of the world such as South Africa. If you are doubtful about the amount of humidity at any time, a hygrometer will show the percentage present; to be safe, try to maintain it above 65 per cent for the majority of plants.

As well as spraying the plants overhead and misting them, moisture can be introduced into the air by standing the plants on gravel in saucers or trays, and filling the latter with water. Trays of water placed on the floor will help; constantly moist peat or other absorbent material is another source. It can be supplied by placing a plant-containing pot inside a larger, empty one, and packing the peat in the space between the two. Groups of plants will make their own localized humid atmosphere; a pool, and perhaps a fountain or a waterfall, is

Retaining moisture and humidity
If you have to leave plants untended for short periods, humidity and moisture can be maintained either by putting the plant container inside a larger container, and filling the space with moist peat, or by standing the plants in a shallow tray of gravel and water (the gravel prevents the base of the plants becoming too wet).

one of the best ways of ensuring constant humidity, as is a permanent water tank for watering the plants. This has the double advantage that water can then be supplied at atmospheric temperature.

Autumn

With the onset of autumn, the management of the environment gradually changes to being more like that required in spring, except that the rapid changes of temperature tend not to occur. The air outside the conservatory will have been thoroughly warmed up; the surroundings will have absorbed the sun's heat, with the result that the temperature usually diminishes steadily. There is no need at this time of year for constant manipulation of the windows or ventilators. Instead it usually suffices to open them in the morning, leave them open, and then close them as evening closes in, gradually opening later, and closing earlier, as winter draws nearer.

Shading can be removed and spraying will be less necessary, depending on the type of plants being grown. At some point in the autumn, artificial heating will become necessary. This will generally be at night at first, and possibly also during the day as autumn moves into winter.

Winter

There are two outstanding environmental factors to deal with in winter: one is the maintenance of warmth, and the other is the need for maximum light for the plants.

One of the conservatory's main functions is to protect the plants from low temperatures – of the order of 4°C (40°F) and less. There are many that will survive provided it drops no lower than this, and there are many more that need a minimum only a few degrees higher, around 7°C (45°F). Both groups remain in better condition if the minimum temperature can be boosted a few degrees more, but they will not die at either of these two temperatures, both of which are relatively inexpensive to maintain.

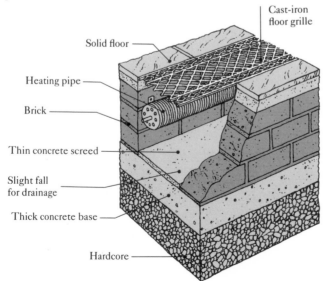

Cast-iron floor grille

Solid floor

Heating pipe

Brick

Thin concrete screed

Slight fall for drainage

Thick concrete base

Hardcore

Underfloor heating
One of the best methods of heating a conservatory is to install underfloor heating at the time of construction, normally around the edges of the room, as the heat is then evenly circulated. Ideally, some form of drainage should be incorporated to deal with any surplus water in the conservatory.

Where a minimum of 10°C (50°F) is required, the difference in cost is of a different order; many of the plants in this category are veering towards the tropical, or are exacting in any case, and the 16°C (60°F) minimum is definitely tropical, and usually means a constant, highly humid atmosphere. To keep up this level of warmth in the depths of winter, when the outside temperature may be –6°C (20°F) for some days or weeks, pre-supposes a considerable outlay on heating.

Heating methods Most of the artificial heating will be needed at night; even if there is no sun during the day, the outside temperature will usually improve to acceptable levels, obviating the need for extra heat inside. The various methods of supplying heat range from paraffin oil heaters specially designed for use under glass with plants, through portable natural and other gas heaters, and electric heating in various forms including underfloor, to radiators extended from the domestic central heating, and coal-fired boilers heating hot-water pipes, of which modern stream-lined and highly efficient versions are now available.

Insulation An obvious way of retaining warmth and cutting down heating costs is to double-glaze the roof of the conservatory, if not the whole of it, although this can make for a very oppressive atmosphere in summer.

An alternative is to use plastic sheet or netting to line the conservatory on the inside. This needs to be put in place early in the winter, or as soon as frosty weather starts, and should be attached so that there is a space between it and the glazing, providing an air-lock to prevent heat escaping. Curtains will also do this when drawn, and provide a good, inexpensive alternative to double glazing.

Insulation materials include plain plastic sheet – there is a kind which is condensation-proof in that any moisture runs down the sheeting to the floor below rather than dripping straight on to plants or humans below. There is also bubble-glazing, which consists of 2.5cm (1in) diameter air bubbles trapped between three sheets of plastic; this can be used as a curtain to divide the conservatory, so that only part of it need be heated.

Netting made of cross-bonded polypropylene polyethylene is fine and lightweight, but surprisingly effective in retaining warmth and, since it is fine, it cuts out little light. Moreover, it can be left in place under the roof all year to act as shading in summer. All these can be attached with drawing pins, tacks, staples or clips (for a metal framework).

Temperature monitoring With all this emphasis on warmth, it is obvious that a method of checking the temperature is essential, so even in an entirely unheated conservatory a thermometer that shows the maximum and minimum levels reached each day will be required.

Knowing the maximum temperature is more important in winter than in summer, as you can then see whether the temperature rose above the minimum necessary for any particular plant, and for how long and how high it rose. This is important, as too long a period at minimum temperatures may damage a plant. Again, it is a matter of experience; in a mixed collection of plants, some will survive, some may not, and you learn to judge when to push the temperature above the minimum.

Light The main reason for using shading in summer is to reduce the sun's heat in the conservatory; the consequent reduction in light transmission is not too important, but during the short and often dull days of winter it is essential to ensure that as much of the light available reaches the plants.

Within limits, the more light there is, the more "active" a plant is. Tropical plants are used to brilliant light for about 12 hours a day all year, so in a cool-temperate winter, the glazing in the conservatory needs to be as clean as possible, and certainly free of shading. Most of the plants in it will be conditioned to good winter light but, surprisingly, most of them will accept the lower light levels; they simply go into a state of suspended animation – more or less – until spring arrives.

Some plants are not worth keeping through winter, for instance, the flame nettle (*Solenostemon*) from Java becomes a sad beige shadow of its exotic brilliant summer self; some become straggly, with sparse, small leaves, and are best cut back hard in spring, or started afresh from cuttings, such as purple heart (*Tradescantia pallida* 'Purpurea').

At the beginning of winter, earlier if possible, the glazing should be thoroughly cleaned, both inside and outside, with hot water and a little household detergent. This is especially important in towns and cities where the grime of pollution can discolour the glass permanently if not removed regularly. Shading painted on the outside should also be washed off.

Leaves may need to be removed, if they have not already been brushed off the roof in autumn. If there is snow, this should not be allowed to lie, especially as there is the risk that it may partially thaw and then freeze, putting an extra strain on the load-bearing capacity of the roof as well as reducing the light. Where insulation is used to cut down the heating costs, it will also decrease the light. On balance, the need to keep out frost is more important than the need to keep up the quantity and quality of light and, even with insulation, the reduction in the light will not be so great as to kill or greatly damage the plants – it is more a case of slight damage or just less good growth.

Ventilation In spite of low temperatures, it is still most important to ensure that fresh air comes into the conservatory in winter. As already mentioned, plants use carbon dioxide from the air as part of their life-processes, so there needs to be a steady renewal of this gas. There is also the fact that they constantly give off water vapour and the atmosphere can rapidly become saturated and much too moist for healthy growth. This will be exacerbated if paraffin heating is used, since 4.5 litres (1gal) of paraffin gives off the equivalent, as it burns, in water vapour.

PHOTOSYNTHESIS
Plants that contain green colouring (chlorophyll) cannot live without light. They need it to carry on a process in which the carbon dioxide and water in the air are combined to form oxygen and carbohydrates; this process, known as photosynthesis, can only continue so long as light is present. The oxygen is given off into the air, and the carbohydrates (sugars) are retained and either used at once or converted to starches and stored. Conversely, plants can only carry on photosynthesis if they contain chlorophyll; plants that are coloured differently do, in fact, contain green, but it is masked by the alternative colour.

LIGHT AND HUMIDITY REQUIREMENTS

LIGHT

During the growing season, from spring until the end of mid-autumn, most plants are happy in the prevailing light in most conservatories. But there are, of course, degrees of lightness, since the area close to the glazing will be better lit than the part close to a back wall; a plant close to the south side of a south-facing conservatory will be better lit still, and will be in direct sunlight for most of the day on a sunny day. Since there are these different degrees of light intensity, the definitions used in the Plants A-Z are given as follows:

As much as possible Requires a position that receives all the direct sunlight that is available. However, in summer it will be advisable to turn the plant a little every few days so that all parts of it receive some sun. In winter, it will be helpful to move the plant to follow the sun around during the day, especially in cool-temperate climates.

Good with some sun Requires a position near to the east, south or west sides of the conservatory where the plant will receive some direct sun at some time every day that the sun shines.

Good Requires a position in the centre or near to the sides of the conservatory, but should not receive direct sun at any time.

Light shade Should be positioned near to the back wall of an east- south- or west-facing conservatory, without any sun, or close to the north side of a north-facing one.

Shade Should be as far away as possible from the source of light, or anywhere in a north-facing conservatory, except close to the glass.

HUMIDITY

Some degree of humidity is needed for all plants, but different genera have adapted to a wide range of climatic conditions. In the cultivation information given in the Plants A-Z I have used the specifications given below.

Very high humidity Above 80 per cent; use all possible means to provide atmospheric moisture, including misting several times a day, or automatic misting, sponging leaves, grouping plants and supplying shallow saucers of water to combat evaporation.

High humidity Above 70 per cent; prevailing humidity should be supplemented to bring it up to a suitable percentage, normally by daily misting.

Normal humidity Around 50 to 70 per cent; this level of humidity prevails in cool-temperate climates without any need for artificial help.

Low humidity Below 50 per cent. No action required.

□ It should be noted that the higher the temperature, the quicker the loss of moisture from the atmosphere; a humidity percentage of 75 at 18°C (65°F) may not need the addition of misting, but at 30°C (85°F) it may well be required.

Again, if you have roof ventilation, open this first, then side windows or ventilators – the lowest ones first. Ventilation should be carried out so that the conservatory is not full of draughts; and if this is unavoidable, vulnerable plants should be temporarily moved out of harm's way. Very little will be required, beyond opening one or two windows or ventilators a crack; in the very coldest weather, and especially if the minimum is being allowed to fall to 4°C (40°F), all can be left closed, but watch the humidity. On windy days, when heat is lost particularly quickly, open the windows/ventilators on the side facing away from the wind, if possible – for example, if it is coming from the north, open on the south side.

MANAGING THE PLANTS

PLANT WHICH is grown outdoors, in the open ground, where its roots have the freedom to range through the soil without restriction, in search of water and nutrient, should be able to grow to its maximum size and health, and to realize its potential for flowering and fruiting. But all sorts of damage can occur owing to adverse weather conditions, from flooding, frost, storms and so on, and to attacks by predators, which range from man and grazing animals to insects, fungi, bacteria and viruses.

A plant confined to a container and the interior of a conservatory is by no means weakened. If it was removed from its container, and had the ability to move unaided, it would probably walk straight back into it and put its roots down very firmly, just as animals captured in the wild and then freed from camp, return to their source of food and security.

Such plants could be said to lead an idyllic life. They are provided with exactly the quantities and type of nutrient and water that they need, at the times they need them; they are protected from damage and predators and, if they are attacked or become infected, they are "medicated" at once. Supports are supplied, regular attention controls their growth, and unwanted vegetation is removed.

You, as their owner, are responsible for all this care; the plants rely entirely on you for their health and life. If this sounds rather daunting, it is consoling to know that, in fact, the care of plants in containers has become very simple and easy, owing to modern research on growing media, nutrients, water needs and container manufacture. Indeed, the latter has diversified and improved so much that there is a form of container suitable for every plant you can think of.

Watering

Water constitutes roughly 80 per cent of the weight of a plant, so its presence or absence makes a great deal of difference to the well-being of the plant. Not only does the water content keep the plant rigid, it contains the mineral nutrients it needs as well as serving as the means of transporting the products of metabolism about the plant, as required. In a container, the quantity of water a plant receives is finite, and is quite quickly lost by evaporation, so frequent replacement is essential.

How to water

The general rules for watering are as follows. At the top of every container there should be a space between the compost and the rim of about 2.5cm (1in). Fill this up with water, poured on fairly quickly. When it has soaked through to the bottom of the container, leave any surplus in the saucer or tray for about 20 minutes. If the surplus is not absorbed by then,

Top watering
Plants are normally watered from the top. Fill the space between the compost and the rim of the pot with water. After 20 minutes, remove any surplus water that drains into the saucer or tray.

Base watering
Plants subject to basal rot are often best watered via the saucer beneath the pot. Add the water to the saucer, refilling as necessary, until all the water is soaked up. If any water remains after 20 minutes, discard it. Do not let the plant stand in stagnant water.

discard it. Another form of watering, base watering, shown below left, is used if plants are subject to basal rot. If there is no surplus with the first watering, repeat and discard ay that drains out into the tray.

Container plant owners tend to belong to one of two groups: those who are heavy handed with the watering and those who keep their plants on the dry side, with the obvious result that certain groups of plants do better with certain people. If you turn out to be a "desert" waterer, lack of any surplus in the tray usually means more is required.

When to water

The need for watering can be determined by a number of different methods, although you can, of course, use a moisture meter, of which there are several different kinds. Most container plant owners judge the need for water by one or more of the following signs: checking the colour of the compost surface – when it becomes dry, it becomes a lighter brown; testing the weight of the container – the difference in weight between moist and dry compost is considerable; tapping the container (clay pots) – a high ringing tone is produced by dry compost, a dull tone by wet compost; poking a finger into the compost to check the lower levels.

Experienced owners can be guided by the appearance of the plant. A plant which is only just in need of water begins to change its overall green very slightly. It has a slightly floppy look and feels limp without having actually reached the wilting stage. In the long run, you learn instinctively when water is needed, and how much, without assessing the compost, simply by checking the appearance of the plant.

CATEGORIES OF WATERING
Conventionally, watering falls into four categories: sparing, moderate, normal and free.

Sparing Usually applies to winter watering, when the plants are either dormant or just ticking over, and therefore absorbing little moisture. Water every two to four weeks, just enough to keep the compost sufficiently moist to prevent the roots from shrivelling.

Moderate Usually for plants with fleshy leaves and stems. Water roughly every week in spring and autumn, every four days in summer, and once a fortnight in winter.

Normal Applies to most plants; the intervals required are roughly twice a week in spring and autumn, daily in the height of summer, and every seven to ten days in winter, depending on the temperature of the conservatory.

Free Usually applies to summer watering for fast-growing plants and those with thin leaves. Water daily and give two applications so that compost is thoroughly soaked. (A plant that suddenly demands free watering, having previously been satisfied with normal watering, may have outgrown its pot – see p. 161.)

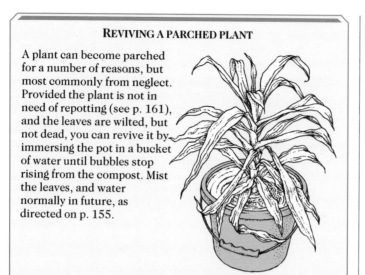

REVIVING A PARCHED PLANT

A plant can become parched for a number of reasons, but most commonly from neglect. Provided the plant is not in need of repotting (see p. 161), and the leaves are wilted, but not dead, you can revive it by immersing the pot in a bucket of water until bubbles stop rising from the compost. Mist the leaves, and water normally in future, as directed on p. 155.

Feeding

Plants have two sources of food: one is the air from which they can obtain the substances needed for photosynthesis (see p. 152), and the other is the soil, from which they obtain a different kind of food, mineral nutrients such as phosphorus, potassium and so on. These are present in the soil as minute particles, or are present in the soil moisture.

One of the functions of plant roots is to absorb moisture from the soil, and by doing so they also take in the mineral foods they require; the process by which water and nutrient pass through the cell walls into the cell is called osmosis. Once in the roots, the nutrients are combined and moved about the plant, together with the products of photosynthesis, as needed to develop leaves and flowers and generally carry on all the functions required to keep the plant alive and growing.

It is essential to grow camellias, citrus and other lime-hating plants in a compost without lime, and to water them with soft water – either boiled or rain water. Alternatively a fertilizer containing sequestrated iron can be watered on to the compost – this special iron is made up in a form which the plant can absorb. The iron in an alkaline compost is "locked up" and cannot be taken in by calcifuges.

Types of fertilizers

All the proprietary composts will contain these and the other minerals needed by plants; the peat-based brands contain nutrients in a form which is easily assimilated by the plant roots, but which lasts for only a few weeks. After that nutrients have to be added in a concentrated form as a powder or as a liquid. The soil-based composts, such as the John Innes range, contain nutrients in a different form, which mostly last during the time a plant is in a particular size of container, so that there is seldom a need to feed the plants as well as water them.

There are a great many variations in fertilizers: some are

general feeds suitable for the majority of plants, while some are specific, say, to chrysanthemums or tomatoes. Others have a high potassium:nitrogen ratio, and yet others have the reverse. Some are liquids that need to be diluted; some are already diluted. Some are inorganic, some organic; some are slow-release, some are "controlled-release". There are fertilizers with only one nutrient and others with a dozen.

The possible combinations and usages could ensure that you stock a special fertilizer for every genus. But in practice you will find that one or two different brands are all you need. However, when you become more experienced in growing container plants, variations can be used to good effect, especially if making up your own compost.

Dry fertilizers These are available in powder or granulated form, and can be applied dry and watered in, or mixed with water and watered in as well. Instructions for dilutions and frequency of application will be given on the fertilizer container.

Liquid fertilizers Most of these are sold in a concentrated form which needs to be diluted with water to a given strength and applied at stated intervals as advised by the manufacturer. A few are for application to the top growth, particularly the leaves, and are known as foliar; they have the advantage that they have an "instant" effect.

Inorganic/organic fertilizers Both types are available for container plants, though the liquid forms of the organic ones are easier to obtain and use; for instance, those based on seaweed or farm manures. Inorganic ones are considered to be "artificial", because they are manufactured from minerals; organic forms are largely derived from vegetable or animal

---

THE PLANT'S NUTRIENT NEEDS

As with animals, particular nutrients are required for particular purposes. There are three which play the largest part in a plant's development, and these are nitrogen, phosphorus and potassium; another which is almost as important is iron. Altogether there are nearly 20 known at present as being essential to plants, and there may be more.

Nitrogen This nutrient is responsible for developing the leaves and stems of plants, and its shortage results at first in pale green colouring, later changing to overall yellow. The plant's growth slows down and ceases, and eventually it dies. There are other reasons for plants turning yellow, but in general where nitrogen deficiency is concerned, the yellow colour will be preceded by pale green.

Phosphorus This is required initially by seedlings and very young plants, and without it they will not carry on developing. Later it is associated with the maturity of the plant and

the development of flowers and fruits. Lack of it is not easy to assess, since various effects are produced, mostly discoloration of the leaves, depending on the species. However, it is hardly ever a problem with container-grown plants.

Potassium Potassium is just as necessary as the other two, especially as it is concerned with water uptake, and it also plays a part in the maturing process, the production of flowers and the ripening of fruit. Its deficiency in container plants is more likely than phosphorus, as flowering can be poor but, even so, it is not often seen.

Iron Lack of iron can cause problems in containers. The youngest leaves of plants turn yellow quite quickly, spreading progressively to the rest of the plant, so that it cannot carry on photosynthesis. It is most frequently seen on plants which need an acid compost, and/or which are being watered with hard water.

refuse, which once had life in them, and they are not manufactured.

There are some useful inorganic dry fertilizers, particularly the slow-release and controlled-release types already referred to. The first ensures that nutrients are slowly dissolved over a certain period, such as over five to six months or over six to nine months; the second allows nutrients to enter the compost moisture according to the temperature of the compost, the idea being that plant roots do not become active until a certain degree of warmth in the compost is reached.

The temperature for release is built in to the make-up of the fertilizer, and the idea is good, provided the compost temperature reaches the same level, and provided the species of plant concerned becomes active at that level. The temperature chosen is one suited to a broad range of plants, so it should work well, and should also be economical.

When to feed

Most feeding is required in summer, and the standard practice is to use a liquid feed, applied at roughly weekly intervals, starting in early summer, and continuing until the beginning of early autumn. However, there are many variations on this, as noted in the cultivation requirements for each genus in the plant list. Moreover, the soil-based John Innes composts should not need additional food; they were planned with the object of supplying a plant with all its needs while it inhabits a container of a certain size and, where a plant does run out of food, it is usually a fast grower and needs more root-room anyway, and should therefore be potted on. If it cannot be potted on, then feeding will obviously be necessary.

In spring, because the majority of plants are repotted into fresh compost, feeding is not required, but again there is a qualification. Some plants grow slowly and do not need annual repotting, so they are top-dressed, and then they are likely to need feeding from late spring or even mid-spring.

In autumn, growth slows down and ceases; at this time, additional feeding is a waste, as it is simply washed through

---

FERTILIZER ANALYSIS

Instructions are given on the outside of the fertilizer packet, bottle or box for applying the feed, and there will also be an analysis of the contents. All the nutrients contained in it will be listed, and the quantities of nitrogen, phosphorus and potassium will be given as percentages in a ratio. A standard analysis for a commonly used outdoor fertilizer is 7:7:7, meaning that there is 7 per cent of each of these three present (as a salt), and that the nutrient content is evenly balanced between them.

However, it may give 14:7:3, in which there is a great deal more nitrogen than potassium; such a fertilizer would be preferable for foliage plants. Where the potassium content is shown to be high, as in 5:6:12, this would be recommended for flowering species. Basically, all you would need is one of each, whether organic or inorganic, dry or liquid, whichever you prefer.

the compost and lost. The time to stop feeding is not arbitrary; the best indication is when the plant's leaves start to yellow and no more flowers are produced. Winter is generally a close season, but the exceptions are noted in the plant list.

If a plant is repotted in peat-based compost halfway through the season, feeding will be needed for a few weeks only.

Composts

When plants grow in open ground, their roots can range freely to find the minerals they need, but in a container such nutrients have to be supplied, partly by application to the compost during the growing season, and partly from whatever growing medium, or compost, is used in the container. With a limited quantity of compost in each container, the mineral nutrients are also limited, and so is the root-room. To remedy both these problems, most plants are repotted each spring into fresh compost (and often into a larger container), of which there are currently two main types.

Peat is an important component of composts and forms a large part of the peat-based kind, but its sources are finite, and the raised wetlands from which it is derived need to be conserved. There is a variety of alternatives to it, such as leaf-mould, cocopeat and cocofibre, composted bark and so on. Considerable research is being undertaken to determine suitable replacements for peat, and composts are already being used that do not contain it. More and more garden centres and shops are supplying these materials, and the composts themselves will be generally available in due course. For the time being, peat can be used as there are still large stocks.

Peat-based compost

The main ingredient here is granulated peat, making up about 75 per cent of the compost, the rest consisting of fine sand, a small quantity of minerals, and some chalk. It is lightweight and easy to handle; it needs watering less frequently than the other type, but dries out completely within a few hours so that some plants reach wilting point unexpectedly quickly.

It works well in plastic containers, and there is generally no need to use a drainage layer in the base of such containers for most plants; however, as always in gardening, there are exceptions to the general rule, and these are noted in the plant list. The main disadvantages are that the food supply is small and, as it is lightweight, plants with a lot of heavy top growth tend to topple over when grown in it.

When using it, be particularly careful not to let it dry completely, even with plants that need to be kept dry in winter, as it takes time to soak it right through to the centre. It doesn't do the plants a lot of good, either. It is possible to overcome the small quantity of food by mixing one of the slow or controlled-release fertilizers with the compost before potting (instead of using liquid fertilizer throughout the growing season) but you will need experience before you do this, so that you know how much to add to a given quantity.

There are various types of composts of this kind: potting, seed, cuttings and so on; some are suitable for both potting and seed sowing, but whatever the kind needed for specific purposes it can be obtained ready made-up from garden supply outlets.

Soil-based compost

Here there is more soil than any other ingredient, and the kind mostly used is the John Innes range of potting and seed composts. The potting compost contains seven parts good loam (sterilized), three parts granulated peat, and two parts coarse sand, all parts by volume. To each 35 litres (1 bushel) of this mixture, 112g (4oz) base fertilizer and 21g (¾oz) chalk is added. The fertilizer should consist of: two parts superphosphate, two parts hoof and horn, and one part sulphate of potash, all parts by weight.

This formula is for the John Innes potting mixture No 1; the next one, No 2, has twice as much fertilizer and chalk, and No 3 three times as much of each per 35 litre (1 bushel). No 1 is suitable for plants in pots up to 10cm (4in) diameter, or other containers with an equivalent amount of compost; No 2 is used for those in pots between 10 and 20cm (4 and 8in) diameter, and No 3 for anything larger than 20cm (8in) diameter.

For seed sowing, the compost consists of: two parts loam, one part peat and one part coarse sand, all parts by volume together with 42g (1½oz) superphosphate and 21g (¾oz) chalk, both by weight, for each 35 litre (bushel) of compost. This is a much finer compost, containing mainly the phosphorus required for seedling development, and should only be used for seed sowing.

If lime-hating plants are to be grown, the seed compost will be suitable if the chalk is replaced by 21g (¾oz) flowers of sulphur, provided plant foods are supplied, starting to use them before the plants become root-bound. Liquid fertilizer solutions are suitable, or the slow-release nutrients can be added.

The soil-based composts provide a good anchor for large and/or top-heavy plants, and are also particularly suitable for clay containers. They are not as sponge-like as the peat composts, and so need watering more frequently, but there is much less danger of sudden wilting.

A drainage layer in the container base is advisable for all forms of compost. It normally consists of broken pieces of clay pot, placed convex side uppermost, broken brick or any similar porous material. For tubs and large containers, a 5cm (2in) deep layer is necessary.

Potting

To ensure that the roots of a plant are comfortable and capable of functioning to their maximum, the plant needs careful insertion into its growing medium and its container. It will inevitably outgrow its container and need a larger one, as well as more fresh compost, and the best time to repot is early

Repotting a plant

Before turning the plant upside down, ensure the compost is moist. Cup one hand around the base of the plant to support it.

Put the plant into the larger pot, firming the compost around the sides of the pot, leaving a 2.5cm (1in) space at the top of the plant for watering.

Water normally and set aside for a day or two in a warm shaded place to allow the plant to settle.

spring, late winter, or whenever growth is just about to start. At this stage, the plant's roots should have developed so that the tips are appearing on the surface of the side of the root-ball, but should not have become unduly elongated and consequently cramped.

In some cases, repotting will be necessary in early or midsummer, if the plants are fast-growing, and the best guide here is to examine the root-ball if you are not quite sure whether a larger container is needed.

Preparation Have a quantity of compost prepared ready on a work surface, and always work with moist compost. Choose a pot or other container whose diameter is at least 2.5cm (1in) larger than the one the plant is in. If plastic, put a little compost in the base; if clay, add a drainage layer and then a little compost.

Sometimes the plant is past the time of repotting, and has grown long roots coiled round at the pot base and emerging from the drainage holes. In this case, unravel them and cut them back level with the base or side of the root-ball, and also loosen the compost a little, to let in air.

Repotting

Make sure the compost of the plant to be potted is also moist and turn the plant upside down; support it and the pot on the palm of one hand, hold the pot with the other and tap the rim on the work surface. This will loosen the root-ball so that the whole plant falls down on to your palm. Turn it the right way up and put it in the centre of the new pot on top of the compost, then adjust the quantity of compost so that the surface of the root-ball is about 2.5cm (1in) below the rim of the pot. This space is essential for adequate watering.

Fill in compost down the side of the pot, and firm it in as you do so, using your fingers so that it is as consolidated as that of the root-ball. Ensure that the plant is always central, otherwise it will have a lopsided root development, and continue until the new compost is level with the root-ball surface. Tap the pot on the work surface to settle the compost and level the surface, then water normally and set aside in a warm, shaded place for a day or two.

Repotting large plants

Plants in containers of 30–38cm (12–15in) in diameter can be dealt with by one person; anything larger will need two people. Plants can be prevented from growing larger by repotting into fresh compost but still using the same size container. To accommodate the compost, the roots have to be cut back, by about a quarter from the base and sides of the root-ball. This may sound extreme, but if carefully done with a sharp knife so as to avoid tearing and pulling, and repotted at once, the plant suffers no harm, though its activity slows down temporarily.

Pruning the top growth at the same time is also advisable, to balance the root pruning.

MOVING PLANTS

Larger plants can be far too heavy for you to move them unaided. If the plant needs to be shifted occasionally into a different position – for example, near a window in winter to take advantage of better light – it pays to construct a simple trolley-style platform from four or five short 2cm (¾in) thick planks, battened underneath, and with castors attached to the undersides of the battens at the four corners.

Alternatively you can, with some help, move the container onto a piece of sacking and then carefully pull the sacking along the floor. It is also advisable to avoid moving the plant after it has just been watered as this can greatly increase the weight to be moved.

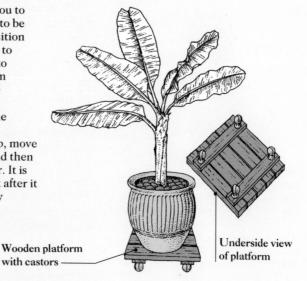

Wooden platform with castors

Underside view of platform

Keeping plants tidy

Regular grooming of plants makes all the difference between an immaculate display and a slightly untidy, rather amateurish-looking one. It also helps to keep the plants in good health, and ensures that the conservatory remains clean.

In the natural course of events, plants shed leaves, buds and flowers, which sometimes lie on lower parts of the plant, or fall on to the floor. Any debris should be removed regularly, otherwise rot may start, or the conservatory floor may be permanently stained by coloured petals. Yellowing, withered or otherwise discoloured leaves need to be removed, as do dead or injured stems, and faded flowers in particular need collecting. The more you deadhead, the more the plant will produce further flowers in most cases.

Large-leaved plants grown for their foliage need to be washed regularly, to remove the dust and grime that collects on them. Use a moist sponge or soft cloth, and tepid water, or alternatively spray and then wipe over the leaves. If leaves are infected with pests, particularly scale insect, remove the bugs as far as possible first, otherwise you are liable to spread the plague. Alternatively you can stand the plants out in a summer shower, which not only cleans them more thoroughly than you can, but waters them and provides plenty of humidity.

Such plants should naturally have a gloss on them, if growing well, but you can improve on it if you wish by applying a proprietary leaf-shine which produces a high polish without clogging the stomata.

Plants steadily change in size and shape, so supports need to be given or extended. Ties need to be renewed and re-sited, and new shoots need to be trained out and tied, to avoid tangled stems, and to show off new flowers and leaves. If the

A hoya supported on a trellis. Make your own support from bamboo or buy them ready-made in plastic

tips of stems have died, they should be cut off, back to living growth, and any completely dead stems cut right back to their point of origin. If a variegated-leaved plant produces a plain-leaved shoot, remove it, otherwise the plant will revert completely.

Pruning

As far as conservatory plants are concerned, there is not a great deal to do; most shrubs need tidying only, and any climbers are simply cut back to fit the space available.

When to prune In general, the time to prune is in late winter or just before repotting in early spring. Another suitable time is in autumn, after flowering and when seasonal growth is gradually ceasing, ready for cold-weather dormancy. For outdoor ornamental plants, a good rule-of-thumb is to prune spring- and early summer-flowering ones immediately flowering has finished, and to prune midsummer- to autumn-flowerers early in the following spring. But conservatory shrubs and climbers mostly flower late, so they are nearly always pruned at the later date, as they flower on the growth produced in the current season, not on shoots produced the previous year.

How much and what to cut With any woody plant, cut off diseased or dead shoots – the latter will have brown bark – weak, stunted shoots and crossing shoots. Thin out the remainder so that they are not crowded, in all cases cutting off completely the shoot to be removed, back to its point of origin. Others need only be pruned to fit the space.

The remainder will need various degrees of cutting back. Light pruning merely removes a few centimetres or inches from the tip of the new shoots; moderate pruning cuts the new

Plant management
Many plants require some form of staking if they are to look their best. The nature of the support depends largely on the needs and features of the plant. Climbers with aerial roots, like monstera, will adhere naturally to a moist moss pole and twining climbers like stephanotis will naturally wind themselves round a wire support or trellis-style frame, but plants that scramble, like bougainvillea or plumbago, need to be tied on to a support, such as a pyramid or trellis, to avoid the stems becoming a tangled mess. Handle any plant gently when you tie it in. Green plastic ties are easy to use – a simple twist or two will hold the stem in place – and can be easily removed and replaced as the plant grows.

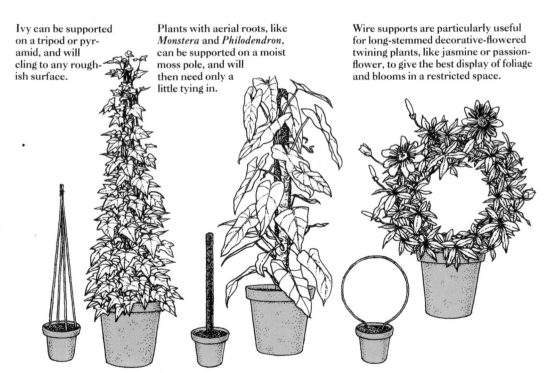

Ivy can be supported on a tripod or pyramid, and will cling to any roughish surface.

Plants with aerial roots, like *Monstera* and *Philodendron*, can be supported on a moist moss pole, and will then need only a little tying in.

Wire supports are particularly useful for long-stemmed decorative-flowered twining plants, like jasmine or passionflower, to give the best display of foliage and blooms in a restricted space.

growth (it does not cut into the old growth) by about half. Hard or severe pruning removes about three-quarters of the new growth. Spur pruning reduces it to leave about 2.5cm (1in) with one or two buds or leaves on the stub.

If the plant is outgrowing its space rapidly, pruning will have to go further back, into the older growth, but it is advisable to treat only some of the shoots at a time, and to do the remainder the following year, to avoid shocking the plant. However, some climbers can be cut back into old growth without harm.

Tipping

This is often done to herbaceous as well as woody plants. Pinching back, or tipping, a plant removes the tip of all the new shoots down to about the second or third leaf or pair of leaves. It is generally done in late spring and early summer, and encourages more shoot production and hence more flowers, but does delay flowering.

Specialist plant care

Certain plants need particular care and attention. Among them are bromeliads, cacti and orchids.

Bromeliads

These plants include the cryptanthus and vrieseas, and are epiphytic (they perch on their support or growing medium, rather than use it as a food source). Many are aerial epiphytes, found on trees; some are terrestrial, largely growing amongst pebbles and rocks. In their natural habitat, there is little rain or food available to them, so they have adapted accordingly to survive in these conditions.

In the wild, the aerial epiphytes grow on the branches and forks of forest trees, where vegetation can pile up and rot. Their roots are vestigial, so most of the water they need is absorbed through the centre of the leaf rosette, often forming

Pruning
Most plants need only moderate pruning (above left) in which the new growth is cut back by about half, while a few, like poinsettias (above centre) require far more radical pruning, taking away three quarters of the new growth. Some need more or less no pruning, taking away only the top couple of pairs of leaves on each new shoot (above right).

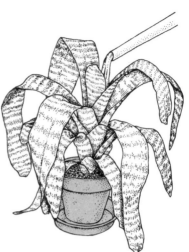

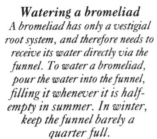

Watering a bromeliad
A bromeliad has only a vestigial root system, and therefore needs to receive its water directly via the funnel. To water a bromeliad, pour the water into the funnel, filling it whenever it is half-empty in summer. In winter, keep the funnel barely a quarter full.

a funnel or "vase", where it collects. Insects often fall into the water, as well as leaves, twigs and other debris, and these provide nutrients. The terrestrial epiphytes differ only in that they have some, not much, soil to root into, and are much more exposed to light.

Compost for bromeliads should be peat-based; a little soil can be mixed into that for the terrestrials, but it is not essential. They do well in hanging containers, or attached to driftwood or dead branches, to which they can be carefully tied with soft string or copper wire. Watering is carried out via the funnel (see above); the compost should be kept just moist, and occasional drying out will not matter. Liquid feeding into the funnel can be done during summer, at half-strength.

Cacti

Cacti grow in some of the driest parts of the world, where rain may not occur for years, and where the sun's heat is great. Consequently they have adapted so that they can conserve the maximum amount of water, and so that they can make the best use of the rain when it does arrive.

The rounded body that many of them have is the one with the smallest area for a given volume, so that they transpire the least moisture possible. The cell tissue is modified to take in the greatest quantity of water, and the hairs or bristles, together with the thick cuticle and waxy covering, further reduce water loss. Their roots, although shallow, are very wide-spreading, to absorb whatever rain – and dew – are available before they evaporate in the heat.

Although cacti do not make the large amount of growth that most other plants do, they are still living plants and need water and nutrients in the same way. Watering from spring to autumn is normal, but sparing to dry in winter; feeding in summer is also normal.

Containers ideally should be shallow but large, with a good drainage layer in the base, and a good compost is one of the

Displaying cacti and succulents
Cacti, being slow growing, are best displayed in groups until they reach a reasonable size. Make sure the plants grouped together enjoy similar conditions of light and moisture, like the ones shown here: Opuntia, Mammillaria, Astrophytum *and* Agave.

soil-based kind, with one extra part of grit added to every three parts of compost, parts by volume. A thin layer of gravel on the compost surface keeps the base of the cactus dry and prevents rotting. Handling prickly cacti can be difficult, so use tongs or a collar of paper wrapped round the lower part.

Orchids

One of the most fascinating groups of plants, orchids can turn into a lifetime's hobby. Their lovely, often bizarre, flowers are curiously shaped and extravagantly and exotically coloured; botanically speaking, they are still evolving and are the most advanced of the plant group that contains reeds, grasses and bulbs. Like bromeliads, they are epiphytic and largely live on trees, and need a special compost, which can be bought made-up. Alternatively a good old-fashioned mixture would contain, by volume, three parts dry, chopped osmunda fibre and one part moist, chopped sphagnum moss.

When repotting, which is usually when the orchid is too big for the container, or the compost has rotted completely, remove the plant by pushing it gently upwards from the back, using a stick. Take off all the old compost and any dead, brown roots; cut off any brown pseudobulbs.

In a clean container, place drainage material vertically to half-fill the container, then put tufts of compost on top, and compost between the roots of the orchid. Return it to the container, towards the back, and work in more compost from the back, half-covering the pseudobulbs, till the front is filled in, too. Firm sideways to avoid compacting the compost downwards, spray the compost surface, but do not water for a week or so. Keep it warm and in a humid atmosphere.

Grow orchids in hanging containers, and a very humid atmosphere; they must have sunlight in autumn, to ensure flowering later.

Repotting orchids
When repotting orchids, remove any dead, brown roots and cut off any brown psendobulbs before transferring the orchid to a new container.

A WORKING AREA

Even if you buy plants ready potted, there is still work to be done looking after them in the growing season, and for this various bits and pieces are necessary. To keep them tidy, it is worth having a special kitchen-unit type work area, with cupboards and drawers, and a work surface on top. A 90cm (3ft) length, with three cupboards and drawers, will do for the average conservatory and has enough storage area to contain the equipment required.

Packets and bottles of fertilizer, string, canes and supporting frames, scissors and secateurs, moisture and pH meters, spare pots, saucers and compost, sprayers and misters, pesticides, vases, catalogues and labels, and watering-cans are the main items that need to be close at hand.

With a good work surface, the unit can be used for potting, sowing seed and general work on the plants. When not in use, it supplies another plant display area, with trailing plants hanging down the back of the unit, which is turned to face the main part of the conservatory. It can also provide a suitable sideboard for a buffet lunch or other meals.

PLANT HEALTH

EVEN IN THE best-run conservatories, plants will have problems. While a conservatory protects and provides them with a near-perfect environment, it also provides the pests and diseases they are prone to with ideal conditions in which to proliferate – hosts and food are there for the taking, without any predators to curb the invasion.

You can prevent this kind of trouble right at the beginning by making sure that any plants you acquire are completely clear of insects or fungus diseases. So much of this sort of trouble is already present on plants when they go into a conservatory, and, if unnoticed, will spread very rapidly. Some pests and diseases – greenfly and grey mould in particular – infect the plants from the garden, but a good deal of the battle is won if you make sure that you start with clean, uninfested and healthy plants.

Another problem can be nutrient deficiencies (see p. 157), but these are much less likely on container plants. The two most likely deficiencies are shortage of nitrogen or of iron, but otherwise failure to feed the plants as required during the growing season or to change the compost are usually the sole causes of nutrient troubles.

While pests and diseases are thought to be the biggest cause of ailing plants, ill-health in fact is much more likely to arise from physiological disorders. These result in turn from faults in the management of the plants and their environment, such as putting them in a light position when they need shade, or watering them heavily when a dryish compost would suit them better.

What usually happens then is that badly managed plants become infested with pests or fungus diseases and, because the plants are already weak, these parasites will finish them off. The appearance of any pest or disease is practically always a sign that the plant concerned is being mismanaged, and its care needs radical alteration. Fortunately for diagnosis, disorders of management all have specific symptoms, and these are listed as follows, with their description, principal causes, and remedies.

Pests and diseases

As can be seen from the following lists, there is a variety of insect and other pests, and diseases, which can invade an equal variety of conservatory plants. Such pests and diseases can be guarded against by checking the plants daily; one obvious greenfly will indicate ten hidden; one mildewed leaf will mean five more the next day, so removal as soon as seen pays handsomely.

The most common problems, their symptoms, causes and remedies are given on the following pages. General symptoms are given first, followed by specific common pests and diseases.

LEAVES/SYMPTOMS	CAUSES	REMEDY
Yellow colouring		
Lowest leaves quickly turning completely yellow and falling.	Sudden drop from normal temperature, or sudden cold.	Maintain even temperatures.
Lowest leaves slowly turning yellow and falling after some time.	Wet compost.	Take out of container, squeeze surplus water out gently and return after a day or two; do not water until compost surface is dry; drainage layer may be needed.
Minute yellow speckling, with which there may also be webbing.	Red spider mite.	See p. 171.
Youngest leaves at tip of shoots turning completely yellow, with yellowing spreading to rest of foliage, but remaining firm and not falling.	Iron deficiency from hard water/alkaline compost.	Use soft water, rainwater, or boiled tap water and apply sequestrated iron; repot in due course in acid compost.
Yellow streaks, rings of mottling gradually spreading, plant stunted and growing slowly.	Virus disease frequently due to aphid invasion. Other vectors may be eelworm, beetles, mites etc.	Destroy plant.
Pale green colouring		
All leaves slowly turning pale green and then yellow, plant slow-growing, with weak, short new growth, and few, if any, flowers.	Nitrogen deficiency.	Repot in fresh compost, or feed with high-nitrogen fertilizer, and improve light.
"Coloured" foliage gradually becoming pale green or fading.	Compost too moist, or light poor.	Keep on dry side for most intense colouring, or improve light in quality and quantity, particularly for leaves with variegations.
Brown colouring		
Leaves with brown spots of varying sizes usually rounded.	Can be cold, minor fungus disease too much fertilizer or dry fertilizer on leaves, drops of water on leaves acting as a focus for sun's heat, or compost with poor structure so aeration and drainage faulty.	See p. 172. Remove all affected leaves if too much spotting.
Underside of leaf with raised brown spots.	Scale insect.	See p. 171.
If reddish brown, on pelargonium.	Rust.	See p. 172.
Leaves with brown tips and/or margins	Dry air, draughts, hard water, alkaline compost, rarely insufficient potassium.	Improve conditions.
Biscuit-coloured, large papery patches.	Sun scald from too much sun.	Move to shadier position.
Biscuit-coloured blisters and tunnelling on leaf surface.	Leafminer.	See p. 171.

LEAVES/SYMPTOMS	CAUSES	REMEDY
Brown colouring (ctd)		
Brown fleshy leaves at soil level, usually affects succulents and/or rosette plants.	Cold, or too much water in compost, especially when cold.	Improve conditions.
White colouring		
White fluffy spots on leaves, especially between leaves and at neck of bulbs or at leaf joints.	Mealy bug.	See p. 171.
White patches that can look like marbling – furry leaves especially prone.	Watering with cold water or cold water falling on leaves.	Use tepid water.
Powdery white patches on upper surface.	Mildew.	See p. 172.
Raised white spots on underside of chrysanthemum leaves.	White rust.	See p. 172.
Grey colouring		
Normally green leaves with an overall grey tone, eventually turning yellow and then brown and falling; sometimes webbing.	Red spider mite.	See p. 171.
Grey fur in patches on leaves, with yellow or brown marking beneath them.	Grey mould (*Botrytis cinerea*).	See p. 172.
Azalea leaves thickened and blistered with grey bloom on malformations.	Azalea gall fungus disease.	Remove completely as soon as seen.
Miscellaneous		
Stickiness	Honeydew secreted by sucking insect pests like whitefly, aphids, and scale insect.	Wipe off gently with a damp cloth and clean well.
Large irregular holes at floor level.	Slugs or snails.	See p. 171.
Semi-circular notches along margins.	Vine weevil.	See p. 171.
Black sooty blotches on upper surfaces.	Sooty mould growing on honeydew – harmless, but blocks stomata.	Wipe off as for honeydew.
Tips distorted, curled and sometimes yellowed.	Greenfly.	See aphids, p. 171.
Sudden leaf fall without discolouration.	Sudden drop in temperature, e.g. at night, or from draughts.	Maintain even temperatures.
Limp hanging leaves or complete plant wilting.	Drought or too much water.	For drought, water thoroughly (see p. 156); see Yellow discolouration.

SYMPTOMS	CAUSES	REMEDY
Flowers		
Few or no flowers.	Lack of light, low level of nutrient, too high nitrogen in compost-fertilizer, especially if plant has a great deal of leaf and shoot growth, low temperature, too large a container – plants flower best if slightly root-bound.	Improve light and warmth, increase humidity, use potash-high fertilizer, keep compost on dry side.
Flower buds dropping before they open, flowers falling before the normal time.	Chiefly dry air, draughts or moving the plant, but also cold, red spider mite or too much/too little water.	Maintain regular temperature, good humidity and careful watering at start of and during flowering.
Pale or discoloured flowers.	Azalea gall (see grey colouring), or mildrew.	See p. 169
Distorted flowers	Virus disease (see also yellow leaf discoloration) or greenfly.	See p. 168.
Brown florets on forced bulbs.	Irregular or insufficient watering while in dark.	None.
Stem or trunk		
White fluffy spots on stems.	Mealy bug.	See p. 171.
Stems with brown rot at compost surface; grey fur may occur on brown areas.	Cold and/or overwatering frequent in winter; grey mould then follows.	See p. 172.
Brown, grey, black, pale green, raised spots, generally rounded, on bark and trunk; stickiness on leaves; slow growth.	Scale insect.	See p. 171.
Whole plant looks "droughty" even if compost kept moist; greyish leaves; poor growth; plant looks sick.	Root mealy bug or root aphis.	See p. 171.

PESTS	SYMPTOMS	REMEDY
Aphids The most common kinds are greenfly and blackfly; they feed by sucking sap from leaves and soft stems, mainly at shoot tips on underside of young leaves.	Leaves below invaded growth may be sticky on upper surface or have patches of black on them; tiny green or black insects are present in large numbers, together with white specks which are cast skins. In compost close to or on roots, root aphis look like white ash; they are generally associated with dry compost.	Remove manually, maintain or improve good light and regular supply of water, humidity and ventilation; spray forcibly with water. Use insecticide such as soft soap or pyrethrum, resemethrin or permethrin if trouble persists, or as soil solution, see p. 173.
Caterpillars Rare, but occasionally found.	Large holes in leaves, buds, flowers and soft stems.	Remove manually.
Leafminer A tiny maggot that lives and feeds within leaf surface tissue. Becomes a pupa after 2–3 weeks. Ten days later it emerges as an adult fly which lays eggs. Cinerarias and chrysanthemums are most vulnerable.	Can be seen as minute dark bumps in pale winding lines on leaf surface. In bad infestations, leaves wither completely and most leaves are affected.	Pick off affected leaves immediately they are seen and destroy them, then isolate plant and watch for further symptoms. Dimethoate is the most effective control.
Mealy bug Feeds by sucking sap from plant and badly weakens it. Plant will eventually die if untreated.	Fluffy white blobs on leaves, leaf-joints and stems. Root mealybugs occur on roots.	Isolate affected plants, and remove as many as possible by hand. Spray vigorously with water, paint with methylated spirits or use chemicals like dimethoate or malathion, as spray or soil solutions, see p. 173.
Mites (red spider & tarsonemid) Sap sucking microscopic pests found on cyclamen begonias and pelargoniums particularly.	The pale red, green, yellow cream or brown specks on leaves are mites; white specks are cast skins or egg shells.	Discard plant if badly affected; spray with derris or introduce predatory mite, *Phytoseulis persimilis* on glasshouse red spider mite.
Scale insects These suck sap from plant, producing a sticky honeydew on which sooty mould grows. Citrus, ferns, palms, ficus and callistemon are all susceptible.	Raised brown spots on lower leaf surface mainly, close to main vein. Sometimes found on stems and trunks.	Scrape off as soon as seen. Wash plant well with soapy water and repeat one week later. Bad infestations may need spraying with dimethoate.
Slugs and snails Rarely a problem.	Irregular holes in leaves near soil level.	Remove manually.
Thrips Minute sap-sucking creatures with fringed wings when adult. Chrysanthemums, begonias and sinningias are all vulnerable.	Silvery patches on petals, buds and sometimes leaf surfaces (upper) in summer.	Maintain good ventilation to prevent temperatures rising too high. Spray with soft soap or resmethrin if badly infested.
Vine weevil Small biscuit-coloured brown or black beetles with forked antennae. They may be present in bought-in plants, so obtain plants from reputable source. Primulas, ferns, orchids, cyclamen and begonias very vulnerable.	Notches in leaf margins but the weevils hid in compost during the day and are hard to spot. White grubs (larvae) feed on roots and crowns of plants, killing them.	Use permethrin, according to manufacturer's instructions, see p. 173.

171

DISEASES	SYMPTOMS	REMEDY
Bacterial soft rot One of the few bacteria-based diseases of plants grown in a conservatory. Bulbs, corms and tubers very prone.	Plant collapses within a few hours. Plant smells very unpleasant, and goes soft and brown.	Discard plant and/or soil/compost, clean container thoroughly, and leave unused for several months.
Grey mould (*Botrytis cinerea*) Fungus disease which spreads rapidly; its spores are constantly present in the air.	Grey fur appears on leaves, buds, stems and flowers. On leaves there is yellow discolouration beneath grey fur; plants eventually rot and fall.	Raise temperature, increase light, ventilate and space plants out. Remove affected parts and destroy. On stems, pare off mould and spray with fungicide like propicanizole or dust with flowers and sulphur.
Powdery mildew Fungus infecting leaves of plants. Rieger begonias, cineraria, schizanthus and chrysanthemums very prone.	White powdery patches on upper leaf surfaces, also on stems and flower buds which discolour and fall. Plants are disfigured and weakened.	Dry hot conditions encourage spread, so reduce temperature and improve ventilation, and humidity. Remove affected parts and spray or dust as for grey mould.
Rust Fungus which takes two forms: red spots which affect chrysanthemums, pelargoniums, primulas, cinerarias and fuchsias; white spots affect only chrysanthemums.	Red/brown raised spots, usually on undersides of leaves, and white raised spots (only on chrysanthemums). Yellow spots appear on upperside of leaves, growth is stunted.	As soon as seen, remove affected parts carefully to avoid spreading spores. Spray with propicanizole if disease continues.
Sooty mould Minor fungus disease which lives on honeydew that sap-sucking pests secrete.	Sooty black mould on leaves.	Sponge off carefully and look for scale insect or other pests.

Control methods

In a conservatory, it is better not to use chemical controls. Apart from all the usual drawbacks, they often smell unpleasant – hardly a suitable attribute for a living area.

However, there are several ways of dealing with plant problems without having to resort to the bottle or the packet, and the first line of defence is to ensure the right growing conditions. Although it would appear impossible to cater for the needs of each plant, in fact there are several general factors common to all of them: good humidity (although desert plants are indifferent to the state of the air, provided it is not heavily moist), light, ventilation, warmth and fairly even temperatures, and space. Watering and feeding *are* factors that can be tailored to each plant, but the rest apply to most of them.

One of the best and most pleasant ways of limiting damage from pests and diseases is to have a good look at all the plants every day. You will then see the crucial first signs of trouble, perhaps one greenfly or a spot of mildew, and will be able to remove it instantly, and make sure there are no more. It is more than likely there will be, hidden under a leaf or at the back of a stem, but you will already have been alerted, and it is removal of these hidden symptoms that is so important. If a plant proves to be seriously invaded, it should be removed and isolated until dealt with and quite clean.

Wiping the leaves and stems with a moist cloth or sponge regularly help to keep problems at bay as does a good wash in a summer shower, or with a pressurized jet of water. Grooming is actually a trouble-shooter as well as a cosmetic process; it gets rid of the dying foliage and flowers that are often the point of entry for disease, or a hiding place for pests.

If a disease like mildew has invaded a plant, or greenfly have had a population explosion, cut back the worst-affected parts to healthy growth.

By using all these techniques, you need only resort to a few chemicals, the most useful and harmless being soft soap, flowers of sulphur and pyrethrum. Resmethrin and permethrin are synthetic analogues of pyrethrum, and last longer; derris is useful too. Dimethoate should really only be used as a last resort; in fact, if a conservatory plant is so badly infested as to need it, it may be better discarded. Where pests have invaded a plant's roots, the best remedy is to wash the roots clean of compost completely, re-pot in fresh moist compost and water lightly with an insecticidal solution. Propicanizole is a systemic chemical fungicide which can be used in the same way, in dire straits. All chemicals, needless to say, should be treated with great caution, applied according to the manufacturer's instructions, and stored safely away.

There are also the biological controls in the form of insects which prey on the plant pests. There is one for red spider mite and another for whitefly; research is continuing to discover others, notably on scale insect, and there will certainly be more in the future. These can be obtained from specialist suppliers, whose addresses are given at the end of the book, and they will give detailed instructions on use. For obvious reasons chemicals should not be used at the same time.

PROPAGATION

ANY COLLECTION of conservatory plants is constantly changing, as some species die off naturally, gifts of plants are received, and you yourself buy plants that take your fancy from conservatory nurseries and garden centres. Some of these plants are particularly good at ensuring the survival of their species, as they produce miniature replicas at the end of stems or on the leaf edges.

If all those produced were potted up, your collection would be rapidly overwhelmed by half-a-dozen species, but the ornamental or rare kinds, which never seem to do their own increasing, are well worth taking the trouble to propagate either to keep or to pass on to friends and relatives. Most plant propagation is not difficult and, with only a little encouragement, most stem cuttings, for instance, will produce roots with surprising alacrity.

Plant propagation will produce two different types of plants, according to which method of increasing them is used. Vegetative propagation involves the use of various types of stem cuttings, leaf cuttings, root cuttings, budding (for roses), grafting, division, offsets and suckers, layering and plantlets. It results in new plants that are exact copies of their parents.

Sexual propagation, in which seeds are used, produces plants which may be like their parents but are usually different, and it is this method which is used by plant breeders to obtain, for example, new varieties of rose, or different kinds of petunias. There are some conservatory plants that can only be grown from seed, such as cinerarias or exacum.

A big advantage of doing your own propagating is that you have complete control over the compost and watering, and you can make sure that the new plants are free from pests or diseases from the start. You can also ensure that they have a healthy start with all the nutrients they need, so that they are inherently vigorous and better able to withstand any problems when mature.

Vegetative propagation

The following forms of vegetative increase can be used for conservatory plants.

Miniature plants

The plantlets that some plants produce are the easiest way to increase plants vegetatively, as they need only be removed when they have produced a few roots of their own, and planted in small pots or other containers of a suitable size to take the roots comfortably.

Offsets

Offsets and suckers are very similar, but instead of being produced at the end of runners, aerial stems or on leaves, they appear at the base of the plant, and root in to the compost if

Miniature plants
A few plants do the work of propagation for you, producing miniature plantlets at the end of runners or aerial stems or on the leaves themselves, as in Saxifraga stolonifera. *Simply detach the plantlets when they have produced a few roots of their own and pot them up in the normal way.*

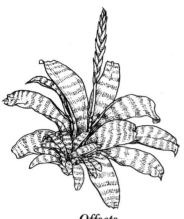

Offsets
A number of plants produce offsets at the base which will root into the compost in time. Once they have developed a few roots, you can detach them carefully and pot them up.

Division
Propagation by division is another simple method of reproducing certain kinds of plants, particularly those multi-centred crowns or those with tuberous roots, like Aspidistra, *which can be split into sections. Division is normally carried out in spring.*

left to their own devices. Bulbs and corms produce smaller bulbs (offsets) and cormlets, and some plants produce these miniatures in the leaf-axils of the top growth, for example, hearts' entangled (*Ceropegia woodii*); such miniatures can be taken off and planted during the growing season. Bamboos grow suckers from their spreading underground stems.

There is no particularly relevant time at which to detach offsets or suckers. It is more a case of waiting until they have produced a reasonable quantity of roots so that they can sustain themselves, and do not need the support of the parent plant. Bulb offsets, however, are planted at the time the parent bulb is potted for the new growing season.

Division

Some plants do not mind being divided, and a few will actually have crowns, (after two or three years) that have several centres instead of one. Division is then easy, as each centre is virtually a separate plant with some roots attached and can be sliced off and potted. Even the remainder will survive, provided each section still has roots. Examples of plants that can be treated in this way are the Italian bellflower (*Campanula isophylla*) and the aspidistra. The stems of some of the rhizomatous begonias can be cut into short lengths and half-buried on the compost surface, and tuberous begonias will survive having their tubers cut into pieces, provided each has an "eye" or bud. In general, division is most successful if done in spring, just when growth is beginning and the plant's "energy" is returning to normal after dormancy.

Stem cuttings

The part of the plant used to make a cutting is usually a stem, and the stem is practically always a young one, from a new shoot produced in the same growing season – in other words, less than a year old. Propagating by cuttings makes use of the principle that an injured stem will react, in the right conditions, by producing roots at the point of injury, so cutting off a piece of stem will stimulate root-cell growth.

Tip or soft cuttings

Of the three sorts of stem cuttings, the one of most use for conservatory plants is probably the tip or soft cutting. A tip cutting is the section of stem at the growing end of the shoot – the end opposite the point at which it is attached to the parent stem. Its length is between 7.5 and 10cm (3 and 4in). Both the inner and outer tissue of such a cutting are still green and soft, not tough and brown.

Because new shoots grow early in the season, tip cuttings are normally made from late spring until midsummer (once the shoot has ceased to extend it starts to mature and a different type of cutting has to be made). To make a tip cutting, or indeed any sort of cutting, the required length of stem is cut off cleanly just below a leaf-joint and the lowest leaf or pair of leaves without tearing the stem; the cutting is then ready to insert into specially prepared compost. The reason for making the cut just below the leaf-joint is that roots are most easily encouraged to grow from that particular part of the stem. There are also internodal cuttings (where the cut is made between two leaf-joints), but few plants require such cuttings.

Ordinary potting compost, preferably peat-based, can be used for the new cuttings, although there are also special cuttings composts. But potting compost has the advantage that you can leave the rooted cutting in it to grow on, rather than being forced to repot it as soon as it has rooted. Containers can be pots, trays (flats), special cuttings bags and so on, and the compost is filled in and lightly firmed so that it is level and below the rim of the container in the usual way.

Cuttings can be placed at the side or in the centre of the container but they are said to root more quickly at the side. Before inserting them, you need to make a hole with a pencil-thick piece of wood deep enough for the cutting to be buried to about half its length, with the base resting firmly on the compost at the bottom of the hole. Then the compost should be firmed closely around the cutting so that it will resist removal if pulled gently by a leaf. Any more leaves that would be buried beneath the compost should be removed, otherwise rotting may start. Finally the compost should be lightly watered to settle the cutting further still.

It is vital to ensure that the atmosphere surrounding the cutting or cuttings is kept moist, because the leaves will still give off water vapour, although there will not yet be any roots to absorb water from the growing medium. So cover with an air-filled clear plastic bag supported on split canes, and keep it in place with tape stuck to both the container and the plastic. If you are taking cuttings frequently, it would be worth investing in a mist propagation unit, which includes a rooting bed and a mechanism that produces a mist of water vapour at pre-set intervals.

Set the inserted cuttings in a shady place, at the temperature recommended for the genus. Leave them there until well rooted, which will be indicated when the stem starts to elongate. Keep the compost moist and occasionally introduce fresh air beneath the plastic. It should then be possible to remove the covering, but spray the top growth regularly for a few days while the cutting or cuttings become acclimatized to the normal atmosphere.

Semi-hardwood or half-ripe cuttings

These are taken later in the growing season and are therefore made from older shoots, though they are still the current season's growth. Again, the end of the stem furthest from the stem's point of origin is used, and the time to make the cutting is usually mid- to late summer, though earlier may sometimes be possible.

The shoots used are generally between 5 and 15cm (2 and 6in) long; the stem of the lower part of the cutting should be starting to become firm and hard, and the skin may even be

Tip cuttings

These are made from new shoots in late spring or early summer, cut off from the parent plant just below a couple of leaf joints from the shoot tip. Insert into potting compost to half the length of the cutting.

The compost is then firmed around the base of the cuttings, which are lightly watered in and covered with an air-filled plastic bag, supported on a few split canes.

Heel cuttings
These are semi-hardwood cuttings taken from the current season's growth, normally in mid-to-late summer. They comprise shortish sideshoots torn carefully away from the main stem, with a small heel of the latter attached, which helps the cuttings to root more easily.

changing from green to brown, but the upper part should still be soft, green and pliable.

Sometimes sideshoots are used which are at a similar stage and, if the plant is less easy to root and the sideshoots are a suitable length overall, about 10cm (4in), they are literally torn off the parent stem so that a sliver of bark and tissue from it are removed as well. This is called a heel cutting, the tongue of bark providing a larger area from which roots can be produced, though there is some debate as to whether it is really beneficial. If used, the tongue should be trimmed a little with a sharp knife, as it will inevitably be ragged.

Then the lower leaves are removed and the cutting inserted as for tip cuttings, but the need for warmth is not so great – normal summer temperatures will be adequate, even if they fall a little below 16°C (60°F) at night. However, rooting may take longer.

Hardwood or fully ripe cutting

These are made later still, in autumn, at which time the stem will be hard nearly to the tip, and most of the skin will be brown rather than green. Such cuttings are between 23 and 30cm (9 and 12in) long, do not need to be enclosed in clear plastic and will root in much lower temperatures, provided these are not down to freezing. The time taken to root can be several months, so that if the cutting is taken in autumn, roots may not appear until the following spring. However, these cuttings are not often used for conservatory plants, as such plants are tender and require warmth for normal growing, as well as propagation.

Leaf cuttings

Not many plants can be increased by using their leaves, but for those that can, it is a sure-fire, easy method. Rex begonias and streptocarpus are two genera that can be treated like this.

For the begonias, a leaf is removed in late spring or summer and cuts made at intervals across the main veins. Then it is laid flat on the surface of moist compost, preferably covered with a fine layer of silver sand, and weighed down with a few small pebbles so that the injured parts touch the compost. There is no need to water, but a very light spray over with a systemic fungicide will prevent grey mould developing, which is often a problem with this kind of cutting. Cover with an air-filled clear plastic bag, tightly secured around the container, keep warm at about 21°C (70°F), and in three weeks or so plantlets will start to appear at the cuts. Once they have good roots, they can be detached and potted. Sinningias can be increased in a similar manner.

In the case of streptocarpus, remove a healthy leaf, cut off the top half so that transpiration is diminished, and push the bottom section upright into moist compost, burying it up to a quarter of its length. The air temperature should be about 16–18 °C (60–65°F), and warmed compost is advisable. Echeveria leaves can be treated similarly, but should neither be watered in nor watered until they are beginning to shrivel. Saintpaulias are treated slightly differently, in that a leaf with its stem attached is used. The length of the stem is reduced to about 4cm (1½in) and then pushed upright into the compost to bury it up to the base of the leaf blade. With humidity and a temperature of about 21°C (70°F), rooting should occur in three to four weeks, when a plantlet will be produced at the base of the stem and grow up through the compost soon afterwards. This is also a suitable alternative method for propagating sinningias, provided that young leaves are used.

Seed propagation

Seed is normally used for sexual, as opposed to vegetative propagation, but in the case of ferns, spores are equivalent to seed (see p. 180). A seed is package of living tissue in a state of suspended animation containing, in effect, an instruction circuit, according to which it can develop to produce a plant of a particular shape, colour and size.

There are many different types of seed and as many different methods of sowing and germinating each, but for the majority of conservatory plants which are satisfactorily increased by seed there are only one or two methods with which you need be concerned.

In order to germinate at all, seeds must have moisture, which can be in the form of water vapour as well as liquid; if they do not absorb moisture for some reason, they cannot even start to germinate. They will also need oxygen in the compost, and tropical plant seed needs warmth, usually above 16°C (60°F). Once germination has started, nutrients will be required, particularly phosphorus and, even if there is some actually present in some part of the seed itself, it must in due course be complemented by external food.

As regards light some seed needs light to germinate, some needs to be in the dark; unfortunately exactly what is required by every genus in cultivation is not yet known. On the whole, it is safe to keep the seeds covered until germination starts, and then to expose the seedlings to a good light but keep them out of direct sunlight to avoid any scorching.

Container preparation

In the past only seed boxes or trays (flats) were available, but now there are half-trays and quarter-trays, pans, cell-trays, 5cm (2in) diameter pots and so on. Large seed can be sown individually in the last named, or in cell-trays, or it can be sown spaced out in seed-boxes, depending on the quantity being sown. Smaller seed can be sown in the smaller trays or shallow pans.

All containers should be spotlessly clean; you need seed compost as opposed to potting compost, and it must be moist. Fill containers to leave a space at the top for watering after germination. If you are using a soil-based compost, firm the corners and the sides first with your fingers, and then the

Saintpaulia leaf cuttings
Take a leaf with the stem attached, trim the stem to about 4cm (1½in) and bury the stem to the base of the leaf blade in moist compost. Keep warm and moist.

Streptocarpus leaf cuttings
Cut the top half of each leaf, and push the base of the leaf into the moist compost, up to a quarter of its length. Keep warm and moist.

Begonia leaf cuttings
Remove the leaves in late spring or summer and cut across the main veins. Lay the leaves flat on the compost surface, cover with silver sand and weigh down with pebbles to ensure contact between the cut veins and the compost. Cover with an air-filled plastic bag and keep warm.

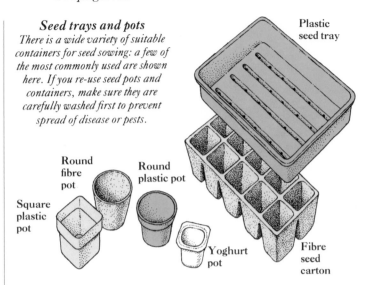

Seed trays and pots

There is a wide variety of suitable containers for seed sowing: a few of the most commonly used are shown here. If you re-use seed pots and containers, make sure they are carefully washed first to prevent spread of disease or pests.

Plastic seed tray

Round fibre pot

Round plastic pot

Square plastic pot

Yoghurt pot

Fibre seed carton

centre; this helps to ensure that it is evenly firm and level. Then give the finishing touch by firming with the base of a pot or a "patter" – a rectangular piece of wood as long as the width of the tray and about 10cm (4in) wide, with an upright handle. Peat-based compost need only be lightly firmed.

If sowing really tiny seeds, put some compost through a perforated zinc sieve, or use a domestic culinary sieve, and riddle it straight on to the compost already in the container. (Sometimes a peat-based compost is recommended for seeds as well as potting, and has quite large pieces of peat in it, not really suitable for seed sowing. If so, sort these out to leave a basically fine, granulated growing medium.)

Then water the compost thoroughly by putting the container in a shallow tray of water and leaving it until the water has soaked up sufficiently through the compost to moisten the surface, which will change colour and become dark. Then set aside to drain. By watering like this, it should not be necessary to water overhead until after germination, thus avoiding the danger of washing the seed into one place.

Seed sowing

The time to sow seed is usually in spring, but this can vary according to when flowering of a particular plant is required. For conservatory displays there are some annuals which are sown in summer so that they will bloom the following spring.

The majority of seed is sprinkled, as evenly as possible, over the compost surface, which is most easily done by taking seed from the palm of one hand with the finger and thumb of the other. It can also be sown direct from a packet but it is less easy to control the flow. The larger seeds are sown at regular spacings; after sowing, cover with sieved, moist compost to a depth equal to the diameter of the seed, and firm it down gently and evenly.

If the seed is so small as to be dust-like, as with begonias or sinningias, mix it with a little silver sand and then sprinkle it. This helps to spread it evenly; it also shows where the seed

Transplanting seedlings
Use potting compost, and a dibber
for moving them – a blunt-pointed
piece of wood like a thick pencil –
much the best tool for digging
underneath the roots without
harming them. Insert them in the
new pots so that the stem is
completely buried, and the lowest
leaves are almost resting on the
compost. This prevents the stem
waving about, which would result
in a weak adult plant.

has been sown. The compost surface must be really fine, and after sowing, there is no need to cover with compost.

Whatever the size of seed, cover the container with black plastic sheet, secured round the edges, and put it in a propagator, perhaps heated to warm the compost. Alternatively leave it in a shaded place, without a propagator, and maintain the temperature recommended for the genus.

Aftercare

Wipe the underside of the black plastic daily to remove condensation, and water the compost with a gentle spray if it shows signs of drying. When germination starts, which may be anything from two days to several weeks (or even months) later, remove the black plastic and provide good light, without direct sunlight.

When the seedlings have one or two seed leaves and two true leaves, lift them out with the roots intact, holding them by a leaf, and transplant (prick them out) to a small pot, or a tray, spaced 5cm (2in) apart, to grow into small plants.

Spores

These, the equivalent of the seeds of flowering plants, are treated slightly differently so that they "germinate". The frond should be shaken gently over the surface of the moist, peat-based compost so that the dust-like spores on the undersides float down on to it. Then the compost container should be covered with a transparent plastic dome or inflated clear plastic bag, to maintain a very humid atmosphere, and put in a shaded, warm place.

To start with, the compost surface will be covered with a green film, then flat, green, leaf-like growths will develop, from which will come miniature fronds. Keep the plantlets really humid, but allow a little air occasionally. When they are about 1.5cm (½in) tall, they can be pricked out into very fine and well-drained potting or cuttings compost, still covered, and occasionally but increasingly ventilated, until the small plants are sufficiently well rooted to survive in a normal environment without a cover.

Fern spores
On the underside of fern fronds you
will see raised brown spots, which
are the spore-cases.

APPENDICES

This section includes lists of plants organized in accordance with their attributes – for example, their temperature requirements, foliage colours, flowering season and so on, as a guide to choosing appropriate plants for particular purposes.

It also includes a short list of suppliers of conservatory plants, including those which specialize in particular groups of plants, like cacti and bromeliads, and of conservatory equipment.

LISTS OF PLANTS

Minimum temperatures

4°C (40°F)

Acacia
Adiantum
Agapanthus
Agave
Aloe
Anigozanthos
Araucaria
Aspidistra
Brugmansia
Callistemon
Camellia
Campanula
Chlorophytum
Chrysanthemum
Citrus
Clianthus
Clivia
Cobaea
Crassula
Cuphea
Dracaena sanderiana
Echeveria
Fatsia
Feijoa
Freesia
Grevillea
Hippeastrum
Leptospermum
Mandevilla
Mirabilis
Myrtus
Nandina
Nerine bowdenii
Passiflora caerulea
Pelargonium
Pleioblastus
Plumbago
Rebutia
Salvia
Saxifraga
Streptocarpus
Tecomaria
Tradescantia (except *T. purpusii*)
Zantedeschia

7°C (45°F)

Abutilon
Aporocactus
Begonia sutherlandii
Billbergia
Blechnum gibbum
Bougainvillea
Camellia reticulata
C. sasanqua
Campsis
Ceropegia
Cineraria
Cupressus
Cymbidium
Dicksonia
Eucomis
Hoya
Jasminum
Lapageria
Lotus
Mammillaria
Maurandia
Nerium
Pelargonium (miniature)
Pellaea
Primula
Punica
Rhododendron
Sedum
Sparmannia
Tweedia

10°C (50°F)

Achimenes
Adiantum
Aechmea
Asparagus
Asplenium
Begonia
Bouvardia
Browallia
Cattleya
Chamaedorea
Cryptanthus
Cycas
Cyclamen
Dracaena
Epiphyllum
Ficus
Gynura
Hatiora
Howeia
Hypoestes
Justicia
Kalanchoe
Monstera
Nephrolepis
Nerine sarniensis
Odontoglossum
Opuntia
Paphiopedilum
Peperomia
Philodendron
Platycerium
Sinningia
Solenostemon
Stephanotis
Streptosolen
Strobilanthes
Tibouchina
Trachycarpus
Tradescantia pallida
  'Purpurea'

13°C (55°F)

Allamanda
Blechnum
Canna
Clerodendron
Columnea
Crossandra
Episcia
Euphorbia
Gloriosa
Hibiscus
Impatiens
Jacobinia
Lantana
Musa
Passiflora
Ruellia
Schefflera
Spathiphyllum
Strelitzia
Thunbergia
Tillandsia

16°C (60°F)

Ananas
Anthurium
Caladium
Calathea
Exacum
Fittonia
Gardenia
Guzmania
Medinilla
Nepenthes
Plumeria
Saintpaulia
Vriesea

There are a few plants which will accept even lower minimums, for instance: *Chamaecereus*, 0°C (32°F); *Echinopsis*, 1°C (34°F); *Fuchsia* and *Hedera*, 2–4°C (36–40°F); *Indocalamus*, −20°C (−4°F); *Narcissus*, 2–7°C (36–45°F); *Parodia*, 1°C (34°F).

Foliage Plants
Adiantum
Aechmea
Agave
Aloe
Ananas
Araucaria
Asparagus
Aspidistra
Asplenium
Begonia
Blechnum
Caladium
Calathea
Ceropegia
Chamaedorea
Chlorophytum
Crassula falcata
Cryptanthus
Cupressus
Cycas
Cyperus
Dicksonia
Dracaena
Echeveria
Episcia
Fatsia
Ficus
Fittonia
Grevillea
Guzmania
Gynura
Hedera
Howeia
Hypoestes
Impatiens
Indocalamus
Kalanchoe
  daigremontianum
Lotus
Maranta
Monstera
Nandina
Nepenthes
Nephrolepis
Opuntia
Pellaea
Peperomia
Philodendron
Platycerium
Pleioblastus
Saxifraga
Schefflera
Sedum
Solenostemon
Sparmannia
Strobilanthes
Tillandsia
Trachycarpus
Tradescantia
Vriesea

Plants with coloured leaves
VARIEGATED
Abutilon megapotamicum
  'Variegatum'
Agave
Aloe
Ananas
Aspidistra elatior
  'Variegata'
Bougainvillea glabra
  'Variegata'
Chlorophytum
Cyperus
Episcia
Fatsia
Ficus sagittata
  'Variegata'
Fittonia
Hedera
Hibiscus rosa-sinensis
  'Cooperi'
Impatiens
Nerium oleander
  'Variegata'
Pelargonium
Peperomia
Pleioblastus
Sedum
Tradescantia

PURPLE/WINE
Begonia rex
Canna
Gynura
Solenostemon
Strobilanthes
Tradescantia pallida
  'Purpusii'

GREY/BLUE
Aechmea
Crassula falcata
Cupressus
Echeveria
Lotus
Sedum sieboldii
Tillandsia

MULTI-COLOURED
Begonia rex
Caladium
Calathea
Ceropegia
Cryptanthus
Cyclamen
Dracaena
Echeveria
Hypoestes
Maranta
Ruellia makoyana
Saxifraga
Solenostemon
Vriesea

Flowering Plants
Abutilon
Acacia
Achimenes
Aechmea
Agapanthus
Allamanda
Anthurium
Aporocactus
Begonia
Billbergia
Bougainvillea
Bouvardia
Browallia
Brugmansia
Brunfelsia
Callistemon
Camellia
Campanula
Campsis
Canna
Cattleya
Chrysanthemum
Cineraria
Citrus
Clerodendrum
Clianthus
Clivia
Columnea
Crossandra
Cyclamen
Cymbidium
Eccremocarpus
Echinopsis
Epiphyllum
Episcia
Eucomis
Euphorbia
Exacum
Feijoa
Freesia
Fuchsia
Gardenia
Gloriosa
Guzmania
Hibiscus
Hippeastrum
Hoya
Impatiens
Jacobinia
Jasminum
Justicia
Kalanchoe blossfeldiana
Lantana
Lapageria
Leptospermum
Lotus
Mammillaria
Mandevilla
Maurandia
Medinilla
Mirabilis
Musa
Myrtus
Narcissus
Nerine
Nerium
Odontoglossum
Paphiopedilum
Parodia
Passiflora
Pelargonium
Peperomia caperata
Plumbago
Primula
Punica
Rebutia
Rhododendron
Ruellia
Saintpaulia
Salvia
Schlumbergera
Sinningia
Sparmannia
Stephanotis
Strelitzia
Streptocarpus
Streptosolen
Tecomaria
Thunbergia
Tibouchina
Tillandsia
Tweedia
Zantedeschia

Shade
LIGHT, DEEP, SOME OF
THE DAY/SEASON
Achimenes
Adiantum
Asparagus
Aspidistra
Asplenium
Begonia
Blechnum
Camellia
Cattleya
Chamaedorea
Cryptanthus
Cycas
Cyclamen
Cymbidium
Dicksonia
Fatsia
Ficus
Fuchsia
Hedera
Howeia
Monstera
Nepenthes
Odontoglossum
Paphiopedilum
Pellaea
Philodendron
Platycerium
Saxifraga
Sinningia

Flower colours

RED
Abutilon 'Cannington Red'
Anthurium
Aporocactus
Bouvardia
Brugmansia sanguinea
Callistemon
Camellia
Clerodendrum thomsoniae
Clianthus
Columnea
Cyclamen
Episcia
Euphorbia
Feijoa
Gloriosa
Guzmania
Hatiora
Lotus
Manettia
Nerine
Nerium
Punica
Salvia
Schlumbergera
Tecomaria

BLUE
Agapanthus
Browallia
Campanula
Clerodendron ugandense
Passiflora caerulea
Plumbago
Tweedia

ORANGE
Abutilon megapotamicum 'Variegatum'
Begonia sutherlandii
Campsis
Clivia
Crossandra
Euphorbia fulgens
Gynura sarmentosa
Strelitzia
Streptosolen
Thunbergia alata

WHITE
Brugmansia suaveolens
Camellia
Citrus
Crassula arborescens
Cyclamen
Echinopsis
Euphorbia pulcherrima
Gardenia
Hoya bella
Jasminum
Mandevilla laxa
Myrtus
Nerine
Nerium
Peperomia caperata
Saxifraga
Sparmannia
Stephanotis
Thunbergia grandiflora

PINK
Aechmea
Bouvardia
Camellia
Cyclamen
Epiphyllum
Euphorbia pulcherrima
Hoya carnosa
Jasminum × stephanense
Justicia carnea
Lapageria
Medinilla
Nerine
Nerium

PURPLE
Brunfelsia
Ceropegia
Cobaea
Eupatorium
Exacum
Maurandia
Musa
Tibouchina

MULTICOLOURED
Achimenes
Begonia
Billbergia
Bougainvillea
Canna
Cattleya
Chrysanthemum
Cineraria
Cymbidium
Eccremocarpus
Epiphyllum
Freesia
Fuchsia
Hibiscus
Hippeastrum
Impatiens
Kalanchoe blossfeldiana
Lantana
Mammillaria
Mirabilis
Narcissus
Odontoglossum
Paphiopedilum
Passiflora
Pelargonium
Primula
Rebutia
Rhododendron simsii
Saintpaulia
Salpiglossis
Schizanthus
Sinningia
Streptocarpus

YELLOW
Acacia
Allamanda
Gynura aurantiaca
Musa
Opuntia
Parodia
Zantedeschia elliottiana

Seasons of flowering

SPRING
Aechmea
Anigozanthos
Anthurium
Aporocactus
Billbergia
Brunfelsia
Callistemon
Camellia
Citrus
Clivia
Columnea
Crassula
Cymbidium
Echinopsis
Epiphyllum
Euphorbia
Gardenia
Guzmania
Hatiora
Hippeastrum
Impatiens
Kalanchoe
Lantana
Leptospermum
Lotus
Mammillaria
Medinilla
Musa
Narcissus
Pelargonium
Rebutia
Ruellia
Saintpaulia
Spathiphyllum
Strelitzia
Tecomaria
Tillandsia
Zantedeschia

SUMMER
Abutilon
Achimenes
Aechmea
Agapanthus
Allamanda
Anthurium
Begonia
Bougainvillea
Bouvardia
Browallia
Brugmansia
Brunfelsia
Campanula
Campsis
Canna
Chamaecereus
Citrus
Clerodendrum
Clianthus
Cobaea
Crassula
Crossandra

Cuphea
Eccremocarpus
Echinopsis
Episcia
Eucomis
Euphorbia
Exacum
Feijoa
Fuchsia
Gloriosa
Guzmania
Hibiscus
Hoya
Impatiens
Jacobinia
Jasminum
Justicia
Kalanchoe blossfeldiana
Lantana
Lapageria
Mammillaria
Mandevilla
Maurandia
Medinilla
Mirabilis
Musa
Myrtus
Nerium
Paphiopedilum
Passiflora
Pelargonium
Peperomia caperata
Plumbago
Plumeria
Punica
Rebutia
Saintpaulia
Salvia
Sinningia
Sparmannia
Stephanotis
Streptocarpus
Streptosolen
Tecomaria
Thunbergia
Tibouchina
Tillandsia
Tweedia
Zantedeschia

AUTUMN
Begonia
Bougainvillea
Bouvardia
Brugmansia
Brunfelsia
Campanula
Campsis
Canna
Cattleya
Chrysanthemum
Cobaea
Cymbidium
Eccremocarpus

Euphorbia
Exacum
Freesia
Fuchsia
Hibiscus
Hoya
Impatiens
Jacobinia
Jasminum
Justicia
Kalanchoe blossfeldiana
Lantana
Lapageria
Manettia
Maurandia
Mirabilis
Myrtus
Nerine
Nerium
Odontoglossum
Paphiopedilum
Passiflora
Pelargonium
Plumbago
Plumeria
Saintpaulia
Salvia
Sinningia
Spathiphyllum
Stephanotis
Streptocarpus
Tecomaria

WINTER
Acacia
Anthurium
Begonia
Browallia
Brunfelsia
Camellia
Campanula
Cattleya
Chrysanthemum
Cineraria
Clivia
Columnea
Cyclamen
Euphorbia
Freesia
Fuchsia
Hippeastrum
Impatiens
Jasminum
Justicia brandigeana
Kalanchoe blossfeldiana
Manettia
Narcissus
Odontoglossum
Paphiopedilum
Pelargonium
Primula
Rhododendron
Ruellia

Saintpaulia
Schlumbergera
Streptocarpus
Tecomaria
Thunbergia
Tweedia

Climbers
Allamanda
Bougainvillea
Campsis
Clerodendrum
Cobaea
Eccremocarpus
Gloriosa
Hedera
Hoya carnosa
Jasminum
Lapageria
Mandevilla
Maurandia
Passiflora
Philodendron
Plumbago
Stephanotis
Tecomaria
Thunbergia

Trailers
Asparagus densiflorus
  'Sprengeri'
Begonia pendula
Campanula
Ceropegia
Chlorophytum
Columnea
Ficus sagittata
Fittonia
Gynura
Hedera
Lotus
Pelargonium
Peperomia scandens
  'Variegata'
Platycerium
Saxifraga
Sedum
Thunbergia
Tradescantia

Cacti
Aporocactus
Chamaecereus
Echinopsis
Epiphyllum
Hatiora
Mammillaria
Opuntia
Parodia
Rebutia
Schlumbergera

Bromeliads
Aechmea

Ananas
Billbergia
Cryptanthus
Guzmania
Tillandsia

Ferns
Adiantum
Asparagus
Asplenium
Blechnum
Dicksonia
Nephrolepis
Pellaea

Orchids
Cattleya
Cymbidium
Odontoglossum
Paphiopedilum

Palms
Chamaedorea
Howeia
Trachycarpus

Potentially large plants
Abutilon
Acacia
Araucaria
Begonia, cane
Boronia
Brugmansia
Callistemon
Camellia
Canna
Citrus sinensis
Clerodendrum
Cupressus
Cycas
Cyperus
Dicksonia
Fatsia
Ficus benjamina
F. elastica
Gardenia
Grevillea
Hibiscus
Howeia
Jacobinia
Medinilla
Monstera
Musa
Myrtus
Nandina
Opuntia ficus-indica
Plumeria
Schefflera
Sparmannia
Strelitzia
Tecomaria
Tibouchina
Trachycarpus

LIST OF SUPPLIERS

Plant suppliers

Abbey Brook Cactus Nursery, Bakewell Rd, Darley Dale, Matlock, Derbyshire DE4 2QS

African Violet Centre, Station Rd, Terrington St Clements, Kings Lynn, Norfolk PE30 4PL

Avon Bulbs, Upper Westwood, Bradford-on-Avon, Wilts BA15 2AT

Blackmore & Langdon Ltd, Stanton Nurseries, Pensford, Bristol, BS18 4JL (begonias)

Blom & Son Ltd., Walter, Coombelands Nurseries Ltd, Leavesden, Watford, Herts WD2 7BH (bulbs)

Burncoose & Southdown Nurseries, Gwennap, Redruth, Cornwall TR16 6BJ

Burnham Nurseries Ltd, Forches Cross, Newton Abbot, Devon TQ12 6PZ (orchids)

Butcher Ltd., Thomas, 60 Wickham Rd, Shirley, Croydon, Surrey CR9 8AG (seeds as well as plants)

Butterfields Nursery, Harvest Hill, Bourne End, Bucks SL8 5JJ (pleiones)

Chessington Nurseries Ltd, Leatherhead Rd, Chessington, Surrey KT9 2NF

Clifton Nurseries Ltd, Clifton Villas, Warwick Avenue, London W9 2PH

Dobie & Son Ltd, Samuel, Broomhill Way, Torquay, Devon TQ2 7QW (seeds)

Efenechtyd Nurseries, Llanelidan, Ruthin, Clwyd LL15 2LG (streptocarpus)

Fibrex Nurseries Ltd, Honeybourne Rd., Pebworth, Stratford-on-Avon, Warks CV37 8XT (pelargoniums, ivies, ferns)

Fleur de Lys, Kemsdale House, Hernhill, Faversham, Kent ME13 9JP

Global Orange Groves UK, PO Box 644, Poole, Dorset BH17 9YB (general citrus species)

Hillier Nurseries (Winchester) Ltd, Ampfield House, Ampfield, Romsey, Hants SO51 9PA (tender shrubs)

Holly Gate Cactus Nursery, Ashington, W. Sussex RH20 3BA

Kingsbury, Noel, Sunbeam Nurseries, Bristol Rd, Frampton Cotterell, Avon BS17 2AU (conservatory plant specialist)

Long Man Gardens, Lewes Road (A27), Wilmington, Polegate, E. Sussex BN26 5RS (conservatory plant specialist)

Oakleigh Nurseries, Monkswood, Alresford, Hants SO24 0HB (fuchsias, pelargoniums)

Palm Centre, The, 22 Guildford Road, London SW8 2BX

Palm Farm, The, Thornton Curtis, South Humberside (general conservatory plants as well as palms)

Peper Harow, Shackleford, Godalming, Surrey GU8 6BG (hanging plants)

Reads Nursery, Hales Hall, Loddon, Norfolk NR14 6QW (conservatory plant specialist, National Collections: citrus, figs, greenhouse grapes)

Simms, Clive, Woodhurst, Essendine, Stamford, Lincs PE9 4LQ

Suttons Seeds Ltd, Hele Rd, Torquay, Devon TQ2 7QJ

Thompson & Morgan Ltd, Poplar Lane, Ipswich, Suffolk IP2 0BA (seedsmen)

Townsend, K. J., 17 Valerie Close, St Albans, Herts AL1 5JD (achimenes)

Unwins Seeds Ltd, Histon, Cambridge CB4 4LE

Van Tubergen (UK) Ltd, Bressingham, Diss, Norfolk IP22 2AB (bulbs)

Wall, B, 4 Selbourne Close, New Haw, Weybridge, Surrey KT15 3RG (begonias)

Wallace & Barr Ltd, the Nurseries, Marden, Kent TN12 9BP (bulbs)

Equipment suppliers

Ann's Garden, Middle Strath, Avon Bridge, Falkirk, FK1 2LA (containers)

Chempak Products, Gedding Rd, Hoddesdon, Herts EN11 0LR (fertilizers)

Conservatory Completion Co Ltd, Kettlestring Lane, Clifton Moor Industrial Park, York YO3 8XF (interior conservatory design and furnishing)

Courtyard Pottery, Groundwell Farm, Cricklade Rd, Swindon, Wilts

Dales Pottery, The, Wetheriggs, Clifton Dykes, Penrith, Cumbria CA10 2DH

Diplex Ltd, PO Box 172, Watford, Herts WD1 1BX (plant care meters)

Erin Marketing Ltd, Astonia House, High St, Baldock, Herts SG7 6PP (lightweight containers)

Fiesta Blinds Ltd, 72–76 Yarm Lane, Stockton-on-Tees, Cleveland TS18 1EW

Haddonstone Ltd, The Forge House, East Haddon, Northampton NN6 8DB (stone containers)

Haws Elliott Ltd, Rawlings Rd., Smethwick, Warley, West Midlands B67 5AB (watering-cans)

Outside Interiors Ltd, Lower Maidenland, St Kew, Bodmin, Cornwall PL30 3HA (interior conservatory design and furnishing)

Rapitest, London Rd, Corwen, Clwyd LL21 0DR (plant care meters)

Thermaforce Ltd, Heybridge works, Maldon, Essex CM9 7NW (conservatory accessories)

Transatlantic Plastics Ltd, 23–27 Kings Rd., Long Ditton, Surrey KT6 5JE

Two Wests & Elliott Ltd, Unit 4, Carrwood Rd., Sheepbrige Industrial Estate, Chesterfield, Derbyshire S41 9RH (conservatory equipment)

Wessex Peat Co Ltd, South Newton, Salisbury, Wilts SP2 0QW (peat, and alternatives to peat)

Whichford Pottery, Whichford, Shipston-on-Stour, Warks CV36 5PG

Conservatories and orangeries (to visit)

Alton Towers, Uttoxeter, Staffs

Belfast Botanic Gardens, Belfast, Northern Ireland (palm house)

Bicton Gardens, Colaton Raleigh, Devon (palm house)

Blithfield, Rugeley, Staffs (orangery)

Carrowhouse, Norwich, Norfolk

Castle Ashby, Northants (orangery)

Chatsworth, Bakewell, Derbys

Chiswick House, Burlington Lane, Chiswick, London W4 (camellia house)

East Cliff Lodge, Ramsgate, Kent

Howsham Hall, Howsham, Norfolk (orangery)

Kensington Palace, London W8 (orangery)

Kew Gardens, Richmond, Surrey (palm house, orangery, and **Princess of Wales conservatory**)

Royal Horticultural Society, Wisley Garden, Ripley, Surrey

Sezincote, Glos (orangery)

Shrubland Hall, Barham, Suffolk (now a health farm, but has retained the winter garden conservatory)

Syon House, Brentford, Middx

Wollaton Hall, Nottingham, Notts (camellia house)

Wrest Park (National Institute of Agricultural Engineering), Silsoe, Beds (orangery)

INDEX

Acknowledgments

The Publishers would like to thank the following individuals and organizations for their help in producing this book:
For allowing their conservatories to be photographed: John Brookes, The Hon R. and Mrs Dennison-Pender, Terry Hewitt of Holly Gate Cactus Nursery, Mrs Forrest, Mrs Haig-Thomas, Mr and Mrs Hugh Johnson, Mr and Mrs M. Lane-Fox, Mr and Mrs J. Merton, Mr and Mrs R. Raworth, Mr and Mrs Relph, Royal Botanic Gardens, Kew, Martin Summers.
Special thanks to Des Whitwell and Chessington Nurseries, Surrey, for their help in providing plants for photography, to Julie Armstrong of Marston and Langinger and Bartholomew's Conservatories for providing locations, and to Joan Phelan for providing conservatory planting plans, to Tony Lord for checking nomenclature of plants, to Hilary Bird for compiling the index, and to Sarah Bloxham for editorial liaison.

Photographic credits
All photographs by Steven Wooster except the following: p 71 (right) Gill Marais/Garden Picture Library; p 78 (left) David Russell/Garden Picture Library; p 88 (right) J.S. Sira/Garden Picture Library; p 114 (right) Harry Smith Collection.